To Harvest, To Hunt

To Harvest, To Hunt
Stories of Resource Use in the American West

Edited by Judith L. Li

Oregon State University Press
Corvallis

The paper in this book meets the guidelines for permanence and durability of the Committee on Production Guidelines for Book Longevity of the Council on Library Resources and the minimum requirements of the American National Standard for Permanence of Paper for Printed Library Materials Z39.48-1984.

Library of Congress Cataloging-in-Publication Data
To harvest, to hunt : stories of resource use in the American West / edited by Judith L. Li.
    p. cm.
    Includes bibliographical references and index.
    ISBN 978-0-87071-192-3 (alk. paper)
    1. Natural resources—West (U.S.) 2. Human ecology—West (U.S.)
3. Social ecology—West (U.S.) 4. Indians of North America—West (U.S.)
5. Immigrants—West (U.S.) 6. West (U.S.)—Environmental conditions.
7. West (U.S.)—Economic conditions. 8. West (U.S.)—Social life and customs. I. Li, Judith L.
                  HC107.A17T6 2007
                  333.70978--dc22
                  2007012366

Oregon State University Press
121 The Valley Library
Corvallis OR 97331-3411
541-737-3166 • fax 541-737-3170
www.osupress.oregonstate.edu

Contents

1. Tahola, WA

2. King Island (Uguivak), AK

3. Prince of Wales Island

4. Siuslaw River, Oregon

5. Santa Cruz Mountains

6. Monterey, CA

7. San Francisco Bay

8. Boise, ID

9. Clifton, OR

10. Nyssa, OR

11. Polk County, OR

12. Gila River Camp, AZ

13. Del Rey, CA

14. Taos, NM

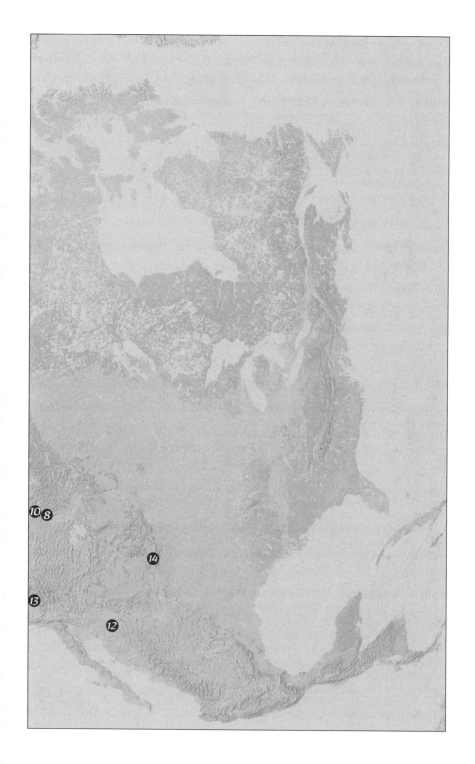

Photograph captions

page 8: The captain and pullers of the Quinault Indian Nation, at sea in the *May-ee*, approach the landing area in the Quileute village of LaPush on their way to the intertribal Canoe Journey held in August 2002 in Taholah, the home of the Quinault Indian Nation. The Quinault crew had paddled up the coast to meet other canoes so that they could come into Taholah with colleagues from other tribes. Photograph courtesy of Debbie Preston, Northwest Indian Fisheries Commission.

page 15: Deanna Kingston and her uncle, Gabriel Muktoyuk, on the slopes of their King Island village, August 2004. Photograph courtesy of author.

page 25: Dolly Garza's uncles, George and Pat Gardner, on their boat. Photograph courtesy of author.

page 35: The Hatch family boathouse in Florence, Oregon, at the mouth of the North Fork of the Siuslaw River. Photograph courtesy of author.

page 38: David Hatch's dad and grandfather after a fishing trip in September 1957. Note the flat flounder, second from left on the string of fish. Photograph courtesy of author.

page 40: Sedge digging at Nicasio reservoir, Marin, California. Photograph courtesy of author.

page 56: Basket made of sedges. Photograph courtesy of author.

page 65: Restored China Camp at San Pedro today. Photograph courtesy of author.

page 69: Historical photo of abalone drying at Monterey Bay. Photograph courtesy of Monterey County Free Libraries.

page 74: Sheepherders and their wagons in southern Idaho, 1901. Photograph courtesy of Idaho Historical Society.

page 87: A family photo of Garamendia family: Lorenzo Garamendia, far right and standing, and Fermina (Achabal) Garmendia next to him on the horse. The other woman on a horse is Agueda Achabal, and the man on the left has not been identified. Photograph courtesy of author.

page 92: Columbia River Packers Association tender towing a gillnet boat on the Columbia, Clifton, Oregon, 1947. Photograph courtesy of Jack Marincovich.

page 100: Kent Martin with fishing net, Clifton, ca. 1978. Photograph courtesy of Terry Norberg.

page 110: Buzz Martin record cover. Courtesy of the Buzz Martin family.

page 135: The northwest section of Camp #2, Gila River, Arizona, November 1942. Photographer: Francis Stewart. Photograph courtesy of the Bancroft Library, University of California, Berkeley. BANC PIC 1967.014 AD-693-PIC.

page 138: Farm work, Gila River internees, June 1944. Photograph courtesy of the Bancroft Library, University of California, Berkeley. BANC PIC 1967.014 AG-614-PIC.

page 142: Irrigating winter pasture at Gila River Internment Camp, November 1942. Photographer: Francis Stewart. Photograph courtesy of the Bancroft Library, University of California, Berkeley. BANC PIC 1967.014 AD-658-PIC.

page 149: Spanish clover is a member of the genus *Trifolium*, illustrated in this old line drawing. This and other botanical drawings for this essay (page 152, Yarrow, *Achillea*; page 153, Puncture vine, *Tribulus terrestris*) appeared in U.S. Department of Agriculture Natural Resource Conservation Service PLANTS database. Original drawings appeared in N. L. Britton and A. Brown. 1913. *Illustrated Flora of the Northern States and Canada.*

page 154: A small ditch that is part of the acequia in Taos, running through town. Photograph courtesy of Judith Li.

page 168: Taos pasture with Pueblo Peak in the background. Photograph courtesy of author.

Introduction

I grew up in the Santa Clara Valley, the granddaughter of Chinese immigrants. We lived in the one-street burg of Campbell when it was still a cannery town, where Mexican, Italian, and Japanese families still worked the land. For millennia Native Americans of the Costonoan tribe hunted and gathered in the wetlands, oak woodlands, and abundant streams of this valley—a region so verdant that the Spanish made it a pueblo in 1782, growing wheat and cattle to support the mission and military fort in San Francisco. After the gold rush in 1849, other European immigrants brought orchard stock for fruit and seedlings for grapes. In the following century Santa Clara Valley became the nation's fruit bowl, rich in fragile "luxury fruits" like apricots, cherries, prunes, nuts, and strawberries. Truck farms, orchards, vineyards, and row crops blanketed the valley when my family settled in a modest ranch-style home in the early 1950s. Our home was on a small tract of three streets, each ending abruptly at a cherry orchard; when the mustard plants grew tall beneath the trees, my sister and I played hide and seek with neighborhood buddies. Down the road from the old grammar school we stopped by the Falcone family farm for fresh chickens, where sometimes Mr. Falcone was defeathering birds in the whirling machine right next to the cash register. Ten blocks from home, Japanese farmers picked strawberries in fields, row on row of plants stretching across the landscape.

The valley of my youth conjures a "story of different but sequential cultures occupying the same space and creating their own succession of places,"[1] what Dan Flores calls a bioregional history. Its multicultural mosaic was a weave of social groups, "cultures," with distinct identities. In this anthology we examine cultures of people organized around resource use in particular—cultures whose communal experiences result in shared values and traditions. Besides their occupational identities, often they share an ethnic identity or tribal affiliation (Mexican rancheros, Basque sheepherders, or Italian fishermen). In time, fidelity to place, local patterns of language, and pursuit of regional arts can make cultures more distinct, as in the linguistically separate tribes of Native California pre-European settlement. But the experience of the last 150 years has trended towards loss of cultural connections; in the Santa Clara Valley changes came quickly and the spirit of the place seemed to slip away. By the time I went to college, we'd lost the orchards, strawberry fields, and sense of separate cultural enclaves. Ford, IBM, and other industries came to town; freeways built over once-productive wetlands, bypassing country roads that led to the old Spanish missions. Del Monte, the last cannery in the Valley, closed forever the year before I began assembling this volume.

A great diversity of peoples across the American West harvested natural and cultivated crops, irrigated its lands, grazed livestock, fished the streams and oceans for centuries before our modern, highly urbanized, world reconfigured the landscape. I gathered the essays for this anthology to recall how diverse cultures have used natural resources in the western United States, and to encourage readers to consider how these legacies could affect contemporary management of the environment. These are stories of Native and immigrant peoples; some are written by those who came from the cultures that created the traditions, others by authors fascinated by particular groups of people or resources. The variety of perspectives gives us multiple lenses for understanding resource use.

To find these historical and contemporary stories, I sought out scholars and writers whose work I valued for their insight into the intersection of culture and resources, beginning with colleagues at my home institution, Oregon State University, and approaching others whose writing on these topics inspired me, including authors who focused on little-publicized or unrecognized uses. Contributors come from diverse disciplines, and their varying expertise and academic interests, blended with passion for particular cultures, provide a range of voices; some tend towards objective, analytical narratives while others are more lyrical. John Nichols' years spent in the arid desert of northern New Mexico and his story of the Taos *acequia* create a very different narrative about community than the essay by ethnic studies professor Patti Sakurai, who reflects about the Gila River Camp in Arizona where her Japanese predecessors were interned during World War II. Contrasting with Dr. Sakurai's reflections in other ways are David Mas Masumoto's poetic letters, firmly grounded in his connection to his family and their land, providing another remembrance of the Japanese experience. Anthropologist Deanna Kingston's account of how her King Island people were alienated from their traditional walrus hunting is very different than biologist Dolly Garza's description of her Haida/Tlingit tribe's modern management of sea otters in southeast Alaska. We learn, from law professor Charles Wilkinson, about renewal among Quinault canoe builders on the coast of Washington, a phenomenon that bears strong resemblance in spirit to David Hatch's Siletz tribe as they strive to develop a marine sanctuary in traditional fishing waters. Life experience, professional and academic training, uniquely inform each essay and provide intriguing contrasts about similar resources and places.

Special places have been illuminated by poets, philosophers, and writers of fiction and prose as part of a strong tradition in Nature writing. Literary greats like Ralph Waldo Emerson, Mary Austin, and Henry David Thoreau wrote of pristine wilderness, arid deserts, idyllic wanderings; natural beauty was integral to conservationist ethics articulated by early environmentalists such as John Muir and Aldo Leopold. Sagas of western pioneers and laborers working the land (such as works by Wallace Stegner, Wendell Berry, and John Steinbeck) broadened our visions beyond pristine nature, detailing how people were using the land's resources. Many of these works are so familiar they help define how we imagine the western U.S. landscape. But our collective memory is fundamentally about the Euro-American experience, leaving on the margins or omitting entirely the role of other immigrant peoples and Native Americans.[2]

Essays in this collection span the North American continent from arctic Alaska, across the timbered Northwest and Mediterranean California, to parched New Mexico, giving voice to peoples of Native and immigrant cultures. All have a spirit of place developed in the context of resource use. For Native peoples that understanding is centuries old, for immigrants it is eagerly acquired. Landscapes, constrained by physical and climatic forces, and characterized by plant and animal communities, become "places" as humans interact with their environments. The volume's emphasis on resource use, rather than on more general relationships with "nature" or "wildness" found in other narratives, tends to focus on cultural adaptations to specific resources—walrus, ferns, Douglas firs, water—and to particular climes—arctic, montane, marine, grassland, or desert. In these particular places, traditional cycles, patterns of harvest and migration, respect for historical legacies, blend as cultures adapt.

In this anthology each story is generated from the relationship of people and resources, and variety in place provides an important source of diversity. Most commonly, monographs or collections in environmental history have focused on particular regions,[3] or on resources.[4] Many volumes consider individual tribes or particular cultural groups,[5] but fewer focus on both cultures and resource use.[6] In her co-edited text *Peoples of Color in the American West,* Sucheng Chan admonishes us that to "neglect histories (of minority groups) distorts the history not only of the groups but also of the American West."[7] As volume editor, I brought together many voices and a mosaic of places, giving readers opportunities to recognize similarities with, and derive new insights about, their own places. This collection is not a history global in scale. Comprehensive histories with economic, social, and environmental views abound. Instead, this is a modest anthology of stories with a personal bent, telling about individuals and particular groups, how they cultivated or harvested resources on which they depended, each contributing to the region's historical legacy.

Despite anthroprogenic changes, our attachment to home places, dubbed "topophilia" by geographer Yi-Fu Tuan, happens most naturally in places small enough to be learned well—local landscapes, familiar plants and animals, intimate details of place.[8] Certainly my longing to find the home place of my youth began with local images. In our stories, we seek what Dan Flores calls a "spirit of place," grounded in "the interaction between humans with local environments,"[9] and encourage the reader to look for patterns across time and regions. We have tried to present essays with strong personal, local roots, which in their sum suggest the diverse, ever-changing contributions of cultures encountering the western landscape.

In the way natural systems are interconnected at many scales, the varied places described by authors telling different stories are interwoven in this anthology. The Spanish presence has been long and significant in much of the arid west (*Shifting Patterns of Land Use in Monterey, California before 1850; Aamodt, Schmaamodt: Who really gets the water?*), yet conflicts with Mexican peoples persist as if in denial of the cultural past (*From Sojourners to Settlers: Mexicanos in Oregon*). How might recognition of our multicultural environmental history and an expanded sense of shared legacy change our perspective? In these narratives the succession of cultures and the interactions between some cultures is obvious, but what part was played by movements of the Basque (*Lorenzo's Letters*) or gathering activities of basketweavers (*California Indian Basketweavers*) across the same landscapes?

Shared resources also link places in our collection. Sea otter were overharvested by Russians and other early nineteenth-century hunters, making way for Chinese abalone fishermen in California (*Lost China Camps*); otter are still highly valued by coastal tribes in Oregon (*Resolution*) and managed carefully by the Haida/Tlingit in southern Alaska (*Comanaging Sea Otter*). What lessons about traditional values and management might be shared between coastal peoples trying to conserve marine mammals today? We believe acknowledging and studying these diverse histories can help us piece together a broader understanding of the larger landscape.

Often transformation of place and cultures leads to confrontations between the ways of traditional and modern worlds. Several essays in this collection explore how conflicts between Native peoples (Haida/Tlingit, Quinault, King Islanders, Siletz, Pomo) and the dominant culture of the United States seem to be moving toward different forms of resolution: political compromise, cultural renewal, relocation, recognition, or resignation. Clashes between majorities and minorities are often expressed as prejudice, and sometimes codified into institutional discrimination. Discovery of riches in the West's minerals, forests, grasslands, and soils opened opportunities for immigrant labor, and created intense competition for labor throughout the region. Discriminatory laws mirrored protestors and riots in the streets. Because of historical violence and legal exclusion, the Chinese I write about no longer fish commercially in California's bays, and the Basque no longer herd their sheep unfenced in the dry plateaus of Oregon and Idaho. Erlinda Gonzales-Berry describes the decades in which Mexican *braceros* brought to Oregon have struggled for legal rights and social justice. But discrimination and outright persecution against immigrants may have been most egregious towards the Japanese Americans interned during World War II. Patti Sakurai and David Mas Masumoto show us how traditions of farming and tilling the land helped their elders survive.

Other conflicts can arise from differences between and within user groups, exacerbated by dwindling resource levels. Groups may come to think of themselves as minorities in a culture dominated by changing priorities. In the case of Columbia River gillnet fishermen that Irene Martin describes, the fishermen's union formed by disparate European immigrant groups now struggles with the competing interests of sports fishermen, Native fishers, and dwindling numbers of salmon. Logging culture, illustrated by Jim LeMonds in songs and poems, fights to survive in an economy where automation and exports have cost many jobs, and timber is no longer king. These are not in the strictest definition stories of minority peoples, but they present a personal side to perspectives rarely heard of groups feeling very much on the margins.

The two sections of this volume illustrate how native peoples, struggling to translate centuries of traditions and resource uses in a contemporary world, face different challenges compared to more recent arrivals who are searching for cultural roots generations after immigration. While diverse in locales and resource uses, the essays from and about Native Americans are quite definitively contemporary. They narrate revival of canoe traditions, restoring marine habitats and basket-weaving plant sites, rebuilding walrus-hunting tradition, recognizing the value of traditional knowledge in managing wildlife populations. Based on cultural traditions and practices, these essays look forward towards greater integration of native rights and traditions into contemporary landscapes.

The historical focus and retrospective in the section about immigrant groups provides an unexpected contrast to the first section in our anthology. These were peoples who brought skills and technologies from the old country, useful in their transition to a new place. The Spanish brought cattle, horses, and traditions of grazing to the West, the Chinese brought their junks and shrimp nets, the Europeans their single-sail boats and drift nets, the Japanese traditions of farming that helped them survive the desert conditions of World War II camps. Many followed the harvest, particularly the migrant *braceros* in Oregon, the Basques of Idaho, and the loggers across the northern forests. As resource levels changed, so harvest patterns and cultural groups adapted. Immigrants struggled to find their place in a changing environment even as they contributed to its transformation. Perhaps because they were less rooted to a place, were ostracized by social forces, and often without legal recourse, immigrants relocated, regrouped, and looked for new roles and places in the rapidly building society of the American West. From one generation to the next, occupational identities, once linked to particular ethnic cultures, faded; memories of early days were easy to erase. In our increasingly urban culture, we have lost many cultural signatures and oral traditions of resources used one or two hundred years ago. Those who participated in those activities are almost invisible on the land or in our literature. These essays help us reconstruct that history.

In the last essay of our collection John Nichols describes the frustrating fight over water allocations among the Pueblo tribes, Old Spanish, New Spanish, and newcomers in a centuries-old ditch system managed by equally old traditions. Distinct cultures, living in communities more than three hundred years old, have very personal attachments to place, and a strong communal commitment to protect their most critical resource, water. The problems are complex, politically and economically charged. Perhaps in other regions the cultural lines may not be as clear, but multi-layered complexity is the reality of natural-resource conflicts; similar dynamics can be detected in other essays. As communities hope for preserving their particular places, cultural traditions and tenacity are contributing to changes on the landscape. Cultural resilience is a common thread among these stories; cultures adapt, summing up old traditions and applying skills in new situations or places.

Resource use inevitably affects people beyond any single cultural group or any local place. We relate to the immediacy of the place around us, but must integrate how our places fit into grander scales. In our contemporary world, the places we identify with are culturally dynamic, spatially expansive, and interconnected with history. Dependent on circumstances of time and place, some cultures are holding firm, some are adapting, and others have dispersed and been transformed. Renewed interpretations of traditions among Native peoples provide models for reintroducing cultural legacies to our modern world. As my memories of California illustrate, physical and cultural transformations may quickly mask historical legacies. Rediscovering those legacies as we have in a number of our essays affirms their importance to our shared sense of cultural identity and place. As we embrace the complexity, conflicts, and diversity of cultural legacies, their lessons can give us the vision of what our place in the world is, and inspire the wisdom to plan into the future.

Judith L. Li, Editor

The little settlement of Taholah lies on the Pacific coast along the south bank of the Quinault River as it empties into the ocean. More rock than sand, this jagged coastline on the Olympic Peninsula receives driving, battering storms for more than half the year. Lodged in a landscape at once harsh and spectacular, furious and giving, Taholah is home to most members of the Quinault Indian Nation.

Return of the Canoe Journey

Charles Wilkinson

In 1953 poverty held a looser grip at Quinault than on most other reservations. To be sure, there was need. No one had indoor plumbing, the cedar plank homes regularly housed extended families of a dozen or more, and family income amounted to less than two-thirds of Washington's statewide average. Nearly half the tribal members, most of them seeking better economic opportunities, lived away from the reservation. Yet standard indicators failed to tell the full story. Pearl Capoeman-Baller, the tailored, soft-spoken president of the Quinault Nation, remembered her youth in Taholah: "We knew, of course, that we were poor. But nobody felt poor. Everybody had the same. We shared. There was no difference in social or economic status."

The wealth of the land played a central role in this. The 200,000-acre reservation provides 26 miles of coastline. The upper, higher end reaches to Lake Quinault, adjacent to Olympic National Park in the Olympic Range. Doused with 70 to 140 inches of rain annually, the reservation, except for the coastal strip and some open prairies, consists of lush rain forest, mainly western redcedar—giant trees rising to canopies two to three hundred feet high—along with hemlock, Sitka spruce, and Douglas fir. The forest floor is a rich, nearly impenetrable tangle of ferns, vine maple, and other vegetation— and fallen behemoths that in time become seedbeds for new growth. The moisture, the vegetation, and the spongy soil make perfect watershed conditions for the Quinault River, one of several big rivers that surge down out of the Olympics.

The reservation produced a modest economic base consisting of some two hundred jobs, almost all in logging and fishing, for a local adult population of fifteen hundred. Beyond that, the ocean and river were virtual cornucopias. Five species of salmon, notably the Quinault blueback, a succulent delicacy found nowhere else, ran in the Quinault. The runs of the early 1950s, depleted by logging but still healthy, provided some commercial returns. A bounty of salmon from subsistence nets spread throughout Taholah, the other reservation town of Queets, and the backwoods reservation homes as families shared their catches. Abundant razor clams and elk also provided staples on the dinner tables.

Traditionally the Quinault were a cedar people as well as a salmon people. They used all parts of the big trees: planks for housing; woven bark and roots for clothing, baskets, and utensils; and leaves for medicines and ceremonies. The redcedars also made possible a hallmark of Quinault society, the elegant canoes that craftsmen carved from downed logs.

The Quinault, then, retained some of their traditional society's basic sources of strength. The Sioux might have lost the buffalo, but the Quinault still had their salmon. Since the 1870s the Bureau of Indian Affairs had pressed Christianizing hard, especially by sending Quinault children off to the federal boarding schools, with their religious and assimilationist orientation, but missionaries had encroached on Quinault tribal land to a lesser degree. Taholah had two churches (some people went to both), the Natives' own Shaker church, which was well attended, and the Pentecostal church, which also had adherents but did not aggressively proselytize. Whatever tender advantages the tribe may have had, by the early 1950s immense forces that threatened to destroy the salmon runs, the forests, and tribal self-governance—the Quinault way of life—had been set in motion.

"America First" pride dominated public sentiment in the postwar years. Reinforced by this attitude, the Bureau of Indian Affairs and the churches drove home the message that Indianness was a thing of the past and assimilation into the larger society was both inevitable and good. Indian clothing and languages were remnants of a lost day. Indians should abandon the reservations and move to the cities that offered a modern American way of life. All the old ceremonies . . . were archaic and pagan. As Alvin Josephy wrote, "Agents of the Bureau of Indian Affairs looked away from, or even encouraged, missionaries who continued to break up Indian ceremonies or interfere with and punish individual Indians and their families when they tried to revive languages, arts, and other aspects of their traditional cultures."

The campaign made its mark. On the Oregon coast the drums went still; no powwow had been held since World War II broke out. Earl Old Person described the direct impact on individual Indian people: "During this time people didn't want to be associated as Indian. They were afraid. People who talked the Indian language didn't want to talk the Indian language. They were afraid. I think they were still afraid from boarding schools. People would go to school and be beat up for talking the Indian language. And that was still with them. People didn't want to show their Indian way of life."

Over the past two generations tribal sovereignty and Indian culture have been reinvigorated in every way—through their governance, health and education programs, and economic development. The story of revival for the Quinault, the Olympic Peninsula ocean and river people, is among the most telling I know.

In the 1980s, with pride in Quinault culture surging, Phillip Martin had a conversation with Emmett Oliver. Both were tribal members, Martin in his fifties at the time, Oliver a generation older. Oliver raised the idea of building an ocean canoe. He said that other tribes in the Pacific Northwest were thinking about bringing back the canoes and that the Quinault ought to join in.

Oliver's suggestion inflamed Martin. All of the Quinault knew about these canoes of legend, hallmarks of coast Indian culture along with the totem poles. Historically, the Quinault had two classes of canoe: large, durable ocean canoes and lighter, lower, more maneuverable river craft. The ocean canoes, in particular, lay at the heart of tribal existence. Quinault people depended on the ocean's bounty of seafood. The coast tribes engaged in a thriving trade economy that, without the canoes, would have been thwarted by the thick forests, with their big trees and dense brush, and the mountains, steep valleys, and deep rivers. Nor would land travel have allowed the extensive socializing among the tribes of the region.

Specialized canoe carvers, trained by their ancestors, built the ocean canoes. They used giant cedar logs, known for their strength, buoyancy, and resistance to decay. The craft, as large as fifty feet long and eight feet wide, could transport up to ten thousand pounds of cargo, such as fish, seal, and whale. Able to withstand the powerful ocean swells, they made it possible to travel up and down the coast, especially north to British Columbia to trade and visit with sister tribes.

In addition to their utility, the ocean canoes were works of art. What a sight they made, gliding into a harbor, manned by eight or more pullers with their paddles synchronized: colorful, finely crafted vessels with sweeping, graceful lines rising up to the decorative sterns and bows.

Yet events took their toll. Whaling declined. Overland routes were constructed to transport freight. The Bureau of Indian Affairs exerted pressure to jettison cultural ways. When Phillip Martin and Emmett Oliver had their discussion in the 1980s, a few Quinault river canoes could still be seen, but not the ocean canoes. Employed continuously for thousands of years, they had gone out of use by the 1940s.

Martin remembered the ocean vessels well. His uncle had taken him, just seven or eight then, out on the waters up and down the Olympic Peninsula in the family sealing canoe. He had seen many others, and the images stuck in his mind.

But he had no idea how to make one, nor did anyone else at Quinault, for none of the carvers was still alive. Along with fellow tribesmen Guy Capoeman and Shakey Jackson, Martin started going to museums to examine ocean canoes on exhibit, even to Ivar's Restaurant in Seattle, which has a fine specimen hung from the ceiling. Then he came across Steve Brown, a curator at the University of Washington's Burke Museum of Natural History and Culture. Brown, a non-Indian, had not only studied the ocean canoes of the Northwest tribes as an academic but actually learned how to carve them. And Brown gave generously of his time, traveling down to Taholah to pass on his knowledge about the intricate process of constructing ocean canoes in the traditional way.

Martin, Capoeman, Jackson, and other tribal members, calling themselves the Quinault Canoe Club, went to work. They found a downed seven-hundred-year-old cedar, split it, cut it into lengths, and let it dry. Intending to build two vessels, with much elbow grease they hollowed out two long sections, for each canoe was essentially one piece. They attached the stern and bow and seats for the pullers. Employing no nails, they instead pounded in fifty to sixty dowels per canoe. Finally, they carved designs into the canoes and painted them, with red the dominant color. Martin had not been counting, but when I asked him, he estimated that in total the labor required about two thousand man-hours.

By this time the Quinault had a clear objective: the Canoe Journey of 1994. Emmett Oliver, who had first presented the ocean canoe idea to Phillip Martin, had been busy with other tribes as well. As newly carved canoes were launched, Oliver and others decided to revive an ancient traditional practice, of having an annual gathering of all canoe tribes. This included the tribes of British Columbia because for millennia—long before any United States–Canada border line—Pacific coastal tribes had had extensive commercial, social, and family relationships. During the deadening years, though, the contacts waned, and did not rekindle until recent times, with tribal nationalism rising on both sides of the border. One part of that renewal took place in 1989: the reinitiation of the annual summer gathering, now called the Canoe Journey, of American and commonwealth canoes. Seattle hosted the event, and it was a wild success.

By 1994 the Quinault had two canoes ocean-ready, the *May-ee* (meaning "the new beginning") and *Tso-Kapoo* ("wolf coat"). That year the Canoe Journey would be held in Victoria, on Vancouver Island. They decided to paddle up on the *Tso-Kapoo*, 39 feet long with ten pullers and a captain, and a skiff that served as a supply boat.

"It was a bright, clear summer morning. Guy Capoeman was the captain, and I was handling the supply boat," remembers David Martin, Phillip Martin's son and former vice-president of the Quinault Indian Nation. "When we got past Queets, the weather kicked up on us. By the time we got to the mouth of the Hoh River, we were facing swells of probably four to six feet. We had to wait off the mouth of the Hoh to see if conditions would get better.

"They never did, so we decided to spend the night on the shore of the Hoh River. But the mouth of the Hoh is rocky, different than down here, different currents. We made one run but couldn't make it in. On the second try we got in trouble, got caught in a sleeper, got sideways.

"We had to abandon the canoe. We all had life jackets, and we all made it in except one, who got caught in a rip current and got knocked unconscious. When we got to him in the skiff, he had no energy to get in, but we pulled him up.

"When we got back to the shore, the canoe came back to the beach in pieces."

The people were distraught, some crying, some walking around retrieving paddles and pieces of the canoe, some just staring out at sea. Capoeman, the captain, was "devastated," carrying responsibility for the voyage, blaming himself, although the events were beyond his or anyone else's control. Finally, exhausted, they lay down on the beach, some people resting their heads on neighbors' backsides. Everyone went quiet, half asleep or contemplating the wreckage.

Then one of the pullers split the silence wide open. An athletic young woman named Phoebe Bryan, "one hundred pounds soaking wet," according to Phillip Martin, jumped to her feet and shouted, "Well! Are we going to go back and get that other canoe or what?"

Two days later the oceangoers headed out on another beautiful summer morning, this time aboard the slightly smaller *May-ee*, fitted out with eight pullers. They paddled up the western side of the Olympic Peninsula and turned east at Makah to the mouth of the Elwah. From there, they rode the "Canoe Trail," a current in the Strait of Juan de Fuca, well known to Indian people, that carries vessels over to the harbor at Sooke, near Victoria. On the way across they hit even worse weather, swells of six to eight feet.

But the *May-ee* made it. When the Quinault paddled into Victoria Harbor, an assemblage was there to welcome them. "What a scene!" exclaimed an excited Phillip Martin, by then in his sixties, as he witnessed a dream he had helped make come true. "There might have been three thousand people out on the docks, screaming and cheering, applauding, taking pictures as we came in. I mean it. What a scene!"

In 2002 the Quinault Indian Nation enthusiastically hosted the Canoe Journey, a three-day celebration with a potlatch, games, and dancing. By then the *Tso-Kapoo* had been put back together with dowels and made seaworthy, and a third ocean canoe was in the water. Carvers would soon be working on a fourth, named in honor of Phillip Martin. An estimated five thousand people from the United States and Canada came to Taholah that year to celebrate the canoes, the ocean, the salmon people. Natalie Charlie observed, "To see the canoes together asking for permission to come ashore in Taholah, it was like for the day time turned back. You were back to when our ancestors were inviting visitors to come eat and celebrate with us. It's really hard to describe that feeling."

And so yet another piece of the old fabric had been woven back together, different now but also the same.

An excerpt from *Blood Struggle—The Rise of Modern Indian Nations*
(W. W. Norton, paperback edition 2006)

Ugiuvak, named King Island, Alaska on western maps, is basically a 1,100-foot-tall basalt rock that juts up out of the Bering Sea. All around the island are steep, rocky cliffs with only a few visible places for paths from the sea to the top of the island. The village where the Ugiuvangmiut used to live was built on the least-steep slope, at an angle between 30 and 45 degrees to the sea. Deanna Kingston describes how her family and tribe used to hunt walrus from this island, and how walrus hunting has changed after their move to the mainland.

Walrus Hunting in a Changing Arctic

Deanna Kingston

My mother grew up on *Ugiuvak*, an island in the Bering Strait, approximately 85 miles northwest of Nome and 40 miles off the mainland Seward Peninsula. This place is called King Island on maps, a small dot right in the middle of the Strait. On August 26, 2004, I flew by helicopter to *Ugiuvak* for the first time; this was a kind of homecoming for me as well as for the two elders (Gabriel Muktoyuk and Agatha Kokuluk) who joined me and a few members of my research/logistics crew. As I searched ahead over the ocean to pick out the tiny island that many *Ugiuvangmiut* (King Islanders) refer to as "paradise," I was surprised to feel more than a little anxious. I had traveled from Oregon, where I am a professor in anthropology, using finely honed skills in communication—reading, writing, speaking, and transcribing words—but at that moment, flying towards the home of my *Ugiuvak* Inupiaq Eskimo ancestors, I felt woefully unprepared in the practical, hands-on knowledge I might need to explore the rugged terrain. I got the first hint of the island's challenges when someone strongly suggested I wear an immersion suit, to keep me alive for at least twenty minutes in the frigid Bering Sea in the event of a helicopter crash.

On that August day, I hiked down to the village from the island top with my maternal uncle, Gabriel Muktoyuk. After he showed me his home, other family members' houses, and the remains of the *qagrit* (semi-subterranean community houses), he decided it might be easier to hike back up by going to the east side of Kuuk, the creek located near the village. As I followed behind him, using basalt rocks as steps and handholds, I suddenly pulled a volleyball-sized rock loose. If I had not caught it, it would have landed right on my foot. After rearranging my feet on the rocks, I let the loose one go and it toppled down about fifteen to twenty feet, taking other small rocks and pebbles with it. Looking down the steep slope to the water below, I realized (with my heart racing) that I was way out of my league. My uncle confidently continued his hike up, but after catching my breath, I decided to leave the steep basalt steps, crossed the creek, and hiked up the steep grassy slope west of the creek. The differences between my uncle's skills and mine were readily apparent; he later told his daughter that I looked "nervous." No wonder many white sailors and explorers called *Ugiuvak* "desolate" and "forbidding." And yet, an average population of one hundred fifty people had lived on *Ugiuvak* for nine hundred years or more. Why? Because people had access to a great variety of food resources, which they stored in a cold storage cave, Qaitquq, located east of the village. In the origin story of *Ugiuvak*, a hunter caught a giant fish, which dragged the hunter out to sea for so long that the hunter fell asleep (Curtis 1970: 105; Ross 1958: 12; Rasmussen 1999:343-44). When he awoke, the fish had turned into the island of *Ugiuvak*. In some versions of the story, people decided to inhabit the island because of its plentiful food resources. Today, the *Ugiuvangmiut* told me, there were approximately fourteen species of edible plants (mostly greens); fourteen species of edible sea birds; king crabs; blue cod; sculpin;

ringed, ribbon, spotted, and bearded seals; polar bears; an occasional whale (beluga or bowhead); and finally, walrus.

Walrus. They were traditionally, and for elders, still are the mainstay of the *Ugiuvangmiut* diet. In the first half of the twentieth century, the annual harvest of walrus averaged around two hundred animals.[4] Shortly after killing walrus, hunters ate the heart, the liver, and raw and partially "cooked" clams from inside the walrus stomach. They took kidneys, "red meat," intestines, stomach, and flippers back to the village, and meat not eaten right away was taken to the cave. Tusks and hides provided other resources; they gave the *Ugiuvangmiut* a prominent economic position in the cross-Bering Strait trade network (cf. Kingston 2000). Walrus. One thousand or more pounds of sea mammal with one- to three-feet-long tusks that could puncture a boat.

Based upon previous ethnographies (e.g., Bogojavlensky 1969; Bogojavlensky and Fuller 1973; Ellanna 1981; Kaplan 1988), I knew intellectually that walrus were important to the *Ugiuvangmiut* and that they were skilled in the taking of walrus. However, my knowledge was gained from books, not through first-hand experience. Now, as I remember my nervous hike, I have gained some understanding of the knowledge, skills, and experiences that *Ugiuvangmiut* walrus hunters needed—knowledge not just of the animal itself, but also of the weather, wind, sea, and ice conditions.

In January and March 2004, a couple of months before the walrus-hunting season, three Oregon State University colleagues (an ecologist, a fisheries population modeler, and a graduate student) and I interviewed nineteen *Ugiuvangmiut* walrus hunters who now live in Nome or in Anchorage.[5] They told us that hunting walrus was dangerous. For instance, Mr. Six[6] reported that a swift current to the west of *Ugiuvak* once carried him and his crew away from the island, with no idea where they were because of heavy fog. They drifted north, no land in sight for thirty-six hours, with limited food and gas in their outboard-powered aluminum boat. A day and a half later when they saw Fairway Rock, near the Diomede Islands, they discovered they'd drifted 70 miles north. Even after drifting in the fog, Mr. Six continued to hunt. As several hunters reported, hunting on the sea was preferred over hunting on land—it was more "challenging." While contending with swift currents, heavy winds, fog, and changing ice conditions, they stalked a large, unpredictable animal. In the view of Mr. Four , "Where's the challenge in hunting an animal that stands there [on land] and looks at you?"

Younger hunters learn how to hunt by watching and observing the older men. It is often years before they are trusted enough to shoot any walrus themselves. In the past, what they observed was reinforced while listening to the older men as they repaired or made their hunting tools in the qagrit. Today, hunters still learn from example. One purpose of this essay is to highlight the hunters' traditional knowledge of walrus hunting near *Ugiuvak*, to discuss why they persist in hunting today, even in the face of great sociopolitical and environmental changes that confront them, and to highlight the importance that *Ugiuvak* still plays in hunting.

The Hunt

Traditionally, the *Ugiuvangmiut* hunted Pacific walrus in cooperative *umiaq* (large skinboat) crews (cf., Bogojavlensky 1969; Bogojavlensky and Fuller 1973). A captain and his close relatives such as brothers, sons, fathers, or brothers-in-law made up a skinboat crew. The captain maintained the boat and hunting implements, and supplied the crew with food and clothing (Bogojavlensky 1969:108-57). Other crew members had specific duties; at least one man was always designated the harpooner. In the first half of the twentieth century, there were two to three skinboat crews, with a total of about thirty hunters.

Annual spring ice break-up is when walrus migrate through Bering Strait— time for the main, and usually only, hunt. First come the females and their pups, accompanied by a few bull "harem" walrus. Females are easier to hunt and less aggressive. The bull walrus and male "teenagers" follow later. Both young bull and "rogue" walrus (loners who do not live with the herd) are more aggressive; they are avoided in the hunt because they will attack hunters in their boats. Hunters can spot rogue walrus because of their discolored tusks, caused by eating seals (instead of the usual clams) whose blubber has a yellowish tint.

Hunters today still prefer to hunt in spring near *Ugiuvak*, where the walrus literally float by on ice floes going north through Bering Strait. Walrus are notoriously aggressive, but even male walrus in the spring are less aggressive as they float on the ice sunning themselves. Earl Mayac said "Walrus are more lazy in spring, laze around in the sun." According to Gabriel Muktoyuk, my maternal uncle, "Walrus are spooky in the fall time, not like spring when they are sunbathing and don't hardly pay any attention to the hunters."

Because currents to the west and north of the island are very swift and can carry a boat away quicker than men could paddle against it, hunters have always preferred to go south and east of the island. Taking advantage of currents that run counter-clockwise in this area, hunters killed and butchered walrus on ice floes south and east of the island, which then drifted back toward the island. Essentially they cut the distance from killing sites to their homes.

To find these ice floes and the walrus, hunters went to the top of the island where they located open leads in the ice, usually within 10 miles of the island. They searched for a reddish or brownish hue, which indicated reflection of walrus skin on the ice. Hunters also made use of how sound travels great distances across water by listening for walrus several miles away. When a herd of walrus was located, the hunters made their decision about whether or not to approach the herd. Mr. Seventeen reported that hunting crews will avoid really large herds that have thousands of animals because it would be dangerous when the walrus rush off the ice after shots are fired. Sometimes a herd might be too small to hunt (approximately ten animals or so), in part because the ice floe is too small for both the crew and the animals, and also because the hunters cannot get many walrus at once. Generally, they like to approach herds with fifty to one hundred animals, as the walrus are more complacent and the ice more sturdy, and hunters can maximize the number of walrus they can take.

Hunters respect walrus as smart animals. Because walrus hear and smell very well but have poor eyesight, walrus herds are approached from downwind so they cannot smell the hunters. Since sound carries well in the air, even further on and in the water, boat motors are turned off several miles away. A strict code of silence is imposed; *Ugiuvangmiut* walrus hunters communicate by sign language. According to Vince Pikonganna, hunters "didn't play around or joke around or waste time to chit-chat . . . They did it [hunted] very silently, respectfully . . . they didn't show any disrespect towards that animal. They . . . would treat it like another human."

The best place to shoot a walrus is on the neck, just below the skull.[7] The bullet cannot penetrate the skull because of its thickness. To avoid ruining the tusks, hunters avoid shooting the walrus's face. Once a walrus is killed, men butcher the walrus, first working on the head and tusks, then moving to other parts of the body—the heart, liver, kidneys, red meat, intestines, stomach, and flippers. Young hunters provide manual labor for butchering and hauling meat and paddling the boat. The men learn certain tricks in butchering a walrus, such as how to extract the tusks from the skull. Mr. Six described how he first opened up the skull, then used an axe to separate and extract the tusks. Older hunters instruct younger hunters to study walrus bones to locate joints for butchering on the ice. A young man just learning to hunt is encouraged to kill an orphaned pup of a female that has already been killed by a more experienced hunter. Young hunters learn technical skills during this relatively easy hunt. To reinforce the value of cooperation and community connections they are taught to share the entire animal with an elder.

Up until the 1960s, the meat was loaded onto walrus-hide skinboats, preferred over aluminum boats because they were quieter, more flexible, lightweight, and could haul a lot of meat.[8] After the hunt, meat and ivory are shared amongst crew members, who distribute the meat to their families when they return home. Female walrus are preferred for food because the meat is more tender and requires less cooking time. I remember eating walrus "milk" at my elder auntie Helen Pushruk's house. Walrus "milk" is the meat taken from the breast of the walrus, which *Ugiuvangmiut* usually prepare by boiling, like they do most of the meat that they eat. As it is cooking, walrus meat has a very strong smell; however, I enjoyed walrus "milk" because it was tender and almost melted in my mouth. Males are about twice the size of females, with larger and longer tusks, but tusks from both males and females are used for carving. In the past, skins of female walrus were desired for making skinboat covers because male skins had holes and battle scars caused by fighting with other males.

Ugiuvak

My description is just a short and undoubtedly incomplete synopsis of the knowledge carried by walrus hunters. For this essay, I term their knowledge a "knowledge of place," which includes not just knowledge of the island, but also of the sea, ice, wind, and weather, and their interactions. Because neither I nor any of my colleagues actually went to *Ugiuvak* to interview these hunters since they now live on mainland Alaska (my visit to *Ugiuvak* took place later), our recordings lack a good portion of this "knowledge of place." In particular, we did not ask: "What does a hunter do when the wind changes direction?" "How do you respond when a walrus attacks you?" "What if the current changes direction?" "What if a fog comes up?" In other words, we did not record all the contingency plans that are needed in this place with highly variable and quickly changing conditions. But, after my only visit to *Ugiuvak*, I realize that it is this very intimate knowledge of place that gives these hunters the confidence to brave the sea and its moods in order to successfully and safely hunt walrus and to bring the meat and ivory home.

Sociopolitical and environmental changes in the second half of the twentieth century resulted in substantially fewer walrus harvested by the *Ugiuvangmiut*, so much so that the *Ugiuvangmiut* are no longer the recognized walrus experts they once were within the region. They moved to the Alaskan mainland, primarily forced by government policy, but some by choice, and the island became deserted. Government policies to draft *Ugiuvangmiut* men for military service during World War II, to stop the spread of tuberculosis by the Public Health Service, to respond to the Indian Relocation Act, and to require all children attend school (including Alaska Native children), all pressured the *Ugiuvangmiut* to move. Individual women often elected to winter in Nome, where they had better access to medical care, to give birth to their babies. When the school population on the island declined, the Bureau of Indian Affairs (BIA) closed its school (which went to the eighth grade) on *Ugiuvak* in 1959,[9] forcing *Ugiuvangmiut* families to move to Nome so their children could attend school. Beginning in the 1950s, *Ugiuvangmiut* students were encouraged to complete a high school education, but the only BIA-run high schools were far away, at Mt. Edgecumbe in Southeast Alaska, Seattle, or Chemawa Indian School in Salem, Oregon. Relocation to the mainland has severely affected their ability to hunt walrus.

No one lives on *Ugiuvak* any more. The last families moved off in 1966. Most went to Nome, but Nome, on the south side of the Seward Peninsula where land-fast ice often extends out 20 miles, is not an ideal place for walrus hunting. Open ice leads are more difficult to find. For a time, hunters traveled to Anvil Mountain (10 miles north of Nome) to find them; now they use satellite imagery accessed via the Internet. To hunt walrus, hunters must travel another 50 or more miles, compared to the 10 miles or less from *Ugiuvak*. Their aluminum boats are faster than skinboats, but they're smaller, less flexible, less easy to patch in case of a walrus attack, and noisier. They must carry enough gas to bring them back home, enough in case of an accident or if the current drifts them away from the mainland; that means there is less room for hauling back meat and ivory, and less room for hunters. Compared to the nine or ten men on the old skinboats, there are only five men on hunting crews today. For the cash required to purchase aluminum boats and gas, hunters need either wage employment or sales from ivory carving. The numbers of hunters today are similar to the past—I estimated that there are at least twenty-five to thirty active walrus hunters today, in about five or six active boats. But modern walrus hunting takes more time and effort in addition to cash. Not everyone hunts every year, but a couple of crews still make the attempt by finding open ice leads south of Nome in the Norton Sound or by driving to Cape Woolley and then taking their boats forty miles west to *Ugiuvak.*

The *Ugiuvangmiut* have endured in part by adapting to modern limitations. Because they cannot carry as much meat in the smaller aluminum boats, they kill only forty walrus in a hunting season rather than the two hundred walrus the hunting crews harvested in the past. Ivory is still in high demand, but boat size restricts how much ivory can be carried. Before, walrus skins were needed for the skinboats, but since they no longer use skinboats, they don't need as many walrus skins. Many hunters told us every part of the animal is used when a walrus is killed, and they complained about men they call "head-hunters," people from other communities who only take the tusks after killing walrus, violating a cardinal hunting rule. These hunters would be banned from hunting all together among the *Ugiuvangmiut,* who choose to limit their take to forty whole animals as part of their respect for walrus.

Climate change also affects hunting: the Arctic is warming at a faster rate than in lower latitudes (Arctic Climate Impact Assessment 2004). Ice forms later in the winter, which means that it is thinner and melts earlier in the springtime. During our interviews, Mr. Four explained, "I don't think [the ice] is that thick 'cause we had a late freeze-up this year (winter 2003-04). So, the ice will take off fast. [We'll] have to chase the ice from here if we leave from here [Cape Woolley], which depends on how good the road conditions are this spring and how fast you can get your boat to camp." As the ice goes out earlier and melts faster, the time to hunt walrus has decreased from four weeks (as it was in the past) to about two weeks in recent years. If the hunters are not ready to go out the minute the ice breaks, they often miss hunting any walrus at all. There have been recent years when the total number of walrus taken by *Ugiuvangmiut* hunters was zero.

No doubt, hunting has declined overall, but the *Ugiuvangmiut* continue to hunt walrus, because *Ugiuvangmiut* elders still prefer walrus and other sea-mammal meat to other meats they can get on the mainland. As Mr. Seventeen reported, "I made a lot of . . . old ladies happy when I brought them walrus meat." Mr. Four concurred: "You can't live without it. I mean, some people can't live without it [walrus meat]."

Since the turn of the twentieth century, the *Ugiuvangmiut* have been among the best of the ivory carvers (Ray 1980). Today, that tradition continues; most *Ugiuvangmiut* men either carve for a living or supplement their wages with sales from ivory carvings. Many of the carvings sold in Nome and Anchorage are produced by *Ugiuvangmiut* carvers. Each is known for a particular style of carving: Teddy Mayac Sr. carves birds, Earl Mayac often carves shamanistic or half-man/half-animal figures; Tommy Tiulana often carves Wolf Dancers; and others carve polar bears or seals.

Although the total number of hunters today is the same as it was in the past (thirty or so), the percentage of walrus hunters has dramatically decreased, from about 100 percent of the able-bodied males to about 10-25 percent.[10] Much of this decline can be attributed to the loss of place, caused by the total relocation of the *Ugiuvangmiut* to the mainland. However, the importance of walrus hunting has not decreased. Boat crews still recruit younger hunters; the youngest walrus hunter is about twenty years old as of this writing. The hunters overwhelmingly prefer to hunt from *Ugiuvak* because it is easier; they often go to great lengths to get to *Ugiuvak*, the island, to hunt, only resorting to hunting from Nome if the road and weather conditions preclude their travel. They continue to hunt at great economic cost, under arduous and dangerous arctic conditions, and they maintain traditional networks of sharing the meat and ivory from the hunt in the community.

In preparation for the 2006 fieldwork in the NSF project (which started in 2004 with the reconnaissance visit and continued with actual fieldwork in 2005 and 2006) mentioned in note 1, it was necessary to hire several King Island men to reconstruct the historic stairways in the village. During the negotiations for this work, stair crew supervisor Jimmy Carlisle made it absolutely clear to us that if walrus were sighted en route to the island, hunting took priority over their commitment to this project, because the men needed ivory for carving and the elders wanted walrus meat. About June 12 or 13, 2006, with a research group of twenty-seven community members, scientists, and logistics personnel on *Ugiuvak* to map place names, one walrus hunting crew (composed of Wilfred Anowlic, Hubert Kokuluk, Eddie Muktoyuk, Jr., and John Kokuluk) arrived on the island after killing eight walrus. The hunters butchered them and distributed some of the meat to the research group, particularly to the elders that were present. A couple of days later, this crew returned to Nome, killing two more walrus along the way. Again, meat was distributed to elders (particularly widowed women) in Nome. Walrus continues to sustain our community.

Acknowledgements

The author would like to thank all of the walrus hunters who agreed to give interviews to our project team, and also to those hunters who did not want to give interviews for various reasons. I want them to know that I respect their choices and also to thank them for helping to preserve and practice their hunting knowledge. I also want to thank the rest of the research team— Jesse Ford, Selina Heppell, and Jessica Cardinal. Finally, for supporting this research, much appreciation goes to the Pacific Walrus Conservation Fund and the National Science Foundation Arctic Social Sciences Program, particularly Anna Kerttula de Echave.

References

Arctic Climate Impact Assessment (ACIA). 2004. *Impacts of a Warming Arctic: Arctic Climate Impact Assessment.* Cambridge, England: Cambridge University Press.

Bogojavlensky, Sergei. 1969. Imaangmiut Eskimo Careers: Skinboats in Bering Strait. Ph.D. dissertation, Harvard University.

———, and Robert W. Fuller. 1973. "Polar Bears, Walrus Hides, and Social Solidarity." *Alaska Journal* 3(2):66-76.

Braem, Nicole M. 2004. Leaving King Island: The Closure of a Bureau of Indian Affairs School and Its Consequences. MA thesis, University of Alaska Fairbanks.

Curtis, Edward S. 1970 [1930]. *The North American Indian: Being a Series of Volumes Picturing and Describing the Indians of the United States and Alaska.* Frederick W. Hodge, ed., 20 vols. New York: Johnson Reprint.

Department of Commerce, State of Alaska. n.d. King Island. Alaska Community Database Community Information Summaries. State of Alaska Department of Commerce, Community and Economic Development. http://www.dced.state. ak.us.dca/commdb/CF_CIS.htm (accessed December 5, 2005).

Ellanna, Linda. 1981. "Ukiuvungmiut: Cliff Dwellers of the Bering Strait." *Alaska Fish Tale & Game Trails* XIII(3):2-4; 44.

Kaplan, Lawrence D. (ed.). 1988. *Ugiuvangmiut Quliapyuit: King Island Tales, Eskimo History and Legends from Bering Strait.* Fairbanks: University of Alaska Press.

Kingston, Deanna M. 1999. Returning: Twentieth Century Performances of the King Island Wolf Dance. Ph.D. dissertation, University of Alaska Fairbanks.

———. 2000. "Siberian Songs and Siberian Kin: Indirect Assertions of King Island Dominance in the Bering Strait Region." *Arctic Anthropology* 37(2):38-51.

Rasmussen, Knud. 1999 [1927]. *Across Arctic America: Narrative of the Fifth Thule Expedition.* Fairbanks: University of Alaska Press.

Ray, Dorothy Jean. 1980 [1961]. *Artists of the Tundra and the Sea.* Seattle and London: University of Washington Press.

Ross, Frances Anna. 1958. The Eskimo Community House. M.A. thesis, Stanford University.

Prince of Wales Island is the third-largest island in the United States; little islands, coves, and inlets edge its 900-mile coastline, providing habitat for northern sea otter. Its climate is more mild than that of other parts of Alaska, but it receives almost 92 inches of precipitation per year. This is ancestral home to Dolly Garza and other members of the Haida and Tlingit. Russians began hunting otter along the Alaskan coast more than 250 years ago, and eventually set their North American base of operations northwest of the island, in Sitka. After more than 150 years of multinational hunting, sea otters were decimated and have been protected from hunting until recent years. Garza's essay describes how her family, with other Haida and Tlingit Tribal members, combine tradition, conservation ethics, and modern technology to manage and monitor sea otter in these waters.

Comanaging Sea Otter:
A Model of Modern Alaska Native Stewardship
Dolly Garza

Introduction

My uncles Pat and George, both living in Craig, Alaska, are modern stewards of sea otter. Instead of hunting the otters with a traditional bow and arrow or a 222 rifle, they are equipped with survey forms and global positioning system units. We are members of the Haida and Tlingit Tribes in Southeast Alaska.

Early each spring Pat and George spend about a week to get their boat ready to conduct sea otter surveys in the Craig and Klawock Tribal territories on the west coast of Alaska's Prince of Wales Island. They check the boat engine and all the gear to ensure they are in good working order after a cold winter. They change the old oil, and test the lines for suppleness. Batteries are checked on the global positioning system (GPS), the hand-held radio, and on the outboard. They arrange to meet with the other two captains, Mike and John. John is the younger captain, and employed as the Tribal Environmental Coordinator at Craig Community Association.

The team gathers at the Tribal office where they receive waterproof survey forms, binoculars, and personal flotation devices. John serves as on-site coordinator, while I provide oversight. We debrief from last year's survey, reviewing transect layouts and otter counts. Where did they see the most otters? Now that we have surveyed for several years, are there transects that reveal no otters in the area? Does it look like otters are moving into new areas, requiring new transects be set up? They discuss plans for this field season. How long will the survey take this year? Does the weather look good for the next couple of weeks? Will they have the same crew members or will they need to train new ones?

These three captains, Pat, Mike, and John, have performed this survey for several years, and they are committed to it for many more. The entire survey requires that each boat commit four to five days, over the course of several weeks. Effective sea otter counting requires surveying only on calmer days, which can be rare in Southeast outer coastal waters. To commit to these surveys, these men are giving up time to fish commercially, hunt for seals, or work on the house in good weather. All are volunteers, and the small honorarium they receive does not compare to wages. Each of the three boats should have a team of three, but crew members tend to change over time. It is a volunteer job and sometimes money to pay bills and provide for family needs overshadows tribal obligations.

Pat, Mike, and John were all born to this island and know their culture and their obligation. As Haida and Tlingit Indians, the Craig-Klawock area is their tribal territory. They grew up listening to tribal and family stories about their island, know where their family set up spring seaweed and fish camps. The older captains, Pat and Mike, know where the important village and camp sites are, and where their ancestors are buried. If you befriend one, they might, over time, take you to where there are petroglyphs or ancient fish traps. These sites are held as common knowledge amongst the old-timers, but they are protected by silence from grave-robbers or photographers who want to make money by taking photos of sacred sites. Both men have fished commercially for decades and gathered local foods to feed their immediate and extended families for decades. They know the west coast of Prince of Wales like the back of their hands. They are perfect leaders for the sea otter survey project. Uncle George is Uncle Pat's right-hand man; having spent as much time on these waters, he is a natural for the job.

John, the younger captain, has learned from his family but through this survey process he is also learning from the older captains. He learns about safe passages during southeast or northerly winds, and where to be wary of submerged rocks at minus tides. There are also lessons about cultural history, and locations of traditional campgrounds. It is an experiential process. He absorbs apparent lessons; other knowledge he will appreciate some time in the future, when he will look back and be grateful for this opportunity.

Southeast Culture

Haida and Tlingit villages were carefully sited to take advantage of regional resources, and a community's size depended on the harvestable surplus from local resources. The villages were generally dominated by one main clan who accepted a main chief as the head of the village. As a village grew beyond a sustainable level, a clan split, and a fraction moved to seek new territories with accessible and unused resources. Through this process the Haida and Tlingit settled primarily along or near all rivers and streams, where plentiful salmon provided the main food staple. Salmon, seal, sea otter, sea lion, halibut, cods, hooligans, clams, cockles, abalone, black seaweed, and ribbon seaweed were critical to the ancient ones for survival and are as important to contemporary Natives for "cultural survival." Both traditional and contemporary Haida and Tlingit depend on the ocean for food, clothing, culture, and travel. Craig is eight miles south of Klawock, and over time both communities are home to both Tlingit and Haida; their territories informally overlap.

Under the Haida clan system there are two over-arching moieties: Eagle and Raven, and below each moiety are clan and house crests. The Haida and Tlingit are matrilineal people: the children follow their mother's crests and belong to her people. My Haida mother is Sgaaláns with the Eagle moiety and frog and sculpin crests. My Tlingit father's clan are the Tinedi with the Raven moiety and dog salmon crest. Clan crests are held in high regard and are often an important part of clan history, alluding to clan survival or dependence on an animal or animal's spirit. Frog may have brought the people to fresh water, or dog salmon may have sacrificed himself to feed a hungry village. When these crests are taken, it is out of respect and may extend to ceremony.

Ceremony

Once a community was established, its survival depended on the proper use and conservation of local resources. Conservation ethics were embedded in daily life skills as well as in legend and cultural practices. Resources were monitored where possible to determine if the returns of salmon were good, if the bushes were loaded with berries, if the fawns were healthy in the fall. Harvests were also monitored and controlled to ensure continued return of resources. Rituals and customs, such as the salmon blessing ceremony, which gives thanks to the first returning salmon, served dual purposes.

When salmon were first spotted going up stream a Haida or Tlingit community began preparations for the first salmon ceremony. No salmon were taken while the community prepared for and conducted the blessing. The salmon were thanked for giving themselves to the people. During the time it took to prepare for and conduct the ceremony, plenty of salmon continued their upriver journey to spawn and provide future generations. Today fishery departments protect the salmon when they first enter a river. They also ensure enough salmon enter the river to spawn and maintain future generations. Both processes allow for salmon escapement upriver, the Natives through respect and ceremony, the government through regulation.

Alaska Natives held ceremonies and exercised taboos to respect and celebrate their many natural resources. Though some of the traditional ceremonies are no longer performed at Native communities, Native people still show their respect with a prayer, a song, or a thank you. Cedar woman is thanked for giving a portion of her skirt to Haida weavers, who will make beautiful baskets and hats. As ceremony and dance are being revived around the Southeast, traditional honor songs are slowly coming back.

Marine mammals are held in high regard by all coastal cultures. A young man's first hunt is still ceremoniously shared. The seal is often given to aunties, uncles, grammas, and grandpas of the clan. A sea lion or whale may be shared more formally with the entire community. The Alutiiq, who live further north in the Kodiak region, traditionally honored the sea otter with beautiful hunting gear and equipment that they believed would attract the sea otter people to them.

Conservation

Each community or culture collectively realized that a season without salmon or seal could make the winter season lean, or in some cases disastrous. While ceremony and taboo interested the early anthropologists, they often failed to see the embedded knowledge base or conservation ethic. The salmon ceremony, that is only a ceremony to the unknowing, embeds conservation simply through the harvest ban during the ceremony. Escapement was ensured as long as the ceremony commenced.

If a young person grows up being taught to respect animals and plants, she will always show respect for them. He will always take only enough deer to feed the family and provide for the Elders. They will keep watch over salmon streams, berry patches, and seal rookeries. Over their lifetime they will hone their conservation ethics and practices. They will become well studied in the fields of ecology, anatomy, botany, ecosystem dynamics, and over time they will understand long-term fluctuations or "decadal oscillations."

Native Alaskans hold a wealth of Traditional Ecological Knowledge (TEK) that encompasses their generational and cultural environmental knowledge. State and federal scientists have other perspectives. A regional biologist has a large area to monitor and may spend only one to two months each year in any management unit, and was probably trained outside of Alaska. Federal biologists often come into an area, learn about the region; then in five years, they are transferred out as a promotion. "Ecological history" is held not by the agencies, but by the community members who are born, raised, and intend to die in their home areas. The community sustains decadal knowledge of its area.

Contemporary Respect

Native hunters, throughout the eleven distinct cultures around Alaska, still take their stewardship obligation seriously. They look over the land and waters wondering what it will be like for their grandchildren. This inherited stewardship is unique to indigenous peoples who are born on the land where their ancestors are buried, where their people originated thanks to Raven. As a culture they have no choice but to stay and tend the land, to respectfully use and protect the resources. Many non-Natives clearly have strong stewardship and conservation ethics, but to them it is not a birth obligation. Local fishermen care passionately about the health of the stock, as it affects their future profits. Many care deeply for the environment and wonder what will be available for their sons and daughters. Yet even deeply committed family fishermen can pack up and move to urban areas where their children have better educational opportunities. Their time in Alaska becomes a youthful adventure, a fond memory.

Alaska Natives are born with the inherent responsibility to protect Tribal territories and resources. It is true that many young Natives do leave and wander the world. Many go off to college, or seek a better life. Yet even those who move away feel the tug of their ancestral home. College students who leave are ready to get out and explore the real world, but cannot make it without their own Indian food, canned fish, venison, freezer boxes of berries and greens. While the "outside world" is new and exciting, it is not home. They know they will end up in their Alaskan home, buried next to their grandfathers.

Contemporary Management

Alaska has state and federal resource management, in a land where natural resources are for the most part fully allocated. Resource boards, such as the Alaska Board of Fisheries, often deal with reallocating resources among user groups based on economic opportunity or benefit. Hypothetically fish and game management is based on recommendations from trained biologists who recommend harvest levels that will ensure conservation of the stock. Managers estimate changes in stock abundance to determine how much can be taken by fishermen, although commercial fishermen often want more. The final decisions are part biological and part political. In this political/policy arena, economics generally rules in decision making. To "maximize benefits," resources are often allocated to those who will receive the greatest return from their use—the commercial fishermen. Another benefit is measured by how much a person will pay to fish, buy gear, and seek accommodations in tourist-related businesses like the fish charter business. These priorities do not protect cultural values or community independence. Native and non-Native communities continue an ongoing fight to protect their ways of life. Because there is no easy way to compare economic benefits with cultural and spiritual values, subsistence and cultural values are often ignored when resources are reallocated. It seems that when Alaska Natives and rural residents use money and labor efficiently, their efforts are not recognized in economic models, and their opportunities are cut back.

Specialized disciplines in science separate the natural world into separate parts, but ecosystem management requires knowledge of entire ecosystems and interconnected relationships over a long time. Baseline data for future comparisons are needed for long-term management, but those studies are rarely funded. As research and management funding is shrinking, so is management's ability to accurately, or closely, estimate stock size. Comanagement between Tribes and governmental agencies offers one solution. Teams like the sea otter monitoring crew combine traditional knowledge and Native conservation ethics with modern technology, to provide critical ongoing, long-term data.

My uncles' sea otter monitoring team is a comanagement project of The Alaska Sea Otter and Steller Sea Lion Commission (TASSC) and the U.S. Fish and Wildlife Service. It fulfills one of the mandates designated in the Marine Mammal Protection Act (MMPA), which specifically provides for comanagement between the U.S. Fish and Wildlife Service, the National Marine Fisheries Service, and Tribal bodies.[1] These funds support the Tribes as they collect data, monitor the health and abundance of marine mammals, monitor population trends, develop cottage industries based on marine mammal parts, or establish local management plans. In addition to sea otter, polar bear are comanaged by the U. S. Fish and Wildlife Service with The Nanook Commission; walrus are managed jointly by U. S. Fish and Wildlife Service and the Eskimo Walrus Commission. These three Tribal commissions represent the interests of Tribal members as they work with the federal agencies.

Besides the small-boat surveys like the ones Pat and John conduct, TASSC trains local Natives to collect tissue samples for sea otter necropsies, and to monitor the health and general condition of sea otters. They train locals to conduct beach-cast surveys to compare natural sea otter mortalities to incidences of high mortality. Based on sightings from boaters, hunters, fishers, and beachcombers, Local Knowledge Surveys estimate the general abundance and expansion of sea otters in southeast Alaska waters. As part of my job I helped The Sitka Sea Otter Commission create one of the first local sea otter management plans for its marine territorial boundaries, a plan that provides for sea otter conservation while protecting important subsistence shellfish beds and ensuring Native hunting rights. Tribal members volunteer time to serve on this commission, taking time away from their jobs, their art, and their family to help formulate policy. Though individually they may or may not have a direct link to sea otter, Natives step forward to meet their tribal obligation.

Tlingit craftsman Boyd makes part of his income from making sea otter arts and crafts that he sells at his art gallery. He knows his people have always held the sea otter in high regard. The fur is one of the warmest in the world, and sea otter blankets were traditionally used for warmth in a 40-foot long clan house that was heated by a single fire in the center pit. Early explorers drew sketches of Chiefs draped in sea otter robes, which were considered a sign of wealth and prestige. Though the population of sea otters has been increasing at 15 percent per year, Boyd has been personally threatened by environmentalists who fundamentally believe no one should hunt sea otter.

As the sea otter populations explode, sea otters continue to expand their range. In twenty-five years the Southeast populations have increased from just a couple hundred planted in the late 1960s to well over six thousand (TASSC, Southeast Alaska Sea Otter Management Plan). The expanding population depends on new sources of clams, crab, sea urchin, abalone, and other invertebrates for food. Large densities of these shellfish provide massive food supplies to feed expanding sea otter groups. Exact population numbers are difficult to estimate. Region-wide surveys by air or boat are very expensive and not conducted on a systematic basis. The small-boat Tribal surveys are important to the federal managers to keep a general handle on large-scale changes in sea otter numbers or movements into new areas.

Other Sitka Sea Otter commissioners, like Reggie, may be more interested in protecting a favorite cockle or clam shellfish bed. As the sea otter populations expand they are getting closer to his traditional food source. Once they reach his clam bed, it will be all over for subsistence harvests. Sea otters will wipe out the entire beach in one winter, then move on to another. Commissioners review sea otter numbers, monitor important subsistence shellfish beds, hear from Tribal members and other interested members of the public, and note changes in seaweed canopies. This ecosystem was substantially over-harvested by early sea otter traders who nearly decimated otter populations, but the otters have recovered following transplants in the 1960s (U.S. Fish & Wildlife Service, Marine Mammal Management Office, various reports). Tribal management is ecosystem-based, and can provide a balance between otters and humans, managing for a stable otter population and providing for harvests and economic opportunities. In comparison, the MMPA is a prohibitive act that does not allow for balancing population growth with other uses or impacts on the environment.

Bringing Stewardship Forward

Alaska Natives were the original stewards to Alaska and they have not relinquished this obligation. Like the Craig sea otter survey crews, Natives will continue to honor their stewardship obligation. Tribes have found new ways to meet this obligation by incorporating traditional practices in research and monitoring programs. Tribal members have been eager to be invited, finally, to work with federal agencies in these comanagement projects.

South of the Sitka Tribe territory, the Craig captains, Pat, Mike, and John, finish gearing up their boats. The three teams decide where each boat will go along the west coast of Prince of Wales Island.

Mike wants to get on with his survey and return to commercial fishing, so he will begin his survey immediately, based on a forecast of good weather. He rises at 5 a.m., checks the marine weather forecast, and the weather from his living-room window. It looks to be a calm day so he wakes his son Raymond and calls his son's friend Scott. They will be ready to leave the dock by 6:00.

The three crews have been trained to conduct the small-boat surveys by TASSC staff, using a survey developed by the U.S. Fish and Wildlife Service. Each participant must use the same protocol for running their boat and entering data. The data belong to the Tribe and will be used to monitor their local sea otter stock. Since other Tribes are using the same protocols, the Fish and Wildlife Service can compare changes in sea otter abundance and distribution from one region to another and over time.

After a half-hour run, Mike's crew idles the skiff down and gets out their gear: binoculars, write-in-rain survey forms, and pencils. Mike marks the spot with the GPS; the first transect begins at 6:30 a.m. Immediately they run into otters. The skiff runs slowly, parallel to the group, about 150 feet from shore, on the outside edge of kelp beds. At 6:50 a.m. they stop the skiff, note their position, and tally their count. Scott counts seventeen otters on the shore side, while Raymond has counted none. Since there will likely be fewer otters on the outside, Raymond fills out the survey form after each twenty-minute transect. As captain, Mike runs the skiff and keeps watch for rocks or unexpected kelp patches, making sure they stick to the twenty-minute survey intervals.

On these trips Raymond and Scott continue learning cultural and natural history from Mike, carrying on an age-old learning process. Mike works to ensure both boys understand respect for these valuable resources. They combine traditional knowledge and practices with new methods of using local knowledge as part of the statewide survey. Their knowledge as local boaters, hunters, and fishermen qualify them to participate in such surveys. For their help, Raymond and Scott receive honoraria that will go into their college funds. My role in this process is purely administrative: I ensure that they stick to transects, use the forms, conduct the survey using proper methodology, and collect their data for the final report. This is necessary to the grant and the value of the data in the future. I must rely on captains Pat, Mike, and John to know where the sea otters are, and to help set up the transects. Given their experience of the water and knowledge of the area, as well as their commitment to protecting their Tribal territories, I know they will conduct safe and high-quality surveys; another year of otter data is secure.

References

The Alaska Sea Otter and Steller Sea Lion Commission (TASSC). 1994. Overview of Programs—February 2004. Anchorage, AK. www.seaotter-sealion.org
U.S. Fish and Wildlife Service, Alaska Marine Mammal Management Office. http:// alaska.fws.gov/fisheries/mmm/

The Siletz tribe fished and hunted in marine and fresh waters along the central Oregon coast. David Hatch shares childhood memories about his family in the central coastal town of Florence, during a time when his tribe lost their reservation lands. In 1977 the official status of the Confederated Tribes of Siletz was restored by the federal government and a portion of their reservation lands was returned to them.

Resolution

David R. Hatch

Whereas, the Siletz Tribal Council is empowered to act upon behalf of the Confederated Tribes of Siletz Indians of Oregon by virtue of its powers set forth in . . . the Constitution adopted by the Tribe on June 2, 1979 . . . and,

I grew up an enrolled member of a tribe that did not exist. I was a year old when recognition of all western Oregon tribes was formally withdrawn by President Eisenhower and a Republican-controlled House and Senate. My little brother and sister could not enroll in our nonexistent tribe.

Whereas, the basis for our economic and social life was the wealth of fish that entered our coastal streams, rivers, and bays providing a principal supply of foods which were shared by all and,

We were good little fishermen. We caught buckets of bullheads from the little boathouse my Grandpa built at the mouth of the North Fork of the Siuslaw. When we had enough bullhead to bait six rings for a day, Grandpa would take us crabbing down by the jetty.

Whereas, our original fish weir sites in the bays and rivers of Oregon were used to harvest the once abundant anchovy, sucker, halibut, white sturgeon, green sturgeon, four types of perch, two type of herring, tomcod, candle fish (ooligan), topsmelt, surf smelt, longfin smelt, two type sardines, starry flounder, chub, blue eels, brown eels, hake, Chinook salmon, coho salmon, chum salmon, steelhead, and trout and the devastation of these fisheries coincided with the degradation of our near-shore habitats and,

On every seven-mile run from Grandpa's boathouse down to the ocean and back, Grandpa told us about the big flounders he used to catch here and the perch he used to catch there. My Dad's story of finding the big skate, rarely seen in tidepools, was my favorite. Dad and Grandpa came back on the next low tide and so did the skate. It did not make good crab bait. My Great-grandpa, Ike Martin, might have been the one who repaired the ancient weir near the boathouse with milled lumber. Ike and my Great-grandma died when my Grandma was eleven. Grandma was the sole survivor of her family. She was shipped to Chemawa Indian School in Salem, where she met an Aleut orphan, my Grandpa.

Whereas, the sea otter is the second most common marine mammal bone found in our middens and the degradation of our near-shore habitats coincided with the extermination of the sea otter and,

In the time called "pre-contact," our fish weirs brought us more than we needed. Every tide released the extra and returned with more. Seals or sea lions are the most common marine mammal bone in our middens depending on where you are on the coast. Only our head men wore robes of sea otter skins so they were never over-hunted. "Managing" the seals, sea lions, and sea otter provided for the abundance we depended on. For thousands of years we practiced what we now call "ecosystem-based management."

Whereas, restoring the estuary and near-shore habitats will provide for the restoration of our traditional fisheries and fisheries which will benefit all Oregonians and,

Dad and his siblings were raised on the allotted land in Florence that Grandma inherited from her father, Ike. In Ike's time individual tribal members had to accept an allotment and give up their 1.1-million-acre Coast Reservation. In high school history class Dad was "taught" Oregon Indians were representatives of "various stages of savage and barbarian culture." In small-town Florence, the family's best bet was to try to blend in. It wasn't a good time to tell the newcomers that the estuaries were changing.

Whereas, the state of Oregon's Statewide Planning Goal 19 is to "conserve marine resources and ecological functions for the purpose of providing long-term ecological, economic, and social value and benefits to future generations" and requires the state to seek comanagement arrangements with federal agencies in cooperation and other governmental agencies to ensure that ocean resources are managed and protected, and

Abundant, balanced, diverse, and sustainable estuary and near-shore ecosystems fell apart when our families were removed or prohibited from practicing our traditional harvest. Our practices were replaced with uninformed over-harvest, extirpation of key species, and management to promote single species, including conflicting species. I participated in the destruction. In high school, I made good summer money (a dollar seventy-five an hour) brushing survey trails, helping the Forest Service build more roads to harvest more trees. I used my machete when the first Giant Pacific Salamander I met slowly opened his mouth to scare me. I am in debt to his spirit. In the winter we did piecework transplanting invasive beach grass to kill the dunes. I learned from my mistakes.

Whereas, in 2002 the Governor's Ocean Policy Advisory Council recommended the establishment of marine protected areas and these recommendations were supported by the Governor . . ., and

Then the Governor's Ocean Policy Advisory Council (OPAC) was terminated and reconstituted by the Legislature. The Governor's ability to select his own advisors was constrained and only a subset of his advisors is actually allowed to vote on issues. Legislative pace stalled action for three years. I am the sole tribal representative on the new OPAC, as I was on the previous council. When I pointed out that asking me to also represent the Coquille Tribe and the Confederated Tribes of Coos, Lower Umpqua, and Siuslaw is like asking France to also represent England and Spain, no one heard.

*David Hatch's dad
and grandfather
after a fishing trip in
September 1957. Note
the flat flounder, second
from left on the string of
fish. Photograph courtesy
of author.*

*Whereas, a National Marine Sanctuary could provide the resources
and tools for Oregon's coastal tribes to work in partnership with local
communities and appropriate state and federal agencies to restore our near
shore and estuary ecosystems.*

We have "managed" the near shore and estuaries of Oregon for thousands of years. Like other OPAC representatives, we know simple access restrictions are inappropriate. Restoring the function of the ecosystems requires concerted efforts to restore missing species, balance the interactions of species and harvest in a sustainable manner. It requires an informed public and the resources to keep track of what we do. We won't have a trail so we need to study and learn as we go.

*Be it now therefore resolved
That the Confederated Tribes of the Siletz Indians of Oregon formally
request the U.S. Departments of Commerce and the Interior initiate the
process of developing a National Marine Sanctuary on the Oregon coast
to restore the near-shore plant communities and restore the historical
abundance and productivity in Oregon's coastal rivers and bays for all
Oregonians.*

We adopted this resolution on April 18, 2003. The Coquille Tribe adopted it on March 27, 2004. Governor Kulongoski met with the nine federally recognized tribes of Oregon on December 12, 2005. Chairman Dee Pigsley of the Confederated Tribes of the Siletz Indians commended the Governor for the National Marine Sanctuary letter he had prematurely mentioned on his Web site. The next day, the Governor mailed a letter to Senator Ron Wyden and the Oregon delegation to inform them that he is asking the Secretary of Commerce to designate an Oregon National Marine Sanctuary to provide for the long-term stewardship of the marine environment using ecosystem-based management.

A generation ago my Grandpa's boat house got away in a flood. We lived in a city and couldn't be there to save it. It would be nice if my grandkids could fish from a boat house in the same spot, but new "management" probably won't allow me to build there. There is hope for my real dream though. Efforts of Oregonians working together may allow my grandchildren or maybe my great-grandchildren to put some fresh sticks in our fish weir and witness the abundance and diversity last seen by their elders seven generations ago.

For centuries Native basketweavers have gathered sedges, willows, grasses, and roots across the valleys, wetlands, foothills, and mountains of the California landscape. In this essay we travel with Margaret Mathewson as she journeys with Native California basketweavers to the stream banks and oak woodlands of the Santa Cruz Mountains, north of Monterey Bay. As they harvest in this place and along other roadsides, parks, and woodlands, we learn about their contemporary struggles to pursue their traditions.

California Indian Basketweavers and the Landscape

Margaret S. Mathewson

A basket is such a simple thing. But is it really? To many people it calls up images of dinner rolls on the table, a thing with pink ribbon on it for Mother's Day, or perhaps something old, precious, and "hands-off" in a museum. To the Native peoples of California, the basket is much, much more. Basketweaving is an ancient artistic skill tied to the very foundations of their traditional lifeways. A basket is something to touch and wear; to give and receive as a gift; to sift flour, dry seaweed, toast pine nuts, and cook in; to dance with and speak to. Modern basketweavers still continue this intricate and exacting art. The natural landscape of California is their gathering place.

None of the traditional roots, shoots, ferns, and grasses can be purchased in craft stores. All must be carefully gathered and processed down into even weaving strands from native plants. The great northern coastal spruce trees provide flexible roots for weaving around strong peeled hazel or willow shoots. Basket sedge or white root is the favored material in central California. Western redbud and bracken fern root give red and black designs. Rush, sumac and deergrass are gathered in damp desert springs and seeps in the south, and the root of the Joshua tree makes a red design element.

Baskets in the past were used in every aspect of traditional life. Babies were born into a basketry cradle carried on the mother's back. Foods such as acorns and baynuts, tarweed seed and camas bulbs, seaweed and grasshoppers, saltgrass and sourberries, all went in baskets—stored, roasted, pounded, winnowed, sifted, leached, boiled, dried, or carried. All these functions were accomplished with traditional culinary baskets. Boats, mats, and houses were also made of twined and bound fibers. But the most spectacular baskets were those made for the special occasions of the annual ceremonial cycle—the "dances"—as well as celebrations of birth, marriage, and the passing of loved ones. Baskets were and are still burned as funeral offerings.

There are two basic basketry types in California. Coiled basketry is done in a spiral like the shell of a snail, with each round sewn onto the row before with the help of a bone or metal awl. Twined basketry is reminiscent of a spider web with two flexible strands twisting around a series of inner spokes. Intricate designs in rich colors adorn the baskets with designs such as "Quail Plumes," "Ant Trails," "Flints," "Salmon Tail," "Butterfly," and "Rattlesnake." Although many weavers today use substitute materials like rattan and raffia for teaching purposes, only the natural materials from native plants lovingly tended and gathered give that true traditional feel to a basket.

A Sunday Excursion

It is a Sunday afternoon somewhere in the Santa Cruz mountains. A perfect day—not too hot, not too cold, with a tiny veil of overcast keeping us from the sun's full force. Old live oaks and pepperwood trees cast dappled shade over the party. A small group of Pomo, Miwok, and Ohlone women, two non-Indian friends, and a husband or two are out for the day. We are digging sedge, called white root by traditional California Indian basketweavers, in an area that needs to be worked. White root needs to be tended to produce the long thin runners or rhizomes needed by central California weavers. The responsibility of traditional Native weavers and their students is to care for the plants in this way or else the beds decline in health and productivity. It is an age-old relationship between woman and plant, deeply rooted in the central California native landscape.

The basket sedge (*Carex barbarae*) grows in seasonally wet plains, streambanks, seeps, and lake shores from Umpqua Valley in Oregon to the coastal bluffs of Southern California. The type specimen was first found in Santa Barbara County, so it is named *barbarae* or Santa Barbara sedge. Although it is not used by the local Chumash there, it is used in the heart of central California by the Yokuts, Mono, Miwok, Salinan, Ohlone, Wintun, Maidu, and Pomo tribes. Each rhizome has a core of flexible woody fiber encased in a jointed golden-brown sheath or skin. The peeled inner core fades from nearly white at the soft growing tip to light brown at the "hard end," which arises from another plant. Baskets of sedge have a warm almost pinky tan color that deepens as they age.

A California Indian basket coiled or twined of sedge root is a perfect masterpiece of technical skill and artistry, so tight it can hold water for cooking acorn soup. Bold patterns in the split shoots of western redbud or bulrush root stand out against the lighter background. Sedge grows particularly well in sandy soil, as it does here in this place, where it has formed thick colonies of crossing and recrossing rhizomes. These roots are crowded, and the soil needs to be loosened and aerated. Older beds are hard to get into. The roots are short, twisted, and brown; leaves are dense and full of thatch. Basketweavers like to dig an area on a two-year cycle. A tended sedge bed is a joy to work in, with long, soft, straw-pale roots and fluffy soil. On this warm spring day, there is a happy mood as people comment on the length of the roots, the size of each others' stacks of roots; they fling soil accidentally into the hair of their companions. It is an age-old scene from the California past acted out by the current players on the stage. Traditional basketry is alive and growing.

Disturbing Questions

In the modern world, this idyllic description of a peaceful art has a darker side. Many problems face modern California basketweavers as Native groups all over the country fight to keep their rights and continue their traditions in the face of the modern onslaught. Fences bar the way to gathering areas, herbicides and pesticides taint the plants, marshes are drained, valleys flooded, and urban development creeps slowly across the countryside. While they simply want to continue in peace and quiet in the old way, weavers have many obstacles. How could such a thing as basketweaving become so complex?

Large-scale problems such as access and spraying can be daunting, but it is often the small encounters with uninvited onlookers that can be the most annoying. By a trail, near a park bench, or under a dam, weavers often find themselves within view of non-Indian people who do not understand what they are doing. A few fishers or hikers walking the dog may stop and ask that dreaded question: "What are you doing?" Sometimes the question has an edge of accusation. "Should you be doing that here?" or "Is that allowed?" The answer may be only a few words. "We're digging roots"—but they mean "We're digging these beautiful white roots, of course, what does it look like we're doing? Please go about your business and leave us in peace." This implied ending is never heard. Then weavers try to explain that what they are doing is an ancient tradition passed down in their family; they're not a bunch of crazy women down in a ditch pulling up weeds. What the weavers really don't want is to draw the person further into their affairs.

That dreaded question pops up again and again: "What are you doing?" When I attend a gathering trip, I often find myself fielding that question, trained in the ancient ways of basketry by a very strict teacher, but also schooled in the jargon of an "explainer." (You have to have this skill after years in graduate school, after all.) And here we are in the Santa Cruz mountains. Mountain bikers whiz by on the packed-dirt trail, up over a log and down hard on the ground. Some of the women feel uncomfortable. The digging continues quietly. A biker comes up from the path, rosy with sweat and youth, pushing his bike, in knee pads, helmet, and a tie-dyed T-shirt. "What are you doing?" A little more information than usual is offered. "We're digging roots to make baskets," says one of the ladies. "Miwok baskets," says another.

"Baskets . . ." There is a long pause from the biker. Perhaps he conjures in his mind a different kind of basket readily available as a foreign import, or roughly crafted ones from local craft stores. Few know all the subtle intricacies of traditional Native American basketry materials, techniques, or designs. They imagine baskets from museums and picture books as things of the past like the image of the stereotypical Plains Indian warrior. Many Americans still cling to old stereotypes. These people in blue jeans can't be authentic Indians. Contemporary Native artists continually struggle to open the eyes of those who would keep them in a generic past of ancient North American culture before the influx of Europeans. There were no feathered war bonnets or bison or tipis here in California. In this gentle Mediterranean climate, grasses and acorns were the annual staples; basketry was and is one of the highest forms of Native expressive art.

The young man continues, looking a bit troubled. "Can't you use branches?" "No, you see . . ." I launch into a shallow explanation of traditional Native California Indian basketry, plant use, history, contemporary management, and so on and so on . . . His eyes get a faraway look and he cuts me off. "You're disturbing the earthworms, you know. They make these, like, tunnels, you know." I am reminded of an article I recently read in a horticulture journal about earthworms and the new popularity of no-till gardening. Maybe the kid is a college student and latching onto a lecture about the importance of earthworms and soil structure. The older woman smiles. "We'll cover them up," she says. No harsh words, no correction, no history of Native American land stewardship, no self-righteousness, passes anyone's lips. All is well today and the roots are content. The biker leaves. The bikes continue all day long. Up over the log and down, hard on the ground. The older woman smiles, "They're disturbing the earthworms."

On a crisp, autumn day I join two weavers on a hillside seep in Marin County north of San Francisco. We are cutting Woodwardia fern fronds on a back road. Because it is a roadside bed, this spot is particularly open to public scrutiny. We take only a few fronds from each clump. The ferns have a long inner filament that will be dyed with alder bark to a beautiful red-orange color. It will be lovely laid over the spruce roots next to the dark glossy black of the maidenhair fern and the bright white of the beargrass leaf. Perhaps a "Snake's nose" design or the "Mountain Hand" mark. Yurok, Karok, and Hupa designs. Strong designs. A weaver likes to speak silently to the plants to let them know how beautiful they will be twined into a basket or medallion, shown and gifted during the annual dance cycle. We are all smiling quietly to ourselves and the fern plants.

A car pulls out from a redwood house across the way. A large deck perches high above the forest floor and cement bags keep the hill from sliding into the churning and eroded creek below. A large pile of firewood adorns the manicured driveway. The car pulls up, a BMW, silver, with a sunroof, and a woman in dark glasses rolls down the window. "What are you doing?" she questions frantically. I launch into the usual explanation of basketry fibers and California Indian traditional uses. My friends are quiet. She is more frantic than ever. "You can't do that! You can't take nature away like that!" I glance over at her neat pile of stacked firewood and interject a note about the sustainability of Native plant management. "We've been coming here for close to ten years," I say. "I've lived here for fifteen years and I've never seen you before!" My comments on the difference between fifteen years and generations of basketmakers are lost. "I'm going to call the cops!" and the BMW zooms away. All this time my two quiet friends have been quickly, efficiently packing up our vehicle; we make a back-road getaway. I assume she didn't get our plate number because my friends and I are still free.

Situations like these drive home the differences between continuing Native California traditions and beliefs, and those of many non-Natives who are often unaware of their own invasive practices. California basketmakers encounter a great deal of hypocrisy on collecting trips. To Native California basketmakers, respect for the natural world is renewed every day, with every collecting trip, each basket created, each time it is used. In the conifer forests, oak woodlands, and valley wetlands of California, Native peoples have been quietly pursuing their ancient skills by gathering as best they can in these landscapes, moving the past forward into the present and the future. It is passed from one generation to another as it has always been transmitted, from aunts and mothers and grandmothers to younger weavers, at home and increasingly in small classes. That is the definition of "tradition."

It is not a public event. It is not meant to be analyzed and laid open to all, although there are a number of public forums where weavers do demonstrate and talk about their work. The California Indian Basketweavers Association (ciba.org) holds an annual event, as do a number of museums and interpretive centers. Weavers are very interested in increasing public awareness of the existence of California's ancient traditions in the modern world, but they do not wish to be disturbed during those more private and often spiritual meetings between themselves and their honored elders—the plants.

The Raiding Party Mindset

Besides the problem of casual onlookers, Native people often have difficulty getting access to areas where their ancestors gathered. In many cases a sort of "raiding party" mentality develops, complete with doses of sadness, fear, and nervousness over being caught, mixed with a good deal of humor and satisfaction. For decades parks and wilderness areas had been viewed as "natural" areas, available for public viewing but not use. "Leave only footprints, take only photographs" has been a common sign in parks and wilderness-designated areas. But prior to Euro-American contact, these were hunting and gathering lands of Native Californians. Recently, regional parks and forests have looked for ways to accommodate Native gatherers. Though permits are now available for traditional gathering, many local branch offices are still unfamiliar with the new laws and forms.

I talked with a group of weavers who decided to apply for a Native use permit rather than simply gathering at the state park in their usual manner. "We wanted to do it right for a change." Before they could find someone who even knew about the permit policy, it took seventeen separate phone calls, with a number of calls rerouted back to those already contacted. Ultimately the weaver sent the proper form to the office herself, as park staff could not find the paperwork. Needless to say, that group of weavers strutted proudly through the park that day, wishing a ranger would stop them with their bundles of fronds and sticks and roots, but they gathered uninterrupted.

The national forests have had a permit policy for "alternative forest products" for a long time. Their personnel generally review products by the ton or cubic yard for the commercial forest-products industry. Collectors of firewood, herbs, mushrooms, and beargrass (for the floral industry) usually want large quantities. But to a Native gatherer, a lot is an armload. I have heard several cases where the permit officer laughed when a weaver applied to collect "a few bundles" of sticks. Nevertheless one may still be ticketed or fined if caught in a park or national forest with unsanctioned sticks. Many Native weavers believe they are not subject to these rules. What they do in their own ancient gathering grounds is no one's business but their own. Many weavers and other gatherers go boldly about their business and refuse to get permits. They are uncomfortable with the lengthy procedures, do not want to be bothered. Complex information is often required, and gatherers feel like their privacy is being invaded by people who have no appreciation for what they are doing. Nevertheless, they are wary and cautious. When one Pomo weaver was a young woman people shot at her on several gathering trips. Her friends and family would stage elaborate picnics, taking turns going under the picnic table to dig for sedge roots while others kept watch. Some weavers have the luxury of using traditional sites within reservations or their own private lands. Others have the permission of landowners.

Sometimes permitting creates conflicts over how preservation and conservation is understood. Once Miwok and Ohlone weavers applied for a permit to gather sedge roots in an area with an endemic species of rabbit—the bush bunny. The rabbit feeds on the sedge leaves. There was a firm "No" to the application. This sparked a series of arguments, proofs, and counter-proofs designed to show that "traditional weavers are also an endangered native species," and gathering plants would not affect the food supply of the rabbit in any way. After a number of emotional and painful arguments, the permit was granted. In the winter of 1996-1997 extreme flooding, on the order of 10 to 12 feet of water, greatly altered the sediment layers and vegetation in this park. Now efforts are under way to "rejuvenate" the area. It will be interesting to see if there are any surviving rabbits or if they will return from higher ground. The sedge plants are still thriving.

Fire and Water

In the past few years, the Forest Service in northwestern California has begun working with Native groups to reinstate not only Native collecting but also burning basketry plants to produce quality materials. Smokey the Bear told us for many years that we are supposed to prevent forest fires; no one wants to see blackened stumps, after all. But many Native California tribes burned every year in a complex seasonal cycle that rejuvenated the land. Burning recycles nutrients, promotes young soft growth that attracts and nourishes game animals, kills disease organisms, and opens up the forest understory to promote air circulation and easy travel for animals. Regular burns also prevent the buildup of dead wood that can fuel huge catastrophic wildfires. The heat produced in these large fires is enough to kill plants outright rather than rejuvenate them as a small cool burn will. Native Miwok people used to manage Yosemite Valley with fire to produce an open oak and grassland mix with huge sweeping views of the mountains around. This vista is what non-Indians saw when they first marveled at the place more than 150 years ago. Now meadows are threatened by encroaching conifers and cottonwoods; the sweeping views are not as apparent. Today there is a great controversy over the restoration of the valley and controlled burns in general. Most foresters now believe in the benefits of burning, but implementation is difficult. After Native burning cycles ended in the 1800s, Indian people in Northwestern California simply followed wildfires to collect good basket material. One woman was arrested for arson when a fire she set to burn the hazel bushes on her property got away. Currently there are some special controlled burns in the Six Rivers National Forest designated specifically for basketry materials but weavers wish this policy were more widespread.

Development still causes major destruction of gathering areas in central coastal and Southern California. One project with enormous repercussions was the Warm Springs Dam project in the 1970s and the flooding of its reservoir, Lake Sonoma. My own teacher, Mabel McKay, was one of those who stood in front of the earthmovers to get the work to stop. The protest was not enough to halt the dam but it was enough to turn heads and open a dialogue. An ancient Pomo gathering area went under water but a great effort was made to document and collect sedge plants from these areas and move them to an area just below the dam where a museum and interpretive center was built. It was an emotional time for many Pomo weavers. The new site has never been as good as the older areas, according to many weavers who gathered at the old sites. It is lower and brushier, and maybe doesn't get the same amount of water. After all, basket sedge knows just where to plant itself. Besides, there are new regulations about who can gather at the new site. Gatherers must contend with a locked gate and close proximity of the public at the visitors' center, as well as interference by center employees. A traditional sedge dig can be a very extensive excavation with the removal of plants and large quantities of sand, as well as the rhizomes. When the new area was used during its early years, management stood around watching to see if gatherers were doing everything right, in their view. The gatherers complained, "They wouldn't let us take out the plants at first." Eventually the officials let the weavers alone. When I went there with Mabel in the mid-1980s, her class was left alone. Over twenty years later, the bed is still there, although it needs occasional clearing of invasive blackberry and hemlock.

Places with established native-plant communities often have very subtle and complex hydrology. Draining waterways, clearing, cementing, and dredging channels have affected basketry plants such as bulrush and *Juncus*. For weavers, it is important that areas that are set aside have provisions made so that adjacent development does not affect their plants. One case involves an area of dogbane (*Apocynum cannabinum*), a cordage fiber plant, in Santa Rosa. This milky-sapped perennial, with pinkish stems and flaming yellow autumn foliage, is commonly thought of by agriculturalists as an invasive weed. It has a beautiful silky brownish fiber that is used in making string and nets. It likes damp areas that may be seasonally flooded, especially along rivers, ditches, and in this case an old abandoned orchard recently bought by developers and slated for the axe. To accommodate adjacent buildings and vineyards the developer wanted to alter the water table. This would kill the already unstable stand of plants and negate the effort of Native groups to save the stand. Many Native people also believed the plants were secretly sprayed during one of the periods when the developer had control of the site. After a legal battle lasting years in which control of the site went back and forth, the stand has finally been set aside, though much reduced in size and health. Now a chainlink fence and locked gates create barriers between collectors and plants even though the site is protected from development. Most weavers do not want to deal with locks and regulations, but wish to continue their traditional gathering practices as they always have.

The spraying of herbicides on natural vegetation is probably the most commonly voiced fear of Native weavers today, especially in the heavily forested northwest of the state and Sierra Nevada. Many of the targeted plants are the basketry plants themselves. Softwood (conifer) management on large tracts of forest land involves discouraging or removing broad-leafed "under brush" such as bigleaf maple, alder, hazel, willow, and buckbrush. All are used extensively in Native basketry. It's hard to believe that some people think of these plants as weeds, so revered are they by Native weavers. Because sprayed materials often do not show immediate death, Native peoples may not know an area has been sprayed if plants are poorly labeled or signs are not clearly posted on roads. Land managers are usually unaware that anyone is gathering targeted plants, and generally don't know the specific details of use.

In other ecosystems, ranching and agricultural activities also involve spraying and dredging willows and bulrushes from drainage ditches and stream channels. East of the Sierras it is common practice for ranchers to spray these plants in ditches. People living off groundwater in these areas tell countless stories about health problems in their families, ranging from sores and rashes to cancers. Effects are often slow and complex, both for those using the water and for gatherers. It is not simply a matter of residues on plants. The potential for toxic contact for Native gatherers is much greater. Basketry materials are often placed in the mouth to hold the strand firm while the weaver splits or cleans the materials. Native weavers developed rashes on their faces or hands from splitting willow. The ends of sticks are also chewed to "brush" the ends for basket weaving. One weaver's "splitting tooth" became diseased and fell out.

In response to complaints from the California Indian Basketweavers Association, the Department of Pesticide Regulation set up a study to evaluate the risk involved in gathering these materials. Such a "risk assessment" is common in evaluating new products or in reevaluating older ones. It assumes that there is an "acceptable" level of risk. However, the basket weavers assert that there is *no* acceptable risk level. The methodology for the assessments used special clothing by a test group of gatherers, and analysis of residues on the clothing, and the plant parts gathered were deemed unacceptable by the basketmakers. They believed the methods were not sufficiently inclusive. A series of news stories on CNN reported that the California Indian Basketweavers Association refused to endorse the study. The basketweavers say that the story was biased against them and the public has again been misled. The controversy and the health problems continue.

Gathering with a Good Heart

But all this worry is not good for the baskets. Back in the Santa Cruz Mountains in the warm spring sunshine we are not worried. The root digging is good today. Everyone is happy. There are no sad thoughts or disagreements to upset the harmony of the day. These will be good baskets with a good heart. Sedge roots are gathered by many different weavers in different ways, following varying degrees of traditional "rules." But the word "rules" is perhaps not the best translation for what this knowledge entails. They are rather unspoken beliefs about how and when to do things correctly and with respect. Weaving has a "power," as do other skills and occupations. That power can be disrupted or misdirected and that can cause harm to the weavers, their families, friends, and others, and even to the very fabric of the world. It is not to be taken lightly.

These are some of the ancient Pomo "rules." Roots will only come to the weaver who is balanced, settled, well, and content. There must be no illness or death in the family of the weaver if she is to gather or work on her baskets. She must think only good thoughts lest bad feelings be woven into the basket and do harm to someone who touches it later. She must not weave on the power of her monthly cycle for the same reason. That power is especially potent and dangerous.

Most weavers today do not follow these proscriptions as closely as some of the elders used to. Among Pomo weavers it is also common to incorporate the quill of a flicker feather into the basket when weaving when she is menstruating. Done in the proper way, this action forestalls any harmful effect and the weaver may then proceed normally with the basket weaving. Older Pomo baskets I have seen in museums show an occasional flicker quill in the weave. Quills are also found randomly in the baskets of other tribes suggesting that this may have once been a more common practice. Among weavers in northern California there is a great deal of variation in the use of the menstrual proscription. Most know of the traditional foundation for this rule but some do not follow it because they are "living in a modern world."

Others follow it closely. By far the most common interpretation of the rule is that a weaver may work on her own projects or for close family members when she is menstruating. If a basket is destined for another person or especially for a ceremonial function, she will not weave on it or touch it at this time. Some non-Indians are particularly uncomfortable with the menstrual rules. They think their personal rights and freedoms are being put down. But those weavers who follow the strictest rules do not see it that way. It is a matter of respect. Each person must be mindful of others and do things in a way that does no harm to others. Following the rules is like that.

There is also a strong sense of the plants as personified individuals with whom one can speak. Many weavers from all areas and skill levels have related stories of the plants speaking to weavers and conveying information and encouragement about the weaving traditions. Wind, water, soil, and rock formations also figure in these accounts, as well as the voices of basketry teachers who have passed away. Human actions and emotions are used in these accounts. One weaver speaks of "breathlessness" in a patch of very tall willows, of the stems "shaking their shoulders" and "reaching out." Others speak of a feeling of joy felt by the plants when they are "told" what they will become after they are gathered. The telling of things to the plants is very important. Most older traditional weavers relate "rules" about the proper addressing of plants. The address need not be vocal but may come in the form of a prayer. Plants must not feel as though they are being simply uprooted and taken away. They must be treated as any other valued member of society. Thoughts must be positive during a collecting trip or the "roots won't come to you." Physical offerings are often but not always part of a collecting trip. An offering may take the form of some beads or tobacco (ancient traditional offerings) or some of the food brought along for the collectors.

Today, on our gathering expedition, each person has done her or his own personal preparation—prayer, for lack of a better word. There is no need for more. There are no altars or complex rituals that might be done "wrong." This is not some great propitious occasion separated out from daily life. It is life, pure and simple. It is a natural part of the lives of these people. They are comfortable with it. Nature is not some unfathomable deity. It is here.

Weavers will often sit and prepare the materials there in the sedge bed, splitting them and peeling the jointed golden-brown skins away from the woody core. The insides are carefully rolled up and tied with strips of cloth to protect the roots as they dry. Materials are seasoned or cured for a year or more before use, to prevent shrinkage and loosening of the basket as they dry. The skins and shavings are traditionally placed back in the natural environment and generally not put in the trash can, where they would go into a landfill. The soil is replaced and leaf cover restored. Fern tops are taken off and scattered where they will make new plants. The gathering places are left clean and healthy. All will be well again for next year.

Not Just Weeds

One person's treasure is another person's weed. Thousands of people come to public Indian events in California, at Native celebrations, educational events, museums, and interpretive centers. According to my own personal survey of these audiences, they tend to think of land in four ways: 1) one's own land or backyard, 2) someone else's land or backyard, 3) a public park, street, forest, etc., or 4) wasteland, generally associated with vacant lots, road verges, ditches, and often most desert habitats. Though not all individuals think this way, they tend to think of plants in a similar way: 1) *ornamental* garden flowers, shrubs, trees, and grass, 2) *wild* flowers, shrubs, trees, and grass, and 3) *weeds* or "scrub" bushes, which they view as useless, ugly, or a fire hazard. Though not a random cross-section of the public, the survey represents people interested in these issues in the first place. In individual cases, knowledge of the plant world was much more sophisticated, but the broad applicability of these categories was surprising.

The mainstream concept of a "weed" comes from generations of dependence on monocrop agricultural systems in which a single strain or clone is planted to the exclusion of all others. Food is delivered in trucks to the grocery store from . . . who knows where? It is beautiful, spotless, and glossy—picture perfect. Gardens must be perfectly manicured and edged. Nothing mars the grass. Disease organisms proliferate and tough, opportunistic plants called "weeds" are sprayed into submission. Some of the most useful and flavorful edible wild plants, both native and introduced, are classed as weeds—nettles, dandelions, lamb's quarter, and chickweed. And the sedge is just such a plant. Useful and nurtured by some; scorned, sprayed, or simply ignored by others. Traditional basket-making plants in California are almost all weeds. These include sedges, rushes, and bulrushes, willows and buckbrushes, dogbane and milkweeds, even bracken ferns. Large forest trees are also basket resources but some of these are also seen as weed trees by foresters. These include maples, alders, and hazels. A few others are thought of as choice ornamentals such as redbud, maidenhair, and chain ferns.

Not surprisingly many members of the general public are astounded to discover that these "weeds" are useful and produce such lovely works of "art." One weaver relates a story of a woman at a demonstration who was associated with the rice-growing industry in the Central Valley. When told that bulrush and sedge had been used to make a beautiful basket on display there, she shook her head and commented, "We spray for that! I'm glad someone can use that noxious weed." She may have also been referring to a number of introduced species of nutgrass sedge or small bulrushes, which are very prevalent and invasive in rice fields. Such a lumping of traditional basketry plants with similar imported plants and their inclusion in the "weed" category is offensive to weavers.

There are broader implications of these different perspectives. Native people often see urban and other wastelands, ditches, vacant lots, and roadsides as traditional gathering grounds. For them, land is land and the plants grow where they grow. The plants do not designate the land, neither do the basketmakers. There is no "wasteland" in Native thought. Modern urban and suburban people are often on the move. They do not generally stay in a place long enough to feel a connection to that place. They are constantly being uprooted. Sounds sort of like "weeds," doesn't it? Even a tenure of twenty years or more is not enough to instill a feeling of "home" akin to that felt by people whose parents, grandparents, and great-grandparents lived on that land. They are the perennial inhabitants.

This is not to say that mobile people do not like the land. There is a superficial liking for places: a sense of beauty, a feeling for the community of people or often historical buildings and natural or human-generated "tourist" attractions. These are the sensational attributes of a place or those which instill an immediate response. In time people who live in these places often find that the thrill has worn off and may look for the next most fashionable place to "put down roots." Areas in the country go "boom and bust" as potential living sites are based for the most part on an economic foundation and popularity.

Most non-Indian people can recite the timeline of their particular family history from place to place, eventually hailing from some other continent. Native people trace their families back not from place to place, but from person to person in the same place. Their sense of place is firmly rooted. They see a longer view of the past. This view is rooted in a culture not in an individual. It includes traditional use and often stories and images associated with particular landforms ranging from individual small rocks and springs to whole valleys and mountain ranges. These oral traditions also include stands of native plant material. Native people use parts of the land in ways that are beneficial to humans and respect the responsibility of the humans living there to take care of that land base in perpetuity. There is no sense of closure to this view of land use. Time is not an issue. The land was taken care of in this way in the past so that the timeline stretches back beyond living memory. The land must be taken care of in the future so that the timeline stretches forward beyond our living comprehension of time.

Many young California Indian people involved in traditional basketry are following this lead and choosing to root themselves in ancestral lands even if they have lived in other regions. Many who do not live in their ancestral areas for reasons of work, family, and marriage between areas, or because of other concerns such as health problems, often return to the ancestral land base to gather materials. This is akin to a sort of "pilgrimage." They feel that the plant materials are connected with their family line in a very real way.

Facing the Challenges

Through all these trials, California Indian basketweavers have risen to the challenge. There is more and more interest every year; the young people are coming up to the teachings of the elders. The players and the tools have changed, but the game is still the same. Ancient life ways and beliefs about land use are still intact even while the land has been altered or carved into blocks. An older traditional basketmaker looks out across the landscape and sees something old, even in the midst of urban development. She will return to a place her teachers gathered even if it is now in a vacant city lot because she sees the past of the plant as well as its present. Young weavers will try to find a patch of plants in an area once occupied by their people even if this means searching in cement channels in the heart of a metropolis.

Environmentalists and botanists show concern over the possible introduction of plants from one area in California to another. Some believe that the plants must not even be transported from one valley to another. Because the genetic makeup of certain strains of native plants will be compromised, the same concerns are often voiced over planting garden varieties of plants such as hybrid irises and columbines, because their airborne pollen will affect wild populations. These concerns are considered over zealous by many people who believe 1) that there never was a fixed unchanging landscape frozen in time, and 2) the introduction of European and Asian plants has irreparably changed the face of the California flora anyway.

Many Native weavers readily transplant plants from areas they know to have good qualities to other areas and their yards. Recently many native weavers have established beds of materials such as sedge, bulrush, *Juncus*, deer grass, maidenhair and chain ferns, dogbane, milkweeds, and redbud. But these are not large enough or old enough to support more than a few weavers. Some plants are difficult to establish, like beargrass, which resents transplanting and grows slowly from seed. Others, like willow, need a great deal of room or water to grow. Many plants are not practical or economical, such as large conifers.

Natural areas are still seen as the best places to get materials both for abundance and spiritual reasons. Some weavers believe that traditional basketry plants should not be grown for weaving. It is considered akin to caging a wild animal, an affront to the spirit of the plant. This is not, however, a common attitude. Others believe that weavers should not have to grow materials. They should be available in the wild as they have been traditionally, without the need for alternatives. If plant propagation is seen as an alternative by public agencies, Native weavers fear efforts to alleviate problems in wild areas may stop. There is also potential for exploitation in the propagation of basketry plants for sale by native-plant nurseries run by non-Indians. This is not seen as correct by some weavers. There are however, several Indian-run native-plant nurseries that propagate and sell basketry and other useful plants. The funds raised are used to promote Indian issues.

Interest in California basketry has prompted a trend in publicly owned parks and forests to restore areas where basketry plants may have grown in the past. New beds have also been created in wild areas that will eventually mature as gathering areas. Public education has been included in these projects in the form of docent training, public schools projects, and traveling lectures. Volunteers donate time, money, and plants to the efforts as well. Most of these restoration projects are run by non-Indian groups such as parks, interpretive museums, botanical gardens, schools, or foundations. As with any large organization involving many and varied participants, there is controversy. If bad feelings arise between the members and participants the feeling of creation that generally accompanies these projects can die. Traditional weavers will not gather in an area that holds any kind of bad feeling for them. Non-Indian groups are generally careful to allow the Native people to have the final say in plant matters but this is not always the case when it comes down to issues of ultimate control.

The Future

In 1990 a group of interested weavers and friends got together and formed the California Indian Basketweavers Association. Since that time, there has been a tremendous increase in the power available to Native basketmakers in California. It has allowed a previously scattered group of people with common interests and concerns to voice some of those concerns as a unified whole. Other  powerful organizations that have often stood in opposition to the concerns of Native groups, such as public land use agencies, do not usually respond to concerns voiced by individuals. When these specific concerns are voiced by another large institution, however, negotiations must be made.

The importance of the California Indian Basketweavers Association to the modern basketry scene cannot be overstressed. It is a vital and powerful organization in a world' where basketry studies in books and museums had been dominated by non-Indians. However, CIBA is still funded by non-Indian funding organizations and in a sense must cater to non-Indian systems of organization. This is a source of anxiety to some Native weavers. Maintaining ancient cultural traditions and the arts are not high priority in this country and it has been very difficult to get funding. There are no clear solutions to all the concerns that are surfacing each day but most Native people agree that the existence of CIBA is a step in the right direction: a forum for continued debate with the mainstream, a springboard for further action, and a means to make this ancient tradition visible to others. The gathering is the last weekend in June and interested people may make donations or join the organization on the Web site (www.ciba.org).

Through all the modern tumult the sedge plants will keep growing. I have a sedge bed in my parents' backyard I planted nearly twenty years ago. Between that, the dogbane, the juncus, and the deergrass, it's a wonder they have a backyard anymore. Whenever we can, we dig the beds and spread the roots around to the basketweavers. It is a nice warm day in mid June. I will be heading to the CIBA gathering soon and I want to have a tub of roots for people. Two of my weaver friends are helping me, here in our suburban yard under the clothesline. They are nice long roots. We are thinking good thoughts. The sedge is happy today. All is well.

Situated along the coast of central California, the Monterey region has a varied topography that structured distinct climates and enhanced vegetational diversity. In the late eighteenth century, when Steven Hackel's essay is set, this landscape between the coast and inland mountains was covered with grasses and woodlands of oaks, pines, cypresses, willows, and cottonwoods. Winters were cool and wet; summers were warm and dry. On summer days, a coastal strip of land some three to four miles wide was often shrouded in fog; yet, further inland, up the valleys of the Carmel and Salinas rivers, days were usually warm and clear.[1] Steven Hackel's essay is the first one in our anthology about immigrant experiences, describing transitions in this place from one Native Californians knew to one remade by Spanish settlement.

Shifting Patterns of Land Use in Monterey, California before 1850

Steven W. Hackel

Since it became a state in 1850, few regions have been as important to the economic growth of the U.S. as California. Corporate agriculture, the cattle industry, and the expansion of mining, logging, and residential construction have brought wealth and comfort to many in California and beyond. But not without cost. Today, few of California's old-growth forests stand, less than 10 percent of its coastal wetlands remain, and only 2 percent of its original interior wetlands exist. Moreover, 17 percent of all plants and 40 percent of all inland fish in California are non-native. To be sure, most of these changes occurred as a result of the enormous influx of people into the state after the Gold Rush and after California's admission into the Union in 1850. But early Anglo-American visitors to California were on to something when they observed that the region in the late 1840s and early 1850s already had "an old and cultivated aspect." Through selective burning, pruning, cultivating, irrigating, tilling, and sowing over thousands of years, California Indians had placed their mark on the land, creating for themselves a region of plenty that appeared to be "a well-kept domain." In this essay, through an examination of ecological change and shifting patterns of land use in the Monterey region during the second half of the eighteenth century, I'll suggest the degree to which Indians, and then Spaniards and Mexicans, modified the California landscape generations before the Anglo-American invasion.[2]

Perhaps as long as twelve thousand years ago humans lived along California's coast in the Monterey region.[3] Little is known about these first Californians.[4] What little evidence remains from their early occupation suggests that these ancient pioneers lived in small groups and exploited a wide variety of resources, especially shellfish and small terrestrial animals.[5] They had few tools and lacked the skills or technologies to exploit either acorns or salmon, both of which were abundant.[6] Over time, as sea levels rose, the coastal zone of the Monterey region gradually was remade and could support fewer and fewer large animals.[7] As a consequence of all of these changes, the early Indians of the region were forced to alter their patterns of settlement and subsistence. How these adaptations occurred along California's central coast is unknown.

Compared to the earliest coastal Indians, those who inhabited the region between 500 B.C. to 1,000 A.D. seem to have had a more diversified economy. They relied on a wide array of plant foods and smaller animals and practiced seasonal migrations, moving from one environment to another in pursuit of food.[8] Constant relocation and seasonal food shortages limited their population growth, for these groups could grow no larger than the number that could survive the lean months of late winter and early spring. At some point—between two thousand and one thousand years ago—the people of the region began to accumulate large surpluses of food by relying more intensively on existing resources that could support larger populations.[9] The key developments, then, were social and technological changes that permitted the intensive collection and exploitation of indigenous plants and animals.[10]

The Monterey region has a mild, Mediterranean climate typical of coastal California. Generally, soaking rains began in the late fall, in October or November. These storms lasted for several days but were usually separated by clear cool days. Fall rains brought the germination of annual plants, and winter rains were accompanied by large flocks of waterfowl. In the late spring, rains diminished and days became warmer. Wild flowers bloomed, and rodents, birds, and small mammals nourished themselves on hillsides and grasslands. By late spring, rains were infrequent, grasses became dormant, and wildflowers produced their seeds. Summer was warm, dry, and often foggy.

Throughout these seasonal changes, deer and elk browsed native grasses and brush, ranging from valleys to mountains, in pursuit of food.

Certainly by 1,000 A.D., Indians of the Monterey region knew how to use a bow and arrow, how to make baskets and nets, and how to gather and process acorns and buckeyes. They collected a diversity of foods—mammals, birds, fish, shellfish, grasses, and seeds.[11] They lived in stable communities for much of the year, but they also maintained smaller seasonal work stations or camps. They divided their work into small groups and stored surplus foods—meats and acorns—for use over the winter. Most importantly, the unit of production shifted from the household to the community. And like Indians elsewhere in California, they used burning, irrigation, and pruning to maximize food sources and production. Around one thousand years ago, the subsistence and settlement patterns of the Indians of the Monterey region changed yet again. But this change was marked more by an intensification and fuller expression of existing practices than by a radical departure in response to environmental change. Settlements became more dispersed, and more sites were occupied seasonally. Specialized crafts developed, the shell-bead economy expanded, and tribal political organization became more complex. Thus, the centuries just before European settlement represented a climax of thousands of years of human efforts that contributed to gradual ecological change in the Monterey region.

Indians of Monterey were part of a complicated human mosaic that made California home to one of the most linguistically diverse and densely settled populations in North America. Some 310,000 Indians lived within the boundaries of the present state in the mid-eighteenth century, and scholars have classified these Indians into six culture areas and identified seven distinct language stocks and at least one hundred distinct languages.[12] Missions, presidios, and civilian settlements established in the coastal region between San Diego and San Francisco most directly and immediately affected some sixty thousand Indians. These Indians lived in semi-sedentary settlements of one hundred to one thousand people, whose language and culture often varied from village to village. Trade, marriage, and ritual connected these communities, but most villages steadfastly maintained autonomy and protected their areas against encroachment.[13]

We do not know the size of the pre-contact Indian population in the Monterey region, but most likely it was between twenty-five hundred and three thousand in the first half of the eighteenth century.[14] They were divided into two linguistic groups, Costanoan and Esselen, and spoke dialects that varied from village to village and were sometimes mutually unintelligible.[15] Costanoan-speaking Indians lived in a broad coastal strip between Point Sur and the Carquinez Straits of San Francisco Bay. Esselen-speaking Indians lived in a smaller, more mountainous area, which included drainages of the upper Carmel River, the Arroyo Seco, and the upper Salinas Valley. Mission San Carlos, which was established adjacent to the Monterey presidio in June 1770, drew Indians from only part of this region, an area roughly circumscribed by the Salinas River in the east, the Pajaro River that runs through modern Watsonville in the north, and Vicente Creek in the south.

By the eve of Spanish colonization, the Indians of the Monterey region had developed a complicated seasonal round of food procurement that was keyed to the region's rich plant and animal resources and seasonal changes in the climate. In the late summer, they labored intensively to prepare for the winter months. Since their activities and resources were so varied, it is thought that they divided themselves into small and temporary groups to more efficiently process key staples. These smaller groups often relocated for weeks or months at a time to camps along the coast or in the interior, where they collected and processed foods. In the late summer and early fall, groups gathered acorns, harvested grass seeds, and collected buckeyes, nuts, and berries. Some ventured to the shore to gather shellfish; others relocated to rivers and streams to catch steelhead; still others headed further inland in pursuit of game attracted to dropping acorns. In the warm California sun, Indians dried shellfish and meat from game. The acorn, a rich source of both carbohydrates and fats, was the most important food gathered and stored, like grass seeds and other nuts. Once the food stores were in place, Indians set fire to grasslands. This seasonal burning encouraged the growth of certain plants, protected grasslands from encroaching conifers, created habitat for large game, and aided harvest of pine nuts and rabbit hunting.

During the winter months, after the acorn harvest and the burning of the grasslands, a period of comparative inactivity settled over the Monterey region. Indians abandoned temporary coastal and interior work stations and returned to their principal villages. For the next four to six months, during the coolest and wettest months of the year, Indians in Monterey collected shellfish and hunted occasionally, but for the most part they subsisted off their stored foods. With the coming of spring, the pace of life once again quickened. Hunting and collecting resumed in earnest to supplement dwindling stores of food, and as the weather improved, small task groups again dispersed from the main village for short periods in pursuit of food.[16]

By the middle of the eighteenth century, Indians of the Monterey region used hundreds of plants and animals for food and medicinal purposes. They traded with their neighbors to obtain luxury goods and basic necessities. Through the use of fire and other techniques, they remade their region to suit their needs. Using their complex social and political organization, they produced, gathered, and accumulated surpluses that allowed them to persist through times of scarcity. All of this changed when Spaniards arrived with their plants and animals in 1769.

When Spain settled Alta California, it brought to the region missions, presidios, and animals. The Spanish military fort, or presidio, at Monterey had horses and mules from its inception in June 1770, and in August 1771 Pedro Fages—the military official in charge of Alta California—delivered to the mission a sow, a hog, and four piglets.[17] Four months later the mission accepted eighteen head of cattle; by then the presidio almost certainly had its own herd.[18] Two years later mules were added,[19] and by 1783 there was a herd of 220 sheep at San Carlos.[20] When introduced to verdant, open grasslands, horses, cattle, and sheep multiplied rapidly, dispersing widely throughout the Monterey region and Alta California. An animal population explosion—in technical terms an "ungulate irruption"—emerged from the earliest years of Spanish settlement in Alta California.[21]

By 1783 Mission San Carlos counted some 874 animals: 500 cattle, 110 sheep, 110 goats, 25 pigs, 18 mules, and 111 horses.[22] As their numbers grew, the mission's animals proved too numerous to keep corralled; most were turned loose to graze the countryside and hunted down only when needed by the mission. For Indians the consequences were dire. Spanish cattle, sheep, and horses overran Indian lands, trampling Indian fields and encroaching on their villages. Indians who killed Spanish livestock risked punishment by the padres and soldiers. Soldiers exacerbated the Indians' problems by seeking to eliminate natural predators, such as bears, which occasionally threatened the growing herds. Cattle and horse herds of the neighboring presidio also grew unchecked.

Year by year, Spanish livestock invaded and then exhausted grasslands farther and farther from the mission and presidio. Into this disturbed environment followed a host of non-native weeds and plants that came with the Europeans and their animals and had proven themselves adept at coexisting alongside European grazing animals elsewhere. Hardier than native grasses and bushes, and more suited to dry, compacted soil, they outcompeted many indigenous food sources. Adobe bricks made in the Monterey region during the 1820s, 1830s, and 1840s recorded how native plants were almost completely displaced by European weeds; these bricks contain much higher pollen counts of European weeds than of native plants.[23] By the turn of the nineteenth century, the hills and valleys of Monterey were covered with alien plants that supported Spanish livestock but few if any Indian villages. In 1800 nearly all Indians of the Monterey region necessarily depended on mission fields, not the surrounding hillsides, for their primary subsistence.

The Franciscans came to California with the seeds and tools—hoes, plows, shovels and picks—to transform the land and prepare it for European agriculture. At first, they had little success. But by 1783 Indians working the mission's irrigated fields produced surplus food. The padres boasted of a "sizeable walled garden [which produces] abundant vegetables and some fruit."[24] In that year, Indians at San Carlos harvested some 4,500 bushels, a huge figure which no doubt explains why in that year more Indians came to the mission for baptism than in any other.[25] According to one of the missionaries, Father Junípero Serra, the more than six hundred Indians already at the mission were maintained "without scarcity."[26] So abundant was the crop that Father Serra sent nearly 200 bushels of wheat to the soldiers at the Monterey presidio. More tellingly, the padres "gave," in their words, some 375 bushels of grain to unbaptized villagers of the region who had worked in the mission's fields during the harvest. The spread of Spanish plants and animals was beginning to threaten the subsistence economies of these more remote villages.[27]

As a result of the growth in Spanish agriculture and its pastoral economy, the natural environment of the Monterey region was in crisis by the late eighteenth century. In the early 1790s, the number of cattle and sheep kept by San Carlos more than doubled, increasing from 1,082 cattle and 900 sheep in 1790 to 2,300 and 1,577 respectively in 1794. That same year, Missions Santa Cruz and Soledad—both founded in 1791—grazed nearly seven hundred cattle and nine hundred sheep; in the presidio, horses and cattle numbered in the thousands. A drought gripped the overgrazed region in 1793, 1794, and 1795; suddenly, it seemed, there was inadequate pasture to support the steadily increasing herds of horses, cattle, and sheep.[28] Soon, the royal herd of cattle grazed in the lower Salinas Valley was declining in numbers and producing far fewer calves, a sure sign of malnourishment.[29] A precipitous decline in the presidio's cattle prompted an investigation by the governor. Soldiers described a region that had not seen rain in years, where the pasturage had become "infinitely" reduced.[30] By the mid 1790s, the native vegetation of the region had been severely damaged if not totally destroyed by drought and the introduced animals. Thousands of horses, cattle, and sheep ranged farther and farther from mission and presidio in search of pasture, scouring the valleys and hills of the region, rooting out any remaining pockets of native grasses. Sheep that can eat grasses down to stubble proved especially damaging to the pasturage in and around Monterey. What cattle, horses, and sheep had not eaten, they trampled.

Indians who had not yet moved to Mission San Carlos, Mission Santa Cruz, or Mission Soledad still depended upon the countryside for their subsistence; they were hit especially hard by the drought and free-ranging animals. When acorns and seeds they depended on disappeared, Indians suffered from what the soldiers described as their great "hunger" and Indians increasingly turned to cattle as a source of food.[31] Various colonial laws criminalized the traditional activities Indians used to create a landscape suitable to their needs and aided Spanish takeover of the land. Most importantly, Governor José Joaquín de Arrillaga made it a crime for Indians in the missions and in the countryside to set fire to their fields, a practice they had long utilized in their hunting and proto-agriculture strategies.

Spanish livestock recovered quickly after the drought of the 1790s; native vegetation and the Indian communities who depended upon those plants collapsed. Once rains returned in 1798, non-native grasses and introduced livestock solidified their hold on the Monterey region; by then nearly all the Indians of the region had relocated to one of its missions.[32] Now, the region looked like a pastoral paradise, with its mild climate of wet but cool winters, and its rich covering of grasses well adapted to both drought and intensive grazing by horses, cattle, and sheep. By 1820 Missions Santa Cruz, San Carlos, Soledad, and San Juan Bautista tripled the number of cattle sheep and horses they grazed. Throughout Spanish California, missions and their animals came to dominate and then transform the countryside. The number of horses in the Monterey region were limited, but cattle and sheep continued to increase in numbers. By the end of the Spanish period, missions in California collectively held some 193,234 sheep, 149,730 cattle, and 19,830 horses.[33] The presidios, a small number of private ranchos, and numerous wild herds held countless more.

For the Indians of California, the arrival of Spaniards with their plants and animals were no less momentous than the direst predictions about global warming are for us today. They were driven from a changed countryside into missions where they were forced to seek a subsistence in non-native crops and European methods of agriculture. Within the compass of a single generation, Indians saw the world around them come undone. Today, in the Age of Global Warming, we are constantly reminded of the role of industrialization in accelerating ecological change. Belching smokestacks, smoldering rainforests, receding ice caps, and rising seas suggest our ability to harness nature and the peril with which we do so. Our preoccupation with finding a solution to catastrophic climate change and our hubris in believing only modern people dramatically modify their surroundings should not obscure our awareness of how peoples of the past made and remade their environment. To be sure, Indians and then Spaniards in California did not usher in global climate change, but their modification of the land was part of a global process of ecological change that has accelerated since the early modern period, when Europeans began to settle and colonize much of the Western Hemisphere.

In the mild Mediterranean climate of northern California, the protected bays of San Francisco and Monterey produced a bounty of fish, shellfish, and other invertebrates for Native tribes, Spanish colonists, and later, the flood of immigrants who followed the Gold Rush of 1849. California's greatest port at San Francisco is the outlet of the Sacramento and San Joaquin rivers that spring from the Sierra Nevada and gather waters of their expansive valleys. Monterey Bay, once prized by the Spanish, is more shallow, but had an equally important fishery in the nineteenth and early twentieth centuries. This essay considers the role of Chinese fishermen in both these places.

Lost China Camps

Judith L. Li

My father's father came from a village of farmers and duck herders in Guang Dong, China, and we had no direct ties to fishing traditions. However Dad was a fanatic fisherman. With him I fished the delta of San Francisco Bay in small wooden boats, and ran along the wide beaches of Monterey Bay after fish caught on his long surf rods. I got to know the foggy mornings, balmy afternoons, changing tides, moonlit beaches of these great coastal bays. During the late nineteenth century in these same places, hundreds of Chinese fishermen from the Pearl River delta harvested a diverse catch of bay shrimp, oysters, bottom fishes, and abalone. In San Francisco Bay a few hidden spots are reminders of their fishing camps: China Basin off the wharf near PacBell baseball park in San Francisco, China Camp in San Rafael.

In search of these landmarks and stories, my Mom, Alice Lew, and I traveled to Marin County on a warm summer day in September 2004. Mom grew up across the bay in Oakland, but this was the first visit to this China Camp for both of us. We drove north from San Francisco, headed east out of San Rafael, then meandered along the marshside road past Turtle Back Hill, Bullhead Flat, and Rat Cove, arriving at San Pedro Point and the state park where the last Chinese shrimp-fishing village in California is restored. Protected from the main channel of San Francisco Bay, where tides ebb and flow out of the Sacramento Delta, this China Camp lies on the shores of San Pablo Bay. A gravel drive led downhill to the few buildings remaining of a village complex that once housed 469 people and seven separate camps. On the left, three small wooden cabins, apparently living quarters, with a white picket fence bearing the sign "Private. No Trespassing." The two structures closest to the wooden boardwalk looked lived in, with signs of modern life— coffee cups, dishes, soap. But the third was overgrown with broad-leaved morning glory, its entry stairs askew, the door not quite fitting its frame. A long pier was still in use but locked at a rusty cyclone fence that looked out onto the planks of the wharf. Tied to the shady side of the pier was a three-quarter-sized replica of a sampan, its mast rocking back and forth in the wind without its single "lateen" sail rigged. A fleet of these small wooden boats tended the shrimp nets set in the bay, dumping the uniquely Chinese "purse bag nets" full of shrimp into their holds, and delivering the catch to larger junks or back to shore.

Norman Scofield visited this camp on July 17, 1897: "The fishermen are occupied solely in the catching of shrimps and nothing but the small meshed purse seines used. Each boat runs a set of thirty nets which are set at low tide and taken in at high tide: thus each boat makes two catches a day" (Scofield, 1897).

Stashed into each sampan were baskets brimming with small fish, perhaps silvery smelt, and shrimp. As the 100-pound basket load was poured out the fish were picked out, leaving only half the catch in shrimp ready to cook in the ovens. These brick structures are still standing along the boardwalk leading away from the pier. After the shrimp were boiled, only the largest went to market to be sold fresh, but most were laid out in the sun to dry. The cove at China Camp was a good place for drying. Its sandy beach is protected from winds and fog by the surrounding hills. On the summer day we visited, a little Chinese boy played in the gentle curl of bay surf under the watchful eye of his young parents; a group of chatty women set up their wooden easels to paint their visions of the blue bay waters and distant East Bay hills.

I turned back towards the largest structure standing—a barn of rough-hewn redwood siding, each board about twelve inches wide, with thicker redwood beams forming the framework. The structure is more than a hundred years old, yet the weather-worn redwood gives it a solid feeling, and my footsteps echoed slightly as I walked inside. While I felt steeped in the fragrance of old wood, cool breezes came through the openings that once were windows, and I could still see the little boy playing in the water.

Leaning in a corner was a wooden roller that looked like a miniature steam roller, about three feet wide and two feet in diameter. More than a century ago workers pushed the roller over dried shrimp spread on the barn floor, gently crushing them. To separate lightweight shrimp heads and shells from the heavier meat, they poured crushed shrimp into a fan mill, which still stands next to the window, facing the sea. The mill was first developed more than two thousand years ago in China to winnow grains. Fishermen turned the hand crank of this mill to propel thin wooden fan blades inside the drum, which spilled separated shrimp out onto round, flat bamboo trays. In the simplicity of the wooden tools and the logical order of the process, I could easily imagine how millions of shrimp were prepared for shipment to China.

While the Genovese, Portuguese, and other Europeans pursued salmon, sole, flounder, and other fish for fresh market and canneries, Chinese fishermen up and down the California coast netted a diversity of invertebrates, algae, and bottom fish primarily to dry for Chinese markets in Asia. A delicacy even more special than shrimp was abalone. The greatest abalone harvest was in southern California, where Chinese fishermen dominated the fishery for abalone meat and shells in San Diego, Los Angeles, and Santa Barbara in the mid-nineteenth century (Chinn, 1969). When I was growing up in Northern California, I heard stories about the abalone whose numbers waxed and waned 150 miles south of San Francisco in Monterey Bay.

Compared to the expansive San Francisco Bay and its delta, Monterey Bay is smaller, more exposed to the ocean, with broad shallow beaches. I grew up playing in the shallow surf, picnicking on wide expanses of white sand, and poking in tidepools for orange sea stars, purple prickly sea urchins, blue-black mussels, and hermit crabs crawling in borrowed snail shells. Monterey's shallow bay provided ideal conditions for a lush kelp forest and an array of marine life. Sea otters grew well in this environment.

In the late 1700s Russians began hunting otter along the North American coastline, shipping highly prized pelts across the Pacific to Asia. The soft, lush otter fur and its luxurious warmth was coveted by Russian and Chinese aristocracy for trimming winter coats and court gowns. The Spanish claimed this region, ruling it from Mexico for more than a century without occupying it. Fearing competition for these lands and the riches of the otter fur trade they made Monterey a Spanish port and home to Mission San Carlos in Carmel, capital of Alta California and the mission system.

Soon Spanish, Russian, and Mexican fur hunters were harvesting twenty to thirty thousand sea otters along the coast annually, making millions of dollars, and drawing Americans around the Horn to grab a share of the trade. By 1825 sea otters were decimated, but their favored prey—sea urchins, abalone, and small fishes—became more abundant: a timely turn of the tides for the arrival of Chinese fishermen in 1853. They were probably Tanka, a Chinese minority from the Pearl River delta. These fishermen had been living on boats for all their recorded history (Lydon, 1985 p. 30).[1] They arrived with their families in junks, simple boats propelled by three sails: one on the main mast in the middle of the boat, one fore and another aft. Though seaworthy, the junks were barely large enough to hold a fisherman's family for ocean travel. When they landed, the Tanka began a Chinese community unique to the gold rush era—a group of families, not simply bachelors.

Earth-shaking events of the mid-nineteenth century wrought great changes in California and Monterey: Mexico declared independence from Spain in 1840, dismantled the mission system, and dispersed remaining Native populations; the United States acquired California in 1848, shortly before gold was discovered, attracting a rush of humanity who overwhelmed the former Mexican majority of Alta California. Yankees moved their capital to San Francisco, then to Sacramento where the economies were booming, far away from Monterey, where the Mexican lifestyle prevailed. In 1850 Monterey's census recorded predominantly Spanish-speaking Californios who tended unfenced cattle herds (Lydon, 1985 p. 26; and see Steven Hackel's essay in this volume). While the old capital became a quiet Mexican backwater, Santa Cruz in the northern tip of the bay filled with Yankees working the limestone mines and redwood timber mill. During this transitional period of California's history, the Chinese were the only ones interested in Monterey Bay fisheries. They were isolated from other fishermen, and the abalone were an unexpected treasure.

Abalone are grand mollusks that can be more than six inches wide. Their shells have a bumpy, rugged exterior, and layers of lumniscence line the interior. Underneath, a great muscular foot clings tenaciously to rocks that get battered by crashing surf. Their name may derive from the Indian name for them, "Aulon," or from the Spanish word "orejones," sea ears.[2] At low tide, the Chinese ventured out across the slippery kelp-covered tide pools to harvest the abalone. Sometimes, they approached the shallows in their boats. Still, prying abalone muscle off the rocks was no easy task. Once, a fisherman accidentally dropped his pry rod, and decided to reach under the shell to pull off the big muscle. Big mistake. The abalone clamped down on the fisherman, who drowned with the incoming tide because no one was around to pry him loose (*New Era* October 3, 1900).

To catch fish the Chinese navigated the shallow Monterey Bay waters in small sampans. These were little 21-foot boats built from redwood, cut from nearby forests in the Santa Cruz mountains. Each boat was decorated to protect the fisherman: "The outside of the craft was normally painted black, with eyes at the prow to enable the boat to see where it was going" (Armentrout-Ma 1979). A single fisherman stood at the back of the boat, sculling with an oar, or steering with the single sail. At day's end the boats were scooted onto flat, sandy beaches near the Chinese fishing camps along the edge of the bay. The "topsy-turvy" camps were fashioned of redwood shakes and driftwood collected on the beaches.

The largest permanent village grew up near the old Spanish settlement at Monterey, between Point Almejas (Mussel Point) and Point Alones (Abalone Point). Chinese fishermen also shared Point Lobos, or Whaler's Cove, with Portuguese whalers until the late 1870s. In a cove of Carmel Bay, just south of Monterey, naturalist David Starr Jordan visited Pescadero Point, named "the fishing place" by the Spanish and Mexicans, where he counted forty Chinese living in eight houses and twelve boats. In total a flotilla of thirty handmade boats were tied up on the rocky shore line (*Monterey Democrat*, July 20, 1872).

Railroads had not yet connected Monterey to San Francisco, and markets for fresh seafood were out of reach. The Chinese turned to their traditional methods of drying so that their harvest could be loaded onto junks bound for China. Abalone were hung on railings and roofs of wooden cabins to dry, their shells stacked in mounds next to the camps. As the harvest expanded, sea urchins, sea slugs, squid, shrimp, "rock fish, cod, halibut, flounders, red and blue fish, yellow tail, mackerel, sardines and shell fish" were added (*Weekly Herald*, Aug. 15, 1874). Drying techniques were adapted. Flounder were hung by their tails to dry; squid were hung from racks; seaweed was spread on the hillside. When the pearly abalone shells became popular for buttons and furniture inlay, the mounds of shells were converted to new income. A dizzying, diverse array of sights and fishy smells.

Fifteen years after the Tanka arrived, the Southern Pacific Railroad built a rail line connecting Santa Cruz and the Monterey region to San Francisco. Chinese laborers laid the track, then blasted tunnels through the mountains to Santa Cruz and over the grade from Salinas to Monterey. The railroads brought other immigrants, particularly Italian, Portuguese, and Greek fishermen. Like the Chinese, they'd immigrated with fishing traditions from their homelands, eager to harvest the bounty of California's bay waters. Suddenly the Chinese were faced with competition for the fishery. With political power on their side, at the height of anti-Chinese sentiment, the southern Europeans claimed the lucrative fresh-fish harvest. Italians used wide-keeled feluccas that restricted them to deeper waters and were not well adapted to shallow waters in the coves and beaches where the Chinese brought their boats ashore. But the fish were plentiful, and sent fresh, on ice, by rail to San Francisco where unfortunately only half the cargo was edible at the end of the overnight trip to market (Lydon, 1985 p. 46).

The Chinese continued to harvest abalone, and agreed to confine their fishing to Carmel Bay. But it was squid that helped the Chinese fishermen hang on a while longer in Monterey Bay (Lydon, 1985 p. 55). In April, when millions of squid migrated into the bay for two months, all the region's remaining Chinese fishermen converged on Point Alones. They harvested squid at night, in three-boat teams. A single fisherman in one boat lit a torch suspended in a small basket or pan over the water. As the squid were drawn to the light, two other boats quietly circled around them with a purse seine. When the net was drawn tightly, the wiggly squid were hand netted into the boats, and rowed ashore. Unlike the shrimp in San Francisco, these squid required little preparation. Larger squid were split open, cleaned, and dried on racks or rooftops, then shipped as big flakes to China. The smaller ones were left whole to dry, and salted in barrels before they were packed. Because salt was a very expensive commodity in China, these poorer-quality squid were exported more for the salt than for the meat stacked within it (Lydon, 1985 p. 57).

Differences in boats, separation in fish species being harvested, and exploiting different markets allowed the Chinese a period of time where their fishery co-existed with the southern Europeans. But intense anti-Chinese sentiments in the mid-1870s created a political atmosphere in California that helped push the Chinese out of Monterey's fishing industry.[3]

While European fishermen initiated limits to the kinds of fish the Chinese could take, tourists, lured by the railroads, arrived. They didn't like seeing shaggy fishing camps cobbled together with driftwood or smelling squid drying in the open air. The beaches where I ran into the surf at Aptos and Capitola, within sight of Santa Cruz on the northern edge of Monterey Bay, used to be Chinese fishing camps. The fishermen had no lease arrangements with landowners on the bluffs, and they were forced to retreat steadily down the beach. They kept moving until sand ran out past the outlet of the Pajaro River. The tides worked to wash away the makeshift camps, and no signs remained one hundred years later when we played in the sand.

Around the southern edges of the bay, the permanent Chinese villages became desirable real estate, but smells of drying fish, squid, abalone, and seaweed were intolerable to the newer immigrants. When Point Alones burnt to the ground in 1906 under suspicious circumstances, the city would not rebuild. The remaining Chinese moved inland to farm or work as laborers. The largest village at Point Alones became the site for sardine canneries; now a few pier pilings in the cove just west of the Monterey Bay Aquarium mark the site. No other signs of these pioneers remain—no buildings survived, no prominent place names. At Pescadero, that "fishing place," there used to be a heavy rusted chain the Chinese fishermen used for mooring boats in the small cove. Nearby their children sold abalone shells to tourists. Today Pescadero is the seventeenth green of the Pebble Beach golf course on the scenic Seventeen Mile Drive.

Shrimp fishermen in San Francisco faced other forms of discrimination. Between 1897 and 1911 legislative acts were directed specifically towards Chinese fishermen, closing the shrimp fishing season except for the poor fishing months of summer, banning exportation of shrimp, and prohibiting their bag nets (Armentrout-Ma 1981). During a similar period, between 1870 and 1915, the shrimp fishery of San Francisco Bay surpassed any other in the United States (Chinn 1969 p. 38). At its peak there were twenty-six Chinese fishing camps edging the mudflats of the bay: at Point Avisadero (near PacBell field in San Francisco), Point San Bruno where the airport is today, Richmond in the East Bay, Point San Quentin and San Pedro Point, that we now call China Camp, to the north (Scofield 1954). Further justification for restricting shrimp fishermen was based on fears that shrimp were being overharvested. But consumer demand for shrimp continued, and restrictions were eased in 1915. At China Camp and in the South Bay a few fishermen renewed shrimp fishing using modern trawlers.

In those days San Francisco Bay was alive with commercial fishing activity and boat traffic. There were no bridges; ferries carried people, crisscrossing the bay from San Francisco north to San Pablo Bay, east to Oakland, and south towards San Jose. Though overfishing may have contributed to the decline of San Francisco's abundant shrimp, siltation, pollution from ship wastes, and urban development also played a role. These environmental factors escalated particularly during World War II, degrading water quality and eliminating bay habitat for shrimp, oysters, clams, and other tideland fauna.

After World War II fresh bay shrimp were still sold by Chinese fishermen and my Mom remembers the shrimp displayed on great circular bamboo trays along bay piers in Oakland and Berkeley. Recently a food connoisseur on one of my favorite cooking shows declared the bay shrimp of San Francisco to be the most special in all the world, and still a rare treat.

These days the road leading away from San Pedro Point's China Camp borders the Bay. As Mom and I drove home I viewed the mudflats along the highway with new appreciation. Flocks of small shore birds flew low over the water, rushes and reeds punctuated the tidal mudflats. Salt-extraction plants, towering apartment complexes, mushrooming housing units, and harbors built on lands "reclaimed" by filling in the flats occupy many of the tidal areas once rich in fish and invertebrates. Restoration has begun to recover a fraction of those lands, but only historical photographs and stories from our elders remind us of the fishermen, their sampans, their camps, and harvests of shrimp and abalone.

References

Armentrout-Ma, Eve. 1979. "Sampans, Junks and Chinese Fishermen in the Golden State." San Francisco National Maritime Museum. Pamphlet.

———. 1981. "Chinese in California's Fishing Industry, 1850-1942." *California History* 60, no. 2: 142-57.

Chinn, Thomas W. 1969. *A History of The Chinese in California; A Syllabus.* San Francisco, California: Chinese Historical Society of America, p. 40-44.

Lydon, S. 1985. *Chinese Gold: The Chinese in the Monterey Bay Region.* Capitola, California: Capitola Book Company.

Monterey Democrat, July 20, 1872. *In*: Lydon, S. 1985. *Chinese Gold: The Chinese in the Monterey Bay Region.* Capitola, California: Capitola Book Company.

New Era, October 3, 1900. *In*: Lydon, S. 1985. *Chinese Gold: The Chinese in the Monterey Bay Region.* Capitola, California: Capitola Book Company.

Scofield, N. B. July 1897. Report to the California Board of Fish and Game Commissioners. *In*: Commissioners 16th Biennial Report (1899-1900).

Scofield, W. L. 1954. California Fishing Ports. California Department of Fish and Game. Fish Bulletin No. 96.

Weekly Herald, August 15, 1874. *In*: Lydon, S. 1985. *Chinese Gold: The Chinese in the Monterey Bay Region.* Capitola, California: Capitola Book Company.

In the words of John Bieter's Basque grandfather the "rough" Idaho mountains where he herded sheep were " bald/sparse but pretty steep in places where [they] worked in summer, totally forested with pines." Bieter describes the struggles of nomadic immigrant Basque sheepherders in this harsh, semi-arid terrain of mountain valleys, foothills, and cliffs, dependent on public domain grazing lands.

Lorenzo's Letters
A Basque Immigrant's Experience in the American West

John Bieter

It looked like a scene from a movie shot in the European countryside—the large extended family gathered alongside the centuries-old farmhouse, surrounded by rich, green sloping fields. Our grandfather, born on May 22, 1885, emigrated from this place almost one hundred years ago. On the eve of my oldest brother's wedding the family gathered here for the first and only time around tables with red-and-white checkered cloths, wine, mounds of freshly prepared food, and non-stop conversation. As the afternoon progressed I asked my great aunt, "*Aitxitxek eskutitzak idatzi ahal dau?*" "Did our grandfather ever write any letters?" "*Ez dakit, ikusiko dot.*" "I'm not sure, I'll check." The next day at the wedding reception she handed me a bundle of fifty-one letters. Blowing the dust off the plastic covering, she pronounced, "*Hauek, zuentzat dira.*" "Here, these are for you."

March 27th, 1912 Deusto [a neighborhood of the port city of Bilbao]
My reason [for writing] is to tell you that earlier they promised me to go to California . . . someone was leaving the 5th of April and if I wanted to go with him I can . . . having good health you can make some bucks in a few years. I also really want to go because the daily wage here [in the Basque Country] between room and board and expenses is all gone.

While working a seasonal job in town, my grandfather Lorenzo Garmendia wrote this letter to his father on the farm in Larrabetzu, Bizkaia, the Basque region of northern Spain. His story of immigrating to Idaho and working in the sheep industry represents thousands of Basques who chose to migrate to the American West beginning with the California Gold Rush of 1849. Their experiences with the land helped shape their identity as immigrant Americans and played a role in shaping the landscape of the American West.

Sadly, little is known about the Basques. History books often misidentify, as either Spanish or French, Basque individuals such as Juan Sebastian de Elcano, who finished the circumnavigation voyage for Magellan, or Ignatius of Loyola, founder of the Jesuit order. The region straddling the Pyrenees Mountains in northern Spain and southwestern France has been occupied continuously by humans from at least the Cro-Magnon era. Even the most conservative estimate places Basques in this area since 5,000 to 3,000 B.C., making them the oldest permanent residents of Western Europe. Traditionally, there have been four historical territories on the southern (Spanish) and three on the northern (French) side. Several lines of evidence support the idea of a lengthy, continuous occupation. Basque anthropologists claim human skulls found in the region's caves have Basque features, and blood-type studies revealed an unusually high proportion of Rh-negative blood type distinctive to Basques. However, it is the language, *Euskera,* which linguists cannot link with any other Indo-European language, that separates the Basques most definitively from other Europeans.

While Basques have an ancient history in this region, they also have a long history of leaving it. Starting in the seventh century, Basque whalers hunted in the Bay of Biscay and fished their way across the Atlantic, eventually reaching Newfoundland. Linguistic and archeological evidence points to a Basque presence there in the second half of the sixteenth century. Basques played a significant role throughout the history of settlement in the New World, from a significant portion of Columbus's crew to colonizing and missionary efforts in what would become Mexico, Uruguay, Colombia, and Venezuela. One Basque explorer founded the northern Mexican province of Nueva Vizcaya, naming its capital after his Bizkaian birthplace, Durango. Another Basque descendant became even more famous: Simon Bolivar, the liberator of South America.

In the 1800s, Basques participated in the earliest developments of the sheep industry in the pampas of Argentina and elsewhere. That was part of a secondary Basque migration that also brought the earliest Basques to California after the discovery of gold. While few had success mining, their efforts in the booming livestock industry provided an opportunity. From California, they fanned throughout the American West, trailing sheep in the open range and recruiting family and friends from the Basque Country. Chain migration created a pattern of settlement with French and Navarese Basques establishing themselves in California, while Spanish Basques predominantly from the province of Bizkaia concentrated in Nevada and Idaho.

Basques' movement into the American West represented a relatively minor portion of Basque worldwide settlement over several centuries. Whereas other movements attracted individuals from diverse economic backgrounds, this latest migration consisted almost exclusively of lower-class laborers. Nearly all Basque immigrants that came to Idaho at the turn of the twentieth century had grown up on farms, where they struggled for subsistence living from a variety of crops. Basques traditionally selected one son or daughter as the sole inheritor of a small farm, often six to ten hectares carved out of a hillside, to avoid fragmentation. The other siblings of the traditionally large families remained single and stayed on the farm, entered a religious community, or went to town for work.[1]

On July 5, 1912, Garmendia wrote to confirm a safe arrival despite news that a ship had sunk. "I received your letter on the 3rd (of July) dated the 13th of May. . . . We found out that a ship wrecked . . . we got here with no problems . . ." Typical of the male immigrants, Lorenzo "came to earn some money and I'll come back in 3 or 4 years . . ." He pledged to help his family: "I'm going to send you that amount and even more because until now I have helped you as best I could now it is my wish that you get along better than until now," and held on to a hopeful return: "[Y]ou tell me that you were sad about my leaving don't worry because if I'm healthy I'll see you again."

Lorenzo Garmendia's journey reflects the common Basque immigration pattern into Idaho and the American West. Most early Idaho herders were single males under the age of thirty with little money and education. On average, the fifty-three Boise-bound Basques who arrived in New York between 1897 and 1902 carried only $36.50 each. In 1910 only 50.9 percent of the Basques in Idaho could read and write. Of the few that were married, half left their wives behind. Lorenzo's letter supports the common intent for a short migration to make money and desire to return to the Basque Country with new opportunities afforded from their savings.[2]

Typical of many newcomers, within days of his arrival Lorenzo and another herder, with their dogs and support from a camp tender, were high in the hills in charge of a band of 2,400 sheep. However Lorenzo, like most of his fellow immigrants, had no prior knowledge of herding sheep. If they had herded sheep at all back home, the flock consisted of small bands that provided food and wool for the family, involving none of the loneliness, financial risk, or danger of the large-scale herding in Idaho. Although held in low regard by most Americans, sheepherding offered one of the few emigrating alternatives for young Basque men with few skills and no knowledge of English. As one immigrant claimed, "The worst is no can talk." Another asked, "What the hell else was I going to do, work in an office?"

Many of the novice herders expected terrain in the American West to be like the Basque Country; however, differences in topography and climate were quite pronounced. Over 95 percent of Basque immigrants to Idaho came from the province of Bizkaia, which averages approximately 40 inches of annual rainfall, four times that of the high country desert. Lorenzo Garmendia described the terrain: "[A]ll of the lower mountains are bald/sparse but pretty steep in places where we work in the summer totally forested with pines and steep terrain with cliffs which in Spain there aren't even any to compare with." He claimed: "[N]o one would even believe that you have to herd sheep in such rough mountains." Moreover, he covered more ground in two months than he had his entire life in the Basque region. "We have crossed more land than all of Biscaya and Gipuscua [two provinces in the Basque Country] 30 days that way and 30 days this way . . ."

October 28, 1912

> *[I hope] you enjoyed festival time . . . for us they were days that make you remember because it started to snow on August 29 until September 6 it caught me on a high ridge with the band of sheep the weather was really bad those days you guys must have been enjoying the heat but we were cold in the snow those days it would have been better to be invited over to someone's*

*home for a nice meal than taking care of the sheep in the snow . . . those days
I thought I was going to lose half of the sheep but I didn't lose any . . . others
lost up to two hundred and three hundred with a bad storm.*

That same day, Lorenzo also wrote his friend Gregorio to update him on
his situation in America and inviting him to come. Thanking God for good
health as he opens each letter, Lorenzo moves into the hearsay of the political
arena that affects his livelihood. "It is the changing of the President . . . if
the one from the Democrats [Woodrow Wilson] wins . . . salaries will be cut
in half cattle and food will also drop by half in price." Accordingly, "a lot of
people are selling sheep afraid of that because the biggest business in this
country is sheep."

Lorenzo was correct about the importance of the sheep industry. In 1850,
over five hundred thousand sheep ranged in mostly small flocks on private
lands in the West. However, the profitability of raising sheep attracted investors
and the industry exploded; by 1880, nineteen million head of sheep grazed
in seventeen western states. As Idaho gained statehood in 1890, officials
counted 501,978 head of sheep and by 1910 that number had exploded to
3,010,478.[3]

Lorenzo warned his friend who worked as a baker: "[F]or your occupation
there are very few bakeries" since "work here is with sheep or in the mines or
on some railway or in lumber where they pay 2 and a half 'duros' [dollars] a
day but they stop some jobs in the winter for 2 or 3 months." He also wrote
of the stark reality of being a herder: "[T]o make money sheep is the best
although it's quite sad you might not even see anyone for 6 days and that
makes for long days . . . to live your whole life it is a sad country."

The intense isolation and loneliness took its toll on many. "I remember
when I got my first letter from my mother," one Basque herder said. "I had
to go behind the trees to read it because I was crying like a baby." For some,
this extreme isolation became too much to bear; they went insane or became
"sheeped" or "sagebrushed" as the herders referred to it. In 1908 the courts
tried a Basque herder in Mountain Home to determine his mental health.
After hearing the results of his examination by a local doctor, the court
declared, "He was so far disordered in mind as to endanger health, person
and property," and the court committed him to an institution. In fact, when
early Basques immigrants to Idaho formed a health insurance organization
in Boise, part of its coverage included return passage to the Basque Country
for any member who suffered from mental illness.[4] Lorenzo also identified a

fellow herder from a neighboring town, who "went crazy about a month ago they have him in an insane asylum" (June 19, 1924).

However, the opportunity to make some money and the chance to return to a better life continued to motivate herders. "I ask you to grease up my tools because I might need them when I come back to Spain because when I make some bucks I'm thinking of coming back. . . " (Oct. 28, 1912). Relatives in the Basque Country also benefited. "I'm sending 200 American "duros" [$4,091 dollars in 2006] with a pledge to send more later." (Jan 21, 1913)

The life of a herder followed a regular rhythm. Sheepherders immersed themselves in the bloody, messy work of the lambing season from January to mid-March, when they helped deliver thousands of lambs and then divided them into bands. They learned how to shear the sheep in March and April and trailed them to the foothills to feed on spring grasses in May. During the summer, herders drove the bands to the mountains, followed the retreating line of snow, steered them from one meadow to another, and descended only to ship the lambs in July. They began to trail down to the valleys in October before the first snowfall, and by December they held the sheep in corrals. They prepared for the birth of the first lambs, and the process started again.[5]

Lorenzo looked forward to the possibility of a bonus of $20 (over $400 in 2006) if he could keep all of the lambs protected. But he acknowledged "lots of predators" and the herders' unending efforts to guard the herd. In the mountain meadows coyotes, cougars, or bears often attacked the herd. "When we get 3 or 4 bands [of sheep] together in the mountains we usually spend time learning how to shoot rifles because here all of the sheepherders use rifles." Supporting their efforts, "our boss pays for all of the shotgun shells when we shoot targets." Meanwhile, "the bands are usually grazing in the open hills while we shoot targets the dogs rest because later it's their turn to work because they have to make up for our mistakes" (Kan. 22, 1915).

Summer months in the hills could be the most dangerous, while winter offered the best opportunities for companionship and comforts, as well as the financial costs connected to being in town and not working. Lorenzo received a letter from his sister Maria. "She tells me that her hope is to come to America," he wrote. Besides opportunity for his brothers to work, "for Maria I also have 2 houses where she can work as a maid." While men came to work as herders, the boardinghouses that responded to the need for temporary housing constantly sought young Basque women to work in them. These "homes away from home" met many of the herders' needs, serving at times as hospitals, employment agencies, and marriage mills where many herders met their mates. They had the chance to speak Basque, eat familiar foods, and enjoy the festive atmosphere. "Out of the hills playing *tute* [a Basque card game] cooking chorizos and eggs and making rice pudding we do everyday." Another herder commented, "for us it was heaven . . . the closest thing to home" (Jan. 1, 1915).

However, being in town meant herders were not being paid. " [B]eing in town living costs are greater. . . . [If] some winter you find yourself without work in town you end up with nothing because it gets spent quickly." But with no readily available health care he had no choice. "I'm in Boise these days because I came to get a molar pulled and to fix another two because I had a toothache for a month I think it will take around 10 days to fix my teeth and go back." On another occasion he lost twenty days pay due to a sickness (December 1, 1915) and, riding bareback, he was thrown and broke his leg, which cost him hundreds of dollars in lost pay in addition to his medical and personal expenses (June 1, 1920).

As opportunity in the sheep industry expanded, the demand for herders grew with it; yet few aspired to sheepherding. Settlers described herders as "outcasts and ne'er-do-wells, shifty characters too undependable to be hired in the mines or by cattlemen." One author noted that the sheepherder, the once-honorable figure of the pastoral ages, now "has only one consolation left, and that is the secure knowledge that he is working on rock bottom." A common adage held that "you could not fire a shotgun into the average crowd in the range country without hitting a man who had at some time herded sheep, but it would probably take the charge in the other barrel to make him admit it."

While many employers preferred Basques, they quickly drew the ire of cattle and farming interests. From its inception, the sheep industry had numerous "tramp bands," which did not operate from base ranches. Rather, the absentee owners of these "tramp bands" hired non-English-speaking immigrants such as the Basques and sent them onto the public domain. These ventures required little or no investment in buildings or land and often resulted in handsome profits. Because these owners paid no taxes, had no community roots, and hired alien herders, they drew the ire of landed stockmen. As these bands flourished and as agricultural pursuits grew, itinerant sheepmen sought less-crowded range conditions. This nomadic search for grazing opportunities resulted in constant friction between land interests,[7] including some landed sheepmen who wanted to remove itinerant herds and foreign herders.

In Mono National Forest, California, nineteen sheepmen and stock owners, who had grazed their flocks for the past few years, were notified of their lost rights "bearing on the point of citizenship which excludes aliens [*sic*] and non-property holders from grazing privileges in the forest." After personally surveying conditions in the West, the chief forester determined "that Basque sheep owners were fast gaining possession of the grazing rights and completely crowding the citizen and property holder from grazing their sheep in the forest." The forester allowed those who had grazed in this area to continue for the year, "but such persons must be citizens of the United States, or, if not citizens, must be bona fide residents of and owners of improved ranch property either within or adjacent to the national forest lands which they have formerly used." He concluded, "Anyone not in the above class will be treated as trespassers."[8]

Numerous papers throughout the western United States regularly reported instances of violence involving Basque herders. The Basque language newspaper *Californiako Euskal Herria* (*The Basque Country of California*) reported on May 30, 1896, and August 14, 1897, shootings of Basque herders in California and Arizona. In Winnemucca, Nevada, on August 4 the paper reported, "Armed men are visiting the sheep ranches near Disaster Peak, shooting the sheep and stealing horses. It is supposed the invaders were cattlemen, who took this method of driving the sheepmen from the country." On September 1, 1905, the *Nevada State Herald* reported that a man named Wallace shot a Basque herder, Simon Salas, in the shoulder. Reportedly, Salas was herding sheep on a mountainside while Wallace remained on a creek below. Wallace claimed he called to Salas to "come down." Allegedly Salas refused, and Wallace shot at him. Wallace, who homesteaded in the region, had shot at another herder in a separate incident a year earlier.[9]

A 1919 Forest Service report revealed the range of sentiments felt towards and by the variety of livestock interests. Itinerant herders were strongly criticized. "[The] public range is fast being destroyed by transient sheep owners who have no thought of preserving the range for future generations. These owners are for the most part Basques, who are not citizens of the United States, and are here simply to get what they can from the natural resources of this country with the least possible expense to themselves." However, the report deemed the few naturalized Basques "good citizens" since they improved the ranch property and developed the country.[10]

Public perceptions of Basques varied with the amount of time they spent in America, their economic success, and their future plans. Some Basques enjoyed exceptional economic success; a few in Idaho grew especially wealthy. In 1893, Juan Achabal survived the sinking of his ship on the way to America, literally landed with only the clothes on his back, but by the early 1900s owned eighty thousand sheep and employed fifty-nine men in southwest Idaho. Jose Bengoechea emigrated in 1897, worked a few years as a herder, but within two decades rivaled Achabal for sheep ownership. He also worked as vice-president of the local bank, and proprietor of the Mountain Home Hotel—the town's finest.[11]

While these Basques gained the respect of broader American societal circles, most of their countrymen toiled further down the economic ladder, many as itinerant herders, in the same way that Achabal and Bengoechea got their start. These herders and their practices continued as the target of much American animosity. Ironically, while most of the settled livestock interests had recently migrated to the area and started their businesses in a similar fashion, they continued to view these "tramp" sheepmen as the epitome of the anti-American. They argued that these rootless wanderers trespassed on their land, cared little to nothing about local affairs, and merely stripped the land of its value and returned with their riches to their homeland. On December 5, 1913, the *Humboldt Star* reported that five Basque sheepmen returned to Spain, some of them to visit but "two of them have sold their bands of sheep and will remain in the old country. Incidentally, these latter took away with them several thousand dollars, which will also remain."[12]

On the floor of the Senate, Key Pittman of Nevada delivered a vituperative description of Basques herders. "[The sheepmen] get that class of labor because they seem to be adapted for sheep herding, and they are lacking in intelligence, independence, or anything else. They are just about as near a slave as anybody could be under our present existing conditions." A local Idaho newspaper echoed similar racially slanderous comments: "The scale of living and the methods of doing business of the Bascos are on a par with those of the Chinamen. However, they have some undesirable characteristics that the Chinese are free from." Although the Chinese had been excluded earlier and generally remained near the bottom of social levels of acceptance, the author sought to place Basques at society's lowest rung, describing the Basques as "filthy, treacherous, and meddlesome. However, they work hard and save their money. They are clannish and undesirable but," the author warned, "they have a foothold and unless something is done will make life impossible for the whiteman."[13]

These prejudiced statements at the local and national level, when contrasted against favorable comments in newspapers and other reports, revealed the era's criteria for acceptance and respectability. Specifically, land ownership and citizenship represented a commitment that allowed Basques to be well received into the larger American community. It also seems to have made them more racially acceptable. The relatively small minority that made these choices tended to be praised, while those that did not were scorned. The *Humboldt Star*, reporting on a recent group of arrivals: "They are expert sheepmen and are an industrious people. Many of them own large flocks of sheep and are landowners and have made this country their permanent home."[14] The changing number of applications for citizenship most likely represented attempts to overcome what was clearly an anti-alien environment.[15] In Winnemucca, Nevada, alone, where only forty-eight Basques had filed for United States citizenship between 1871 and 1906, an additional one hundred eight did so between 1906 and 1912. In Ada County, Idaho, only thirteen Basques filed a Declaration of Intention between 1888 and 1903, yet between 1906 and 1909 at least forty-eight filed for citizenship.

After two years of herding sheep, Lorenzo contemplated going into business for himself. On October 26, 1914, he wrote that he had "changed jobs mid September" and "squared up the accounts with my former boss and I left him money with the condition that he would pay me 7 percent interest per year." Apparently, he had enjoyed a good year: "[S]heep owners make a lot of money because wool and the lambs were worth a lot." Consequently, "I and another friend as well are thinking about buying some sheep on our own some way if we can work it out."

While Lorenzo contemplated going into business, wider national and international events—Prohibition, World War I, and immigration acts—drastically affected the context in which he made these decisions. "A bachelor can make more money than in Spain if you can withstand a little calamity," Lorenzo wrote, ". . . and since the first of the year more [tough times] are coming because they have taken away the drinking in all the states of America starting the 1st of next year." This resulted in fewer celebrations: "[Y]ou hear very little guitar playing and very little music here there is a little happiness when sheep and lambs start 'baaa' ing." In a letter dated September 12, 1915, Lorenzo predicted that he would not go to Boise until Christmas when he was "thinking of spending some 15 to 20 days because starting New Years day drinking will be prohibited." His boss from Boise had written, "asking me to come a month before the New Year because he has lots to drink at home and he says he wants to finish all the booze by new year." He added, "that's because of women who in this country can vote and have as much power as men do in Spain."

"I'm getting more and more tired of this sheepherding job and the doctor said that I'm not helping myself out much with this job he said that you can lose your health working in the mountains and that I look like an old fifty year old [he's actually thirty years old] because I'm already a little hunchbacked and I'm starting to get a little bald" (Dec. 1, 1915). Nevertheless, he took the time to have a portrait taken and sent back to the Basque Country.

"Enclosed I send you my portrait and place this gentleman on a special table on Christmas day because he looks like quite the handsome gentleman there." He continued, "but in the mountains he is usually very grimy and with a long beard like the homeless on the corners of Bilbao with their dirty pants." The reaction of friends and family to the portrait was that Lorenzo was "thin and getting old." He countered, "[W]ell in the portrait I seem young and fat if those people could see me in the mountains they would say that I'm not the same as before because even I'm afraid to look in the mirror." He described how the filth worked at times in his favor. "[W]e had some pretty big cloudbursts of rain but not even a drop soaked through my shirt because . . . when our shirts are completely grimy we wear them untucked and it works like a raincoat."

He ended the letter with his constant refrain, "someday I'm going to head out to Spain" (June 15, 1916), but in the following letter noted that "I have a better job than before as camp tender and [make] 5 or 10 dollars more salary per month" (Dec. 2, 1916). Despite the wishes of his family that he return at least for a visit, a "friend and I together have bought some sheep [twelve hundred] with subsequent profitable offers to purchase them" (March 5, 1917). Much of the profit came from demand caused by World War I.

Economically, the war meant a substantial increase in demand for wool, and consequently greater demand for herders at the same time that conscription called many into military service. On March 27, 1917, the *Idaho Statesman* reported that the "National Council of Defense Will Confer With Growers on Supply Needed for War." Concerned over the increased need for wool during wartime, the secretaries of war and navy instructed the National Defense Council to secure for the government "at a reasonable price, an adequate supply of raw wool and manufactured woolens that may be needed for military purposes in event of war." Two weeks later the government anticipated buying 60,000,000 pounds of clean wool for military uses. Equivalent to 140,000,000 pounds of raw wool, the government's demands represented nearly half the total American clip, which would significantly impact the industry. On behalf of western woolgrowers, a committee offered to furnish the war department all the wool required at current market prices. Lorenzo commented on the impact of the war in one of his letters. "Last year sheep owners made a lot of money and this year they are going to make even more it's because of the war because this war is good for this country because they ship a lot of meat and wool to England" (Jan. 22, 1915).[16]

The war also brought out differences within the Basque community, between itinerant herders, who saw in the war an opportunity for greater financial compensation, and those who had established themselves and wished to assure the larger public of their loyalty. On August 26, 1917, the *Idaho Statesman* reported that in some sections of the state, "sheepherders, mostly aliens, . . . have formed a combination and virtually gone on strike, demanding wages of $100 a month and board." The president of the Idaho Woolgrowers' Association countered that "the industry could not afford this increase in pay, that sheepherders generally were receiving $60 and board, and that the item of board was growing large on account of increased costs of food stuff." Moreover, he maintained that this action of "alien employees" merely represented the beginning of an ever-increasing problem for the livestock and farming industries as more men were drafted for the war effort. "The presence of large numbers of aliens in some of the range counties threw an increasing likelihood of being drafted on the American employees in the industries in those counties, and that these Americans in many instances formed the nucleus of skilled employees for sheepmen, cattlemen, and ranchers."[17]

Naturalization made no difference according to the National Woolgrowers' Association, which informed its Idaho division that "a great many Idaho sheepmen do not understand that their Basque and Spanish employees between the ages of 21 and 30 years have to register." The woolgrowers' representative explicitly asked officials about registration requirements and was advised: "The fact that they are not naturalized citizens does not exempt them from the registration."[18] Amid discussions of alien laborers and the draft, those Basques with residency worked hard to assure the public of their loyalty. In resolutions sent to the mayor of Boise and Idaho's governor, Basques asserted their desire to be an asset to the "Greatest Nation Beneath the Sun." Signed by prominent members of the Basque community, the resolution stated that "the Spanish-born citizens expressed their desire to participate in any patriotic rally held in this city." Even more explicit, these "natives of Spain, who are now residents and citizens of the United States," took the unprecedented step of issuing a jingoistic resolution designed to represent "their duty to manifest their loyalty to the government of their adoption during the present international crisis." The group pledged full support and strongly asserted the desire to demonstrate their value as "an asset and not a liability." They maintained their "undivided allegiance and loyalty to this great, free government," and promised to "uphold this government, and to help sustain it in any controversy or armed conflict in which it may engage." They hoped to participate "as freely, loyally and cheerfully as if we were native-born citizens" and cited the purchase of "liberty bonds" as further evidence of their loyalty. The Chairman of the Liberty Bond drive stated, "It is gratifying to see these representatives of a great industry respond so freely in the country's hour of need, there isn't a class of people anywhere who are more loyal." For financially conservative Basque immigrants, these bonds and stamps represented an ideal investment. They could demonstrate their loyalty while securing a low-risk investment.[20]

Lorenzo did not write of being drafted but did comment on Spain's involvement and the effect of the war on increasing demand for workers. "They are saying here that Spain is going to war against Germany this country has already declared war against Germany about a month ago here they say that the Spanish will have to go back to Spain or [report] to the army to help out the Americans." He laments the increase in prices caused by the war but acknowledges "this country is better than ever for the worker because salaries are good." The war not only created demand for laborers, and consequently higher wages, but also resulted in higher profits for owners. Lorenzo commented, "[I]t's all because of the current war all of the sheep owners got rich and they all buy automobiles and come in automobiles to see the sheep" (Oct. 16, 1917).

In the midst of relative prosperity, tragedy found its way to Lorenzo. "I had pretty bad news about the death of my brother Julian," Lorenzo wrote, "may his soul rest in peace in Heaven with the grace of God" (May 16, 1917). Later he made arrangements to send money to his orphaned nieces. In subsequent years the Spanish flu epidemic would kill thousands. "I knew there were lots of epidemics in Spain and that's also what all the news [coming from Spain] says . . . and lots of people have died here lots of Spanish guys all of them from 25 to 35 years old." In Boise, one young Basque recalled six

A family photo of Garamendia family: Lorenzo Garamendia, far right and standing, and Fermina (Achabal) Garmendia next to him on the horse. The other woman on a horse is Agueda Achabal, and the man on the left has not been identified. Photograph courtesy of author.

funerals in one day. One boy served as an altar server at five of them but was sent home exhausted and missed the sixth—that of his own brother.

Predators and unseasonable weather proved challenging as well. "On the first day of going up to the forest we made out pretty well then for 4 days we had to trek across snow without seeing ground to [feed the] sheep," Lorenzo wrote, ". . . without eating in 4 days nothing more than what they could grab from some greenery from the pines in those few days around 3,000 sheep were lost [died] some lost more than others one lost up to 1,200 head that guy ended up going bankrupt we didn't lose more than 40 and thanks to the change in the weather and a little bit of growth of grass" (June 22, 1918). These busy times left little opportunities to write "since morning until sundown we had to stay on our feet by the time we got to sleep it was always about 11 at night." Moreover, a railroad strike resulted in "thousands of lambs that are sold and waiting for wagons" and a drought meant "the lambs haven't fattened up as much as they should have."

The war and shifting attitudes towards immigrants resulted in a drastic change of immigration policy. Lorenzo wrote of the labor shortage due to the war and that "they have stopped the entrance for foreigners into this country for 5 years and the few that are here are leaving for their homelands especially Spanish men." Consequently, "many that have sheep are selling them because they can't find the workers to take care of them" (April 29, 1919).

Tough conditions made the possibility of success more difficult, but the fear of failure drove many to persist. "It was unthinkable," one author stated, "that a Basque emigrant could return to his village without having succeeded in his immigration efforts." Lorenzo claimed, "I wouldn't go to Spain to be like a 'poor man' with pants torn in the seat and to be called poor American [one who failed in America]." A few of his countrymen presented a striking contrast to the average Basque experience. In 1925, the highly successful John Archabal, who had changed his name from Juan Archabal, returned driving an automobile purchased in Detroit and shipped to Europe to tour the Basque Country while hosting dinners for family and friends. He paid each of his siblings $500 so that they would not have to work while he was visiting. In a country where oxen and donkeys prevailed, children ran alongside the car, helped clean and polish it, no doubt dreaming of how they might go to America where they might purchase one for themselves. Lorenzo knew a different reality. "Many who have come to America they think that they will be living like royalty here the one who has the biggest hopes gets the biggest disappointments" (Oct. 9, 1922).

Despite consistent claims about returning to the Basque Country, Lorenzo Garmendia wrote his father that he had a girlfriend and was likely to be married soon (Oct. 9, 1922). Two years later he wrote he would get rid of his nickname "*mutil zarra*" (old single guy), and on June 21, 1924, he married Fermina Achabal, a niece of wealthy John Achabal. For many this decision sealed their fate. Lorenzo's instructions to his father about what to do with his carpentry tools signaled the change. He pledges to "let you know about the tools . . . you can use them whenever you need them because being here I don't need them." But he leaves the door open, if only in his mind: "[W]e'll see how it turns out."

Lorenzo sent money home for them to celebrate the wedding with "a little wine and a *bacalada* [codfish] and a little meat." After getting married, he and Fermina vacationed for the first time in their lives—three weeks along the coast of California (July 27, 1924). The letters became less frequent and described a much more settled lifestyle. In a July 23, 1925, letter, they inform Lorenzo's father that "you also have a very beautiful grand daughter," and promise that "Fermina says that we will come to Spain when our daughter is old enough to work and then we will visit you." The next letter is written by Fermina to her father-in-law. "From what Lorenzo's letter says you haven't had news from here for a long time well I'm telling you that Lorenzo has been really busy with his farm work."

When one of Fermina's brothers who emigrated to Peru came to visit her in Boise, Lorenzo recounted, "I've gotten real lazy about writing." After filling his father in on the latest he writes, "[O]ur little girl is saying a few words in Basque and a few in English. . . . My wife and I are always arguing about this issue [returning to the Basque Country] since we don't have lots of money." On June 20, 1927, a second girl was born and sealed the thought of returning for some time. Letters continue sparingly, separated by great time gaps.

Post World War I, America became increasingly suspicious of its ability to absorb the flood of immigrants pouring into the country. Nativism maintained that southern and western Europeans or "new" immigrants (over twenty million had entered the United States since the 1880s) had polluted the race. This attitude, coupled with the xenophobia of World War I and initial stages of the Red Scare of McCarthyism, created an urgency to stem the tide of immigration. In 1921 the United States established an immigration quota law and the Immigration Act of 1924, which reduced the number of Spanish nationals allowed annually to just 131, ending the Basques' large-scale legal entry into the American West.

In the next decade, economic depression and most especially the Taylor Grazing Act of 1934 permanently changed land use in the American West and subsequently the lives of Basque immigrants. Although grazing fees and regulation had been established earlier by the U.S. Forest Service, the future of millions of acres still in the public domain was bitterly contested. A growing conservation movement, an image of land abused by transient herders, and an East Coast publicity campaign blaming antiquated grazing practices as the cause of land abuse, resulted in the passage of the Taylor Grazing Act in 1934. The bill and subsequent legislation placed 173 million acres in federal grazing districts, where fees and grazing schedules were required. By requiring ownership of base property for eligibility to grazing rights, the Taylor Grazing Act closed ten western states, including Idaho, to itinerant herding. Basque sheepmen could no longer run their sheep freely on public lands. They were forced to make a much larger commitment if they wanted to continue in the business. No other piece of legislation affected Basques' involvement in the sheep industry like this one. "Basques tend to reckon time in terms of before and after 'Taylor Grazing'" wrote anthropologist William A. Douglass. He described it as a "kind of New and Old Testament in their group life in the American West."

Conclusion

That significant portions of western America remained open land well into the twentieth century signified one of the central differences between the Basque Country and the American West. In their homeland, unless Basques inherited it, they were not likely to own any land. Early immigrants such as Lorenzo Garmendia emigrated with the hope of returning, at least creating a better life, and perhaps purchasing a farm. As they worked in America, each had to decide for him/herself what they would do. Many returned, a number stayed. For most the decision did not come in any one moment but rather as it did for Lorenzo—gradually, over time, always with the intent of returning while focused on the work and life at hand.

The land and its uses remained central on both sides of the Atlantic, often providing the very essence of identity. By tradition, the land gave Basques their very name. For instance, Garmendia (Lorenzo's surname) means "volcano" in Basque, Urberuaga means "next to the hot spring," Goikoetxea (sometimes spelled Goicoechea or other variations thereof) means "of the upper house," and Zelaia translates as "plains." Rather than occupation identifying the last name as is common in many European traditions (Shoemaker, for example), geographic location names that person. However, in America these names often changed. "Enrique" Alegria wrote that soon after his family moved to America, "we began calling ourselves American names, [instead of Enrique] I became Henry." My grandmother's uncle Juan became John. Other Basques with the surname Uriaguerica became Uria, Malaxechevarria became Berria and, no doubt to the relief of his future teachers, Estaquio Garroguerricaechevarria became Ed Garro.

These name changes symbolized a larger shift in identity. No longer living in the land from which they had been given their name, Basques changed and altered their names to more fully assimilate into the Anglo-American environment. Was it worth it? It depends on whom you ask. "Forty years later," one Basque man said of his emigration, "you realize that what you gave up is more than what you gained. For a few dollars, you sold your soul, you sold your family, you lose everything. . . . Forty years later, I'm still a foreigner, an immigrant. You give a lot more than you gained." Another woman emigrant commented after a return trip to the Basque Country that the trip "was like a lovely dream. . . . But I like to get back to the United States. This is my own country now and it is better." Another put it even more succinctly: "[T]his is the greatest country on earth."

Although his wife returned with two of their adult daughters after Lorenzo died, he personally never had a chance to return to the Basque Country. Did he forget about the Basque Country? Did he find his place in the American West? At the end of each letter to his father Lorenzo signed "your son who never forgets you." While he was trying to establish himself, return addresses changed regularly, but he adapted to some local customs, suggesting letters be addressed to "Mr. with an *m* and an *r* which means '*senor don*'." When he left the Basque Country in 1912, he expected he would return, but opportunities, responsibilities, and incremental decisions added up to a life spent in America.

At our family celebration decades later, we gathered to celebrate the next chapters of his legacy. Lorenzo's daughter, my mother, stood alongside Lorenzo's sister, speaking to her of stories from the past. What would Lorenzo think? Nephews and nieces from the Basque Country, one a lawyer, later to run for a political office, others teachers, accountants, painters, came to the Garmendia farmhouse that day. One of them aimed to return to the family farm that had been dormant for over a decade. They joined with Lorenzo's Idaho grandchildren to celebrate the marriage of another grandson who would marry a woman from the Basque Country the next day. Our connections with both the landscape adopted by our grandfather and the Basque Country remain strong.

•

The mighty Columbia River enters the Pacific Ocean in the far northwest corner of Oregon at Astoria. Clifton, the fishing community Irene Martin visits in this essay, is thirty miles upriver on the southern bank. Before Euro-American immigration, the Chinookan peoples fished here on the lower Columbia. The river was rich in salmon, its banks forested by conifers spread over surrounding coastal mountains. Runs of salmon supported one of the densest populations of people in North America: half of the fifty thousand Native Americans on the Columbia River lived in the river's lower reaches. When westward-migrating European immigrants, like those described by Irene, arrived at this edge of the continent they quickly began to harvest its rich resources.

Clifton Gillnetters:
Their Ethnic and Occupational Identity

Irene Martin

The drive to Clifton leads down a narrow steep canyon with a salmon stream rushing a hundred feet below the road. There are no guardrails, no warning signs. In the past we've traveled by gillnet boat to Clifton from Skamokawa, our home on the Washington shore of the Columbia. It's a pleasant trip by boat across the main Columbia River ship channel, through Big Slough to Clifton Channel and Clifton, where usually someone has heard us coming and is waiting to help us tie up at the netrack. Today my husband Kent and I are driving, and once the road bends west, we are in the shadow of the high rocky hills and cliffs that earned the community its name.

Jack Marincovich is waiting for us as we pull up to the house he grew up in. "Free coffee," says the sign on the door, and sure enough, coffee and cookies are waiting on the chrome-legged kitchen table that overlooks Clifton Slough. Jack's family has had a home in Clifton for over a century, although the village goes back even further, to the earliest days of the salmon-canning industry. In 1866 a New England family named Hume began the first salmon cannery on the Columbia River at Eagle Cliff, Washington. Their immediate success attracted other entrepreneurs to the canning industry. The Clifton Cannery was founded by brothers James W. and Vincent Cook in 1873. Mont Hawthorne, who worked in the cannery in the 1880s, described it: "I had a lot of fun there fixing over the machinery and moving things all around inside the cannery. Why, we made it a show place. The river boats stopped there, and folks would go through and watch us canning fish."[1]

Four species of salmon—Chinook or Kings, coho, chum, and sockeye—and steelhead trout ran up the Columbia. These fish lay their eggs in freshwater tributaries or the mainstem Columbia, migrate to sea when young, spend years maturing in the ocean, and return again to the streams of their birth to spawn and begin the cycle anew. The spectacular runs of salmon entering the Columbia on their homeward migration were an ideal catch for the Native peoples who speared, dip-netted, and beach-seined them for centuries, and for the immigrant gillnet fishermen who began to arrive in the mid-nineteenth century. Before the invention of tin cans, in the early nineteenth century, the Hudson's Bay Company and other trading companies who participated in the early salt-fish trade purchased salmon from Native fishers. During this period, preceding the actual arrival of most Euro-Americans, disease epidemics of measles, malaria, and smallpox decimated much of the Native population. With the advent of salmon canning, the labor needed for catching fish and operating the canneries led to an influx of immigrants.

Enticed by cannery owners such as the Humes, who encouraged friends and family to emigrate from New England, the earliest fishermen were almost entirely transplants from the eastern seaboard.[2] By the early 1870s, labor shortages forced canneries to widen their search. At the same time, harsh agricultural and economic conditions in the Scandinavian countries and

Finland forced desperate emigrants to take the long voyage by sailing ship around South America to the west coast of North America. They searched for work in the occupations they knew best: fishing, farming, and logging. The lower Columbia offered all three options, attracting successive waves of immigrants from northern Europe, who began fishing, working in canneries, working in logging camps on a seasonal basis, and homesteading small farms.

Emigrants from the Dalmatian Coast also abandoned their European homes. After Italian nationalization they were forced out of traditional fishing grounds in the Adriatic Sea off the coast of Italy; they too were searching for new shores to fish. Salmon cannery owners saw their opportunity to employ a desperate and docile work force, and encouraged them to settle along the lower Columbia, particularly in Brookfield, Washington, and Clifton, Oregon.

The town of Clifton comprised three major immigrant groups. As John Vlastelicia, an old-time Clifton resident, explained, "The Italians were at the lower end, the Yugoslavs were in the center, and the Greeks were in the upper town. The three nationalities, they all got along pretty well together. They're all gillnetters, that's all they ever done . . . In those days they all fished the same . . . They used single nets, shallow nets . . . linen nets."[3] Before he came to Clifton in 1894, John Vlastelicia's father fished in the Adriatic Sea, on an island named Vis. The family continued the fishing tradition; besides John, one of his brothers also fished, the other worked for Bumble Bee Seafoods.[4]

Jack Marincovich, whose family also emigrated from Vis, was born in 1932 and worked as boat puller for his uncle, his father, and grandfather in Clifton, as well as fishing there himself. When he and his wife Georgia returned to Vis in 2004, Jack went fishing in the Adriatic with family members. "This was the greatest part of our trip, fishing as our grandparents had fished and enjoying the life of a family from Vis," including picking grapes from family vineyards. When they left on the ferry, they saw a relative waving a dishtowel from her house in farewell to them. Jack remembered, "It gave me the shivers when she was waving that dish towel . . . I thought that it must have been the same when our ancestors left, and they knew they'd never come back."[5]

Though it evolved over time, Clifton is an ethnically based community that still retains its fishing identity. Gillnetters from Clifton who fished on four main fishing areas or drifts—Quinn Slough, the Cottonwood, the Manhattan, and Ketcura (or Stump Drift)—banded together to pull snags from the river bottom that might entangle or tear their nets. In its heyday as many as thirty-three boats fished here, a situation that caused overcrowding of the fishing grounds and considerable tension, particularly with fishermen on neighboring fishing grounds, such as Puget Island, Cathlamet, and Skamokawa.

Early immigrant fishermen used single-wall gillnets that had a line of floats hung on the upper edge and a line of lead weights attached to the lower edge to help the net hang straight in the water. In the late nineteenth century they developed the diver net, which fishes along the bottom of the river, and is particularly useful in muddy water or high river conditions. Trammel nets, aprons, and strung nets, that deployed several mesh sizes, expanded their ability to capture fish of different sizes.

Gillnetting on the Columbia is embedded in an egalitarian culture. Fishermen are fiercely competitive while fishing, but they overlook animosities to band together to maintain the fishing grounds by pulling snags or debris such as logs that might foul their gear. They form "snag unions" to spread the cost of the equipment and the diver needed to pull snags, and to divide up the labor inherent in such work. According to the custom known as the "drift right" that emerged in the nineteenth century, those who bore the cost and responsibility of maintaining fishing grounds had a preferential right to fish there. Members of the drift developed rules, so that no one fisherman could take advantage of another; for example, lotteries or "drawing numbers" determined who laid out the first net, an example of the strong egalitarian ethic that prevailed. Gillnetters of different ethnic origins, politics, and religions learned to compromise and cooperate as a unit to maintain access to the resource.

In an early case decided by the Supreme Court wildlife (and fish) are "common property" until they are caught by the hunter (or fisher). Thus salmon on the Columbia are considered a common property resource. In contrast, numerous European countries considered salmon as belonging to the owner of the stream to which the fish returned. European fishermen arrived on the shores of the Columbia with backgrounds in fishing technology and customs that they had to adapt both to catch fish and to live in a new polyglot, multi-ethnic pioneer society. European immigrants and Euro-Americans, Native Americans, and Asians formed the labor force in different parts of the fishing and canning industry along the river.

By the mid 1870s the fishing immigrants were forming ethnic communities, such as predominantly Finnish Deep River in Washington. In Astoria, ethnic communities existed within the larger and more diverse township. European immigrant fishermen gathered around their common interests to form the Columbia River Fishermen's Beneficial Aid Society in 1876. My husband's great-grandfather, John Strom, an immigrant from Sweden, was a charter member of this organization.

The Beneficial Aid Society organized to provide a widow's benefit after a fishing death. In the nineteenth century, mortality rates for fishermen were very high, and fishing today is still considered one of the country's most dangerous occupations. After its inception, the Beneficial Aid Society reorganized several times and changed its name to the Columbia River Fishermen's Protective Union (CRFPU). This fishermen's union—one of the oldest on the West Coast—concerned itself with fish prices and established better working conditions for fishermen. Rules for fishing in certain areas, placement of buoys and lights, and struggles with competing gear, such as traps and seines, all came under the Union's purview. But the Union also served to unite fishermen into a kind of "supra-ethnic identity." It organized the various ethnic groups speaking different languages, strung out along a hundred miles of river in two states, with no telephones and no roads, into a cohesive whole by transforming people's mental images of themselves. Their identity as gillnetters became an identity that transcended their national backgrounds. The CRFPU published a pamphlet in 1890 that described the ethnic backgrounds of the fishermen, and contained the following description of the Mediterranean émigrés:

> *There are next about three hundred men from Austria. They are as a rule a happy and generous race, and it can be said to their everlasting credit that it is very rarely that any of them are ever known to commit a criminal act. Coming, as many of them do, from the Dalmatian coast, where they early in life learned the art and profession of the fisherman, they become first-class salmon fishermen.* [6]

One of the purposes of our visit to Clifton is to pay our Union dues. Jack Marincovich, the descendant of Dalmatian coast immigrants, is Executive Secretary of the CRFPU. By maintaining our occupational identity we increase the likelihood that our fishing community will survive. As my husband once wrote, "The maintenance of this ethnic identity may be important as a solution to the problem of supporting a commitment to an occupation which is characterized by low incomes, long hours, often wretched working conditions and high financial and physical risks."[7] We know fishermen also need to band together to combat societal forces that threaten salmon and our way of life. Our coffee discussion revolves around current threats: pressure from sport-fishing groups to take more fish from our allocation, dams on the Columbia that have reduced the salmon runs to a fraction of their former size, and water pollution, an issue that dates back to the 1870s. The CRFPU filed the first anti-pollution lawsuit on the Columbia River in the 1930s, and we recall the pulp slime problems of the 1950s. Now the Willamette River is a Superfund site, and consensus around the table is that problems with water quality are not yet over.

When the Columbia River Packers Association (CRPA) formed in 1899, the Cook cannery at Clifton became part of the operation. Shortly after its assimilation into CRPA the cannery closed, but the facility retained its function as a receiving station for the firm, which eventually became Bumble Bee Seafoods. Clifton itself became a company town. Jack remembered:

When CRPA and Bumble Bee owned [the town], everything was taken care of—if the dock needed repair, they'd repair them. If there was something wrong with the water system they'd repair it . . . when we were kids growing up here it was all company, it was all company boats, the houses were all company. I think they charged you a dollar a year to show you didn't have ownership, the store down there was company . . . and everything you bought you went to the marine store, you billed it to the company you fished for.[11]

When several fishermen arrived at Jack Marincovich's house to take him up on the free coffee offer they reminisced about those days:

We lived in company housing . . . Mrs. Earhart used to bring up fresh vegetables in a boat from Brownsmead . . . We'd exchange fish with farmers for corn, potatoes, chickens, eggs . . . There were other itinerant peddlers who would make needles [for net mending] and sell other stuff . . . The Barendse family had truck gardens and sold or traded fresh vegetables for fish . . . Some families had gardens and grew lettuce, peas, carrots, chard . . . There was a cheese factory on Tenasillihe Island [across Clifton Slough] and we'd get milk and cheese and stuff from them . . . and each October every family made wine when a railroad carload of grapes arrived . . . We all used Zinfandel grapes, but each nationality made a different kind of wine . . . Marko Radich made the best wine . . . Women baked their own bread . . . Children put out setnets for subsistence fish, especially for Friday's meals, since we were nearly all Catholic . . . Church was held once a month in the schoolhouse . . . Nearly all the boats were company boats . . . The company took care of us, but if you sold to anyone else, they cut you off.[8]

The only transportation until nearly the middle of the twentieth century was boat or train; the gravel road that finally connected the village with the outside world in 1937 was narrow and dangerous, and few people had cars. As Jack Marincovich put it, their isolated waterborne society "didn't know what the rest of the world was doing."[9] In tight-knit places like Clifton, with their overwhelmingly fishing population, communities retained their ethnic identities, but overall there was the supra-ethnic identity of fishermen. Clarence Demase remembered two families who made the decision that they did not want their children to follow the fishing occupation. They left the village and moved to Portland to get their children away from the fishing influence, a kind of reverse proof of the town's strong fishing identity.[10]

When Bumble Bee decided to sell Clifton, the company sold the town to the fishermen. John McGowan, former president of Bumble Bee, remembered: "I insisted that we give our fishermen there an opportunity to buy it because we were getting offers from developers . . . that had ideas of . . . making a summer-home community there and putting in a kind of a marina . . . And I thought, geez, these guys have fished for us not only on the Columbia River but a lot of them in Alaska, for not one generation but in many cases, a couple, three generations, and we owe it to those guys to give them an opportunity to acquire that and that's what we did."[12]

The walls of the Marincovich house display numerous photos of Clifton, and Jack shows us his scrapbooks, with pictures of the old school, the CRPA tender, and fishermen's houses. The population of Clifton has shrunk, although several fishermen still fish out of it. And, in memory of the Adriatic ancestry, some Astoria descendants of the village now market Gillnetter's Delight, a red wine, "made in exactly the same manner . . . with descendants of Clifton fishermen . . . a commemorative of that village and all intrepid fishermen."[13]

The Clifton story is only one that could be told of different ethnic groups that came to the Columbia River in the nineteenth and early twentieth century and took up a fishing identity. In order to successfully adapt to constant change, gillnetters developed a culture of memory, with a strong oral tradition that relied on passing down traditions through generations of extended families. In our technological age it is difficult to imagine an occupation that has no technical manuals, no policies and procedures except broad general legislation refined by occasional administrative rules. Young fishermen learn the craft by watching others, asking questions, and by experience. There are no college classes offered, except possibly in the area of marine-engine maintenance, and no textbooks. It takes years to accumulate the knowledge base needed to successfully fish on the Columbia River. Fishermen are in frequent contact, hanging out together on net racks or gear lofts, meeting for morning coffee in order to talk business. My gillnetter husband Kent elaborates: "[T]he fishing experience, owing to its intensely competitive nature, is never static. The development of new gear materials and the ever-changing bottom topography of the fishing grounds make the fisherman's occupation, unlike that of the factory worker, a continuous learning experience which is based upon his own discoveries and those he learns from other fishermen . . . [Fishermen form] a commitment to a totally different life experience which is so demanding and pervasive that the fisherman finds that he has little in common with the remainder of the community and even less with the wider society."[14]

When the coffee break is over, we follow the fishermen back to the warehouse facility. The high hills cast a chilly shadow over the road, although the day is sunny. We pass the old post office and railway station, now roofless and about ready to fall over. The net rack is still solid, however, and the warehouse is extremely well built and maintained. Inside is a Columbia River bowpicker in mint condition, although it is no longer used for fishing, having been replaced by a newer model boat. Neat piles of nets of various sizes are stored in areas marked off for individual fishermen. Delwin Barendse is attaching a corkline to the web of a net, a process known as hanging a net. We stop to visit for a moment, looking at the net and talking about the upcoming spring chinook season. We're all hungry for fish, not just to sell but to take home to eat. The warehouse is unheated; men work for hours there on their gear. No wonder the free coffee is so welcome.

In recent years, fishermen have been experimenting with tangle nets, which fish more selectively for hatchery-raised salmon, while releasing fish that are listed under the Endangered Species Act. Success with new gear like this depends on strong personal connections with others in the industry. Finding out what works and what doesn't would be an insurmountable task for one person, but spread over the fleet, the risk is reduced and a vast database develops. Younger fishermen frequently rely on older ones who have long experience in fishing and gear technology.

The gillnetters' view of themselves is that they are in a minority. While the larger society is an overwhelmingly urban culture, fishermen are a small

fraction of the rural population, with occupational demands that set them aside from everyone else. The net rack and coffee break discussions reveal their frustration in dealing with fisheries agencies managers who have no experience with gear and do not live in their communities. "They think they can learn this out of a book and they don't listen to us."[15] Fishermen, whose culture is rooted in oral communication, commonly believe they are not treated fairly by managers who communicate at a distance, by written and electronic directives. Modern fishermen band together to combat the societal forces that threaten salmon, their harvest, and their way of life. Their interests may induce them into political activism, forming uneasy alliances with environmental groups—uncomfortable arrangements not because they don't have common causes, but because of differences between urban and rural values.

As Jack, Kent, and I leave the Clifton warehouse and head back to our vehicle, we reminisce about a protest in Portland in fall 2004. The Save Our Wild Salmon Coalition organized sport, Native, and commercial fishers to speak out about problems with the Snake River dams. In the commercial fleet were a cannery scow formerly known as the "Marmot," now owned by fisherman Ralph Peitsch; an old lovingly restored bowpicker that had belonged to Bruce Hansen's grandfather; and a couple of newer boats, including our wooden sternpicker, the "Floozie," and Alan Takalo's aluminum bowpicker. After the protest was over many of us thought, "We'd have had a lot more fishermen out if we'd had a protest in Astoria, where there are more gillnetters." But if we held a huge protest in Astoria, would anyone in urban America pay attention?

We head back up the narrow road, on the way home to our own fishing village across the river. The gillnetters' numbers are a fraction of what they once were, because salmon runs have declined dramatically due to continuous assaults on their habitat, among other causes. Many fishermen left this occupation or sought other fisheries, particularly at sea or in Alaska, where they can make a better living. But there are still families like the Takalos who can now claim they are the "sixth generation on the river." Each year in Astoria the Fisher Poets gathering brings in fishers from around the country, particularly the West Coast, who remember their heritage in poems and songs. Each spring, fishermen continue the long-standing custom of bringing in the first spring chinook salmon they catch as a meal for their families and friends: a connection with the past and present and a claim upon the future.

From the beginning of European immigration, logging played a role in building the United States. White pine forests in New England and the Great Lakes, hardwoods in the Midwest, Douglas firs in the Pacific Northwest, and pines in the Southwest built homes, expanded the rail system, and established industrial infrastructure. Diverse forests created by climate, geology, and glacial histories also fashioned a culture with "harvest" as its single objective. Jim LeMonds' essay focuses on the distinctive occupational culture that permeated these forests and the colorful songs and poems that tell the story of the men of Timber Country.

Logger Poetry and Music:
The Culture of Harvest

Jim LeMonds

> *We were the monarchs of the forest, to the west of the great Cascades,*
> *South of the Queen Charlotte Islands, north of the Oregon glades,*
> *Sinking our roots in the hillside and deep in the canyon's shades.*
> *Hundreds of millions our numbers, kings of coniferous clan.*
> *Ours were the valleys untrodden, unspoiled by the hand of man.*
> *Ours were the slopes of the mountain, before the big cut began.[1]*

For more than two centuries, logging has served as an odd kind of American melting pot. It has taken fiercely independent men— immigrants and outcasts relegated to the margins of society—and welded them together, creating a distinctive brand of occupational ethnicity with deep roots. The men who brought down the "monarchs of the forest" described by Robert Swanson in "The Vanished Forest" came from vastly different backgrounds, but logging melded them into a race of their own. It's not that Swedes or Germans or French-Canadians gave up their history and heritage when they signed on as loggers. But there is little doubt that the job itself—the isolation, the danger, the language, the physicality, and the pride—fashioned a unique culture out of common experience. Nowhere is the culture and history of logging and loggers more clearly revealed than in the poetry and music that have spoken for them and about them.

Origins

During the first half of the nineteenth century logging camps were scattered through the woods of New England, the Great Lakes region, and southeastern Canada. In these isolated outposts, French-Canadians, Swedes, Greeks, Slavs, Norwegians, Finns, Russians, Germans, English, Irish, Scots, and others lived in bunkhouses called shanties, where logging songs and poems originated. Their music imitated the work songs of French-Canadian voyageurs and the ballad tradition of northern Europe.

On Saturday nights, each logger took a turn at providing entertainment by dancing a jig, telling a story, or playing or singing a song. Fiddles, harmonicas, dulcimers, and mandolins accompanied them. After the Civil War, guitars and accordions were added. The bunkhouse variety show entertained loggers from different cultures and religions and bonded them in a singular fraternity. The bunkhouse was their domain, and it was free of women, religion, and societal constraints.[2]

The collective "we" and the "Come, all ye" invitation were common in early logger songs. Loggers recognized their alienation from society and even reveled in it. "Falling of the Pine" (1825) emphasizes both the apartness of loggers and their pride in living on the edge:

Come all young men a-wanting of courage bold undaunted,
Repair unto the shanties before your youth's decline.
The spectators they will ponder and gaze on you with wonder,
For your noise exceeds the thunder in the falling of the pine.[3]

The value of music as a unifying force was not lost on company owners. In some camps, a popular balladeer might be kept on the payroll even if he was a poor worker. Subject matter ranged widely, though working conditions, weekend reveling, death, pride, and closeness to nature were—and have continued to be—the best-loved topics. "The Logger's Boast" (1851) is representative of the boisterous logging songs of the 19th century.

Come, all ye sons of freedom throughout the State of Maine,
Come, all ye gallant lumbermen, and listen to my strain;
On the banks of the Penobscot, where the rapid waters flow.
O! we'll range the wild woods over, and a lumbering will go.[4]

Because the turnover rate among employees could exceed 500 percent per year, music spread quickly as men moved from camp to camp. Several songs, including "The Maidens of Ontario," "The Pinery Boy," and "The Farmer's

Son and the Shantyboy," tout the superiority of free-spirited loggers over ignorant, "mossback" farmers and city slickers. As described in "The Festive Lumberjack," the logger was part beast and part super-masculine icon:

I've been around the world a bit, an' seen beasts both great an' small.
The one I mean to tell about for darin' beats 'em all.
He leaves the woods with his bristles raised the full length of his back.
He's known by men of science as the festive lumberjack.[5]

Logs harvested upstream were dumped in ponds formed by splash dams and held there throughout the winter. When spring brought high water, the dams were intentionally breeched, and the logs routed to mills downstream. The result was the closest thing loggers had to a cattle drive. Armed only with pike poles or peaveys, the shantyboys rode the logs downriver to the mills, fighting hang-ups, logjams, rapids, and whirlpools along the way. It was common for crowds to gather along stream banks to watch the spectacle. It was equally common for loggers—many of whom were unable to swim—to drown on the journey. A number of songs eulogized loggers killed on the job. "The Jam on Gerry's Rock," perhaps the best-known logging song of the nineteenth century, details the attempt by six shantyboys and their foreman, "young Monroe," to break up a logjam. All seven die in the attempt.[6]

Initially, the melodies of logging songs were borrowed from popular tunes of the day. However, songwriters such as Joe Scott, W. N. Allen (Shan T. Boy), and Larry Gorman changed that trend during the second half of the nineteenth century by composing original music and lyrics for many of their songs.[7]

Gorman, from Maine, was the best known and most widely admired of the three, in part because his lyrics portrayed loggers less as mythic figures than as vulnerable, exploited human beings. Unlike those before him who focused on maudlin accounts of accidents or romantic renditions of loggers' pastoral existence, Gorman satirized greedy bosses, conniving women, and dishonest bartenders. In "The Hoboes of Maine," he described the cycle that loggers fell into when they hired on:

They'll come by the hundreds, those hardy young bloods,
All neatly attired in their own native goods,
In search of employment and earthly enjoyment,
They'll find it no trouble to hire for the woods.
They'll send them up stream then, to chop and drive team then,
In hopes that their wages will all be clear gain;

But by those man traps they are all handicapped,
And their names are enrolled with the Hoboes of Maine. [8]

Despite his focus on the seamy side of the industry, Gorman's songs failed to generate much political response among loggers. That would be left to Joe Hill and the Industrial Workers of the World (IWW).

The Wobblies

Logging songs changed tone when the IWW—the Wobblies—emerged at the beginning of the twentieth century. For the Wobblies, songs were anthems that inspired and informed. In addition to a union card, new members received a copy of the IWW's *Little Red Songbook: Songs to Fan the Flames of Discontent.*

The Wobblies boasted a number of outstanding lyricists, including Ralph Chaplin and Valentine Huhta, a.k.a. T-Bone Slim. However, Joe Hill was the most widely known. He once said, "A pamphlet, no matter how good, is never read more than once. But a song is learned by heart and repeated over and over."[9] Although the majority of his songs—such as "Everybody's Joining It," "There Is Power In a Union," and "We Will Sing One Song"— were aimed at the working class in general, Hill's words resonated with loggers who were underpaid, subjected to vile camp conditions, and routinely exposed to incredible risk.

Hill spent time in the Pacific Northwest and Canada organizing loggers and mill workers. In 1912, construction workers laying track in British Columbia struck against the Canada Northern Pacific Railway. To support them, Hill wrote "Where the Fraser River Flows," using lyrics that focused on the same issues he preached to timber workers:

Where the Fraser River flows, each fellow worker knows,
They have bullied and oppressed us, but still our union grows.
And we're going to find a way, boys, for shorter hours and better pay, boys.
And we're going to win the day, boys, where the Fraser flows. [10]

When IWW supporters gathered for a street-corner rally, town fathers— often the same men who owned local mills or logging outfits—sometimes sent out the Salvation Army Band to drown the Wobbly chants. Wobbly lyricists fought back by writing words to match the band's inventory of familiar hymns. When the Salvation Army Band launched into a number, the Wobblies responded with union lyrics. "The Lumberjack's Prayer" (1910s) by T-Bone Slim was sung to "Praise God From Whom All Blessings Flow":

I pray dear Lord for Jesus' sake
Give us this day a T-bone steak.
Hallowed be Thy Holy Name,
And don't forget to send the same.
Oh, hear my humble cry, oh Lord,
And send us down some decent board,
Brown gravy and some German fried
With sliced tomatoes on the side. [11]

A favorite among Northwest timber workers, "Fifty Thousand Lumberjacks" was written during an IWW-led strike in 1917 that reduced U.S. timber production to 15 percent of the previous year's total. It provides a glimpse at both the conditions loggers were protesting and the solutions they proposed.

Fifty thousand lumberjacks goin' in to eat.
Fifty thousand plates of slum made from tainted meat.
Fifty thousand lumberjacks all settin' up a yell
To kill the bellyrobbers an' damn their souls to hell.
Take a tip and start right—plan some cozy rooms,
Six or eight spring beds in each, with towels, sheets and brooms,
Shower baths for men who work keeps them well and fit,
A laundry, too, and drying room, would help a little bit.
Tap the bell for eight hours' work; treat the boys like men,
And fifty thousand lumberjacks may come to work again. [12]

Despite efforts by government and business leaders to brand the Wobblies as radicals who were completely out of touch with working people, the IWW successfully laid the groundwork for better pay and working conditions. Attitudes about logging and loggers began to change early in the twentieth century. The public decried the razing of forests in New England and the Great Lakes region, and—following the politicization of the industry by the IWW—was less inclined to view the logger as a romantic figure. In a book titled *Ballads and Songs of the Shanty-Boy*, published in 1926, Franz Rickaby claimed that logging was a "destructive" occupation. He said that loggers, unlike cowboys, had not been a "constructive factor in our national development." [13]

Enter Paul Bunyan.

Bunyan Shapes Loggers' Image

James Stevens and William Laughead, both public relations specialists for timber corporations, set out to create a character that represented the strength, fearlessness, individualism, and pioneer spirit of woods workers. In 1914 Laughead introduced Paul Bunyan's persona in a series of stories, but Stevens is most frequently associated with the spread of Bunyan lore.[14] Lyrics from a 1958 Disney feature about Paul Bunyan effectively summarize his larger-than-life role as land-tamer and spokesman for Manifest Destiny:

North America was a great big land
With a great big job to be done,
A job that needed a great big man.
Paul Bunyan was the one. [15]

In 1951, Pete Seeger and the Weavers recorded Stevens' song "The Frozen Logger." Although not specifically about Bunyan, its lyrics reinforce the image of the indestructible, charismatic logger that Bunyan had come to represent:

As I sat down one evening in a timber town café,
A six-foot-seven waitress these words did say:
I see you are a logger, and not a common bum,
For no one but a logger stirs his coffee with his thumb. [16]

Although Bunyan was instrumental in transforming loggers into mythic figures, many loggers derided Bunyan as a public relations gimmick, corporate timber's version of a super-worker—both union-proof and injury-proof—that employees were expected to emulate. While Stevens was busy doing all he could to romanticize loggers and logging, Woody Guthrie offered a more realistic glimpse of the future in a 1941 song titled "Lumber Is King."

The big trees are falling, and us lumberjacks,
With high power saw, and with double blade axe;
It's fast diesel cats that's a bringing her down,
Cause Lumber is King in a Lumbering town.
But think of the day when the land is cut o'er
And what of King Lumber when Timber's no more? [17]

Stevens and other purveyors of Bunyan stories had one thing in common with the Wobblies: both attempted to speak *for* timber workers. Throughout the second half of the twentieth century, loggers—especially those in the

Pacific Northwest, where the logging culture was strongest—turned to artists who could tell their story in a way that carried more truth than Bunyan could provide.

Robert Swanson

During the 1940s and 1950s, British Columbia's Robert Swanson maintained a large following among West Coast loggers in California, Oregon, Washington, and Canada. A forestry safety inspector, Swanson gathered his knowledge by traveling from camp to camp. His four volumes of poetry— *Rhymes of a Western Logger, Rhymes of a Lumberjack, Bunkhouse Ballads,* and *Rhymes of a Haywire Hooktender*—sold more than eighty thousand copies, mainly via word-of-mouth recommendation.

Although Swanson spent very little time working on the rigging or cutting timber, his work, like that of photographer Darius Kinsey, was accepted by loggers, who believed Swanson's verse effectively portrayed them and their labor. Swanson wrote of bed bugs, donkey punchers, snooze chewers, and big timber, and poked fun at Paul Bunyan's hyperbolical deeds. He endeared himself to loggers with "The Ballad of the Pencil Pusher":

> *He's a mile above the average and a little bit high-hat—*
> *Quite a bit above the boys that hit the camps.*
> *Educated—highly polished—he's a real aristocrat.*
> *And he won't associate with lowly tramps.* [18]

In poems like "The Vanished Host" (excerpted at the beginning of this essay), Swanson captures an ongoing conflict that was beginning to dominate loggers' attitudes: a love for forests that was in opposition to the damage they inflicted upon the landscape.

Buzz Martin

Oregon's Buzz Martin is unquestionably the most respected logger songster of the modern era. Martin, who gained regional acclaim during the 1960s and 1970s, used his experiences as a riggingman, timber faller, and truck driver to create music that garnered significant radio play in Northwest communities. While earlier singers often performed with little or no accompaniment, Martin was backed by a band that included drums, keyboard, and an electric guitar. He appeared with Johnny Cash at the Grand Ol' Opry and represented Oregon in the Festival of American Folk Life at the Smithsonian Institute in Washington D.C.

Part humorist and part bluesman, with a voice reminiscent of both Woody Guthrie and Cash, Martin's blue-collar lyrics struck a chord with loggers and logging communities and earned him regional renown. "Sick of Settin' Chokers" was included on the soundtrack of *Sometimes a Great Notion*, a movie about a logging family that starred Henry Fonda and Paul Newman:

Well, I come up here to these big north woods
To try and make a killin'.
I heard the wages in the woods was good
And a logger's life was thrillin'.
I've been here quite a while
And I ain't been thrilled.
A couple of times I was darn near killed.
And I'm plumb sick of settin' chokers in this doggone rain. [19]

Paul Bunyan was nowhere to be found in Martin's lyrics. His songs tell of blown paychecks, hard-working cat skinners, dilapidated log trucks, cocky timber fallers, and prized chainsaws. Poet and songwriter Otto Oja of Cathlamet, Washington, said Martin was successful because "he knew more about the yarding and rigging part of logging than other writers. Logging really came out in his songs." [20]

One of Martin's best-known songs, "Where There Walks a Logger, There Walks a Man," remains an anthem of pride in many timber communities. Others, like "Fire Danger," simultaneously bemoan and satirize a life filled with financial uncertainty and too often controlled by government agencies:

I'm just a poor old gyppo logger,
Trying to make ends meet.
Got equipment I've got to pay for,
And a family that's got to eat.
But these guys from the Forest Service,
Every time they come around,

All they do is look for something wrong
So they can close you down. [21]

Although he is recognized as a musician, many of Martin's songs are actually spoken poems with minimal instrumental accompaniment. He sometimes groused about unnecessary regulations, but his music primarily relied on humor to describe the danger and uncertainty of loggers' lives.

After Martin's death in 1983, logging music and poetry took on a more strident political tone. Under attack by a growing urban population that regarded loggers as chainsaw-wielding enviro-paths eager to clearcut forests in exchange for money, timber workers responded with songs and poems that expressed their confusion, frustration, anger, and resentment.

Art Revival Meets Contemporary Politics

Folklorist Jens Lund of Olympia, Washington, was instrumental in resuscitating logger poetry and music in the Pacific Northwest during the 1980s and 1990s. He saw that festivals at places like Elko, Nevada, had legitimized Wild West poetry and encouraged cowboys to take the stage. "That was what I was trying to do in the Northwest with logger poetry and music," Lund said. But when he proposed adding logger poets and musicians to the bill at several Northwest timber carnivals during the 1980s, organizers were incredulous. It was the ultimate irony: even in the heart of logging country, the people who were putting together timber festivals were interested only in cowboy poets. "I don't think they believed there was such a thing as logger poetry or music," Lund said.[22]

Eventually, he helped provide a stage for many of today's best-known logger poets and musicians, including Alaska's Hank Nelson, Les Looney, and Gary Shwaver; Washington's Otto Oja, Lon Minkler, Woody Gifford, Linda Marcellus, and Virgil Wallace; and Oregon's Craig Jenkins and Terry McKinnis.

Lund is well aware that environmental pressures and two decades of lay-offs have dented his hard work. "Timber communities have obviously been stressed by mechanization and preservation issues. Things have changed, and it's reflected in the music," he said. "Some of the music is to celebrate heritage, but some of it is an expression of us-against-the-world. It's bitter stuff in many cases."[23]

In "Endangered Species," Oregonians Jenkins and McKinnis express the helplessness and resentment felt by loggers and millworkers forced to absorb the financial impact of environmental regulations enacted during the 1980s and 1990s:

> *There's been enough time and money spent on our fair feathered friend*
> *To feed a lot of hungry and homeless folks and put them back to work again.*
> *Makes you wonder where the importance lies, mankind or the speckled fowl.*
> *Were we created in God's own image, or was it the spotted owl?*[24]

In a poem called "Ode to the Spotted Owl," Sunny Hancock sums up the anger prevalent among residents of Northwest timber communities who blame their plight on liberal urbanites with little knowledge of forests:

> *But if there is one species in this whole wide world around,*
> *That for the good of humankind must be extinction bound,*
> *The one that most folks I know would put highest on their list*
> *Is that large-mouthed, loose-lipped bird*
> *They call environ-mental-ist.* [25]

Loggers weren't the only ones who used lyrics and verse to air their views. In northern California, several members of Earth First! produced songs that criticized the actions of timber giants Georgia-Pacific and Louisiana-Pacific. Todd Cinnamon's "Timberman," released in 1992, attacks G-P and its CEO, T. Marshall Hahn:

> *Now I worked in the mill since I was a young man*
> *Like my dad and his dad and his dad before him.*
> *But they busted the union and the forest is gone.*
> *You can place all the blame on T. Marshall Hahn.* [26]

"Potter Valley Mill," by Earth First! activists Darryl Cherney and Judi Bari, blasts Louisiana-Pacific for overcutting surrounding forests, and then laying off workers and moving the mill to Mexico while reaping record profits:

> *And they're closing down the mill in Potter Valley*
> *Leaving all us good folks in a bind.*
> *They're closing down the mill in Potter Valley*
> *And I can't believe the mess we'll leave behind.*
> *The company says it's environmentalists*
> *Crampin' up their style,*
> *But as I look out on the Mendocino forest*
> *I can't see a tree for miles.* [27]

Hank Nelson Looks Back

He's in his early seventies, but Hank Nelson still considers himself "one of the young ones" among logger poets and musicians. Nelson, who now lives in southeast Alaska, has performed with or been acquainted with virtually all of the modern era's best-known yarn-spinners and songsters.

He grew up in North Bend, Oregon, a coastal logging town near Coos Bay. Beginning at fourteen, he spent summers working as a chokerman in area logging camps. "Those camps were the melting pots for all those guys from different cultures and backgrounds," Nelson said. "They were the places where all those colorful characters who were living on the edge of society were hanging out." He cut timber by day and played country music by night at bars in northern California and southern Oregon. During the 1960s he met Martin. "Buzz was the original," Nelson said. "He did everything in the woods that he wrote and sang about. That's what made him so authentic and so popular. The rest of us are mere saplings compared to Buzz."[28]

When Martin died in 1983, Nelson performed several of Martin's songs at a memorial service. The experience motivated him to write poems and songs on his own, often from ideas that came to him while working in the woods. "I'd write stuff on pieces of my lunch sack or on the band of my hard hat," Nelson said. With the encouragement of Jens Lund, Nelson began performing regularly at timber carnivals and folk festivals throughout the Northwest during the 1980s and 1990s. He has produced three albums— *Old Dogs, Old Cats, and Old Lumberjacks; It's a Picnic Every Day;* and *Tall Timber.*

Nelson's performances include verse from Robert Service, Robert Swanson, and Woody Gifford, a couple of Buzz Martin songs, and Nelson's own poetry and music. "I feel like I have an obligation to keep their stuff alive," Nelson said. "It's a part of our heritage that goes way back to before the start of our nation. But it's getting tougher to keep it going."[29]

The number of available venues has been reduced, and there doesn't seem to be nearly as much public interest as there once was. Nelson points to several factors, including a precipitous fall-off in logging employment that coincides with an increase in mechanization. He also acknowledged that it doesn't make sense for artists to produce work for which there is no demand. "It's one of those sad realities," Nelson said. "There just isn't much interest out there anymore." [30]

Conclusion

Logger poetry and music have never received as much public attention as lyrics dedicated to miners, sailors, railroad men, or cowboys.[31] Bob Walls, an expert on logger culture at Lafayette College, does not believe this disparity is the result of editorial oversight. Walls says logger poetry and music have not reached the level of "romance" necessary for acceptance in our national mythology. "I suspect that when the passion of current forest politics begins to cool, more people will recognize these occupational traditions for what they are—artful expressions of a way of life."[32]

But is Walls being overly optimistic?

"There was a flare up of logging poetry in the 1980s and 1990s," said Otto Oja, "but I haven't seen or heard of any new guys in the last few years." He suggested that investigating the future of logger poetry and music is the equivalent of "looking for something that is no longer there."[33]

Jens Lund agrees: "If there are any new guys out there writing music or poetry, they're staying in the closet." [34]

With the death of Buzz Martin in 1983, logging songs disappeared from play lists of Northwest country music stations. Logger music and poetry remain unnoticed in a country enamored with cowboy mythology. With due respect to Bob Walls, few people believe that will change any time soon. With few new performers on the horizon and limited public interest, there is little reason to believe that logger poetry and music will regain even the modest attention it previously enjoyed.

Logging no longer dominates employment and culture in rural communities of the Pacific Northwest. From 1989 to 1999, more than three hundred mills closed in Washington, Oregon, California, Idaho, and Montana. Thousands of loggers and millworkers lost their jobs. [35] Today, tree plantations meet the needs of a market geared for small-dimension logs. Few mills are equipped to handle trees larger than 32 inches in diameter. And mechanization has taken a huge toll. Roto-saws, feller-bunchers, processors, and mobile shovels are replacing timber fallers and riggingmen at a rapid rate.

Logging poetry and music once told of toughness and danger, of physical prowess and nature's magnificence, of men from different worlds pulled together by an occupation that delivered both pride and respect. Little of that lifestyle remains.

And the voices that once told the stories have nearly fallen silent.

The fertile Willamette Valley, with its mild climate, nutured by abundant rain, contrasts dramatically with the semi-arid Columbia River plateau in the eastern part of the state, but both are important agricultural regions that have attracted farmers and Mexican farm workers, who harvested the myriad of crops produced. The history told by Erlinda Gonzales-Berry narrates the difficult lives of mexicano *farm workers who began arriving early in the twentieth century—many migrants, and some who became residents.*

From Sojourners to Settlers:
Mexicanos in Oregon

Erlinda Gonzales-Berry

Mexicano Pioneers

Under the flags of Spain and Mexico, a robust *vaquero* culture in California formed the foundation of contemporary U.S. cowboy culture (see Hackel, this volume; Boyd 1995, 31); when some of these *mexicano* Californios came north in the mid-nineteenth century, they became Oregon's first cowboys. Mule packers, who were support troops with the Second Regiment Oregon Mounted Volunteers in the Rogue River Wars of the same era were also among the earliest *mexicanos* in Oregon (Gamboa 1991, 45). But for a long time the Northwest remained a peripheral "frontier" region to which selective individuals migrated from the core of Mexico or the Southwest (Saenz 1991, 135). In the early twentieth century a continual migration stream from Mexico to the United States found its way to California and the southwestern states, while only a few intrepid souls ventured into less familiar territory in the Pacific Northwest. Given the nature of Mexican migration patterns—undocumented entries running invisibly parallel to documented migrants—exact numbers of migrants reaching the Northwest are illusive. Excluding the Southwest, Oregon ranked seventh among states with Mexican-born residents by 1910 (Gamboa 1990); the 1930 census recorded more than fifteen hundred people of Mexican descent in Oregon (Peterson del Mar 2003).

Mexican workers recruited from Colorado and Texas to work in the beet fields in Idaho often made their way across the Oregon state line to work and eventually settle in Malheur County. Malheur County in far eastern Oregon is an arid landscape, perched on the edge of the West's Great Basin. Sagebrush blankets the plains, and farming requires irrigation. According to Dority Elguezabal, "Mexicans immigrated into Malheur County as early as 1918 but the majority came around 1937" (1980, 1). The Vale irrigation project was completed in 1930, the Owhyee in 1932, and the sugar factory in Nyssa opened in 1937; Mexican immigration followed (Elguezabal 1980). The Jaramillo family was the first to settle in Malheur County. Leaving Guanajuato, Mexico, by train in 1918, they traveled to St. Louis, where Mr. Jaramillo worked for the railroad for a short time. They hitched a ride west and ended up in Juntura, Oregon. Their granddaughter and her husband, whose family settled in the area in 1943, opened the Gonzales Tortillería in Ontario in 1954. Grandson John Jaramillo owned and operated a farm in the Treasure Valley for many years, and he eventually opened another restaurant in Ontario, Casa Jaramillo. Today these family members figure amongst the prominent Hispanics in Nyssa (Elguezabal 1980).

There are more details to the story of Lupe Rivera Castro, whose family settled in the same area (Hispanic Oral History Project [HOHP]). The family came by train to the United States, where her father began mining in Montana. He migrated with eight other men to Nyssa, a town next door to Ontario in Malheur County. Initially he worked with a machete in the sugar fields before moving to Nyssa's sugar factory, where there were at the time only three Mexican workers. They recruited friends and relatives one by one, and the Mexican population gradually increased. In the labor camp at Adrian their family of eight, which eventually reached eighteen, lived in a cabin with two bunk beds. Lupe's parents set up a stove by the field and would leave her with her sisters to watch over a pot of beans. At lunch break their mother came out of the fields to make tortillas, and together the family would enjoy their lunch break. When asked if she felt discrimination growing up, Rivera Castro was magnanimous in her reply: "We are all discriminated. Humans make errors. Growing up and in school, I felt it. Maybe it was just a lack of cultural understanding" (HOHP). When she was a child Mexicans lived on the east side in Nyssa. They didn't have money to buy property in other parts of town. By the 1990s, when she was interviewed, three quarters of the Nyssa population was Hispanic and they lived throughout the town.

Rivera Castro recalls with pride that if there was one lesson she learned from her parents it was this: "[T]hey taught us to work hard."

While Mexican migration to Oregon was scant in the early twentieth century, the restrictionist and quota debates of the 1920s still affected Oregon. In 1929 the Oregon legislature drew up a memorial urging the United States Congress to establish quotas for Mexican migration that read in part:

> *Whereas under present conditions many thousands of Mexicans are entering the United States without any restrictions, and the cheaper labor of Mexico is rapidly coming in competition with American labor, and if this condition continues the standard of the American worker will be greatly lowered . . . be it* Resolved by the Senate of the State of Oregon [italics in original] *that . . . the memorialists, respectfully request and petition the Congress of the United States to promptly pass the legislation hereinabove referred to, placing Mexico under the same quota provisions concerning immigration as apply to other nations* (Senate Joint Memorial 5; Latino Oral History Project [LOHP]).

Mary Thiel's family migrated to Idaho in 1929 (Gamboa and Buan 1995). By the time she was in high school they had moved from Adrian to Vale, Oregon, where the family of seven worked as a crew in the beet fields. Her mother died of tuberculosis when she was in high school, and Mary herself was forced to leave the fields because of illness. When hers was one of only two Mexican families in Vale, locals didn't pay much attention to them. But as more and more Mexicans moved there during World War II she recalls that "people started focusing on the Mexican people" (Gamboa and Buan 1995, 134). Discrimination became much more apparent, and Mary remembers "being deeply hurt by things people said and did," and going home in tears (Gamboa and Buan 1995, 134). Her life-long engagement with her community began when she started teaching English in a labor camp in Adrian. Wistfully, she recalls that her class was soon taken over by a ministerial association. Feeling displaced, she dropped out, only to see her program abandoned after a short time.

Though some Mexicans settled out in eastern Oregon in the first half of the twentieth century, the more usual pattern was one of seasonal migration. Closure at the Mexican border, massive deportations, and repatriation of Mexicans during the Depression did not greatly affect this pattern. At the same time New Deal social programs, designed to rehabilitate displaced

Midwestern farmers, also declared Mexican seasonal workers ineligible for benefits (Gamboa 1990); but as long as there were crops to be picked, Mexican labor in the Southwest came and went with the seasons. Oregon served as an overflow delta for surplus migrant labor from California. For those most adept at stringing the crops together—tomatoes and grapes in California, on to cherries, hops, and pole beans in Oregon, over to Washington to pick apples—in a work pattern resembling a beaded rosary, jobs could always be had on Oregon farms, even during the Depression. Some of these migrants became permanent residents, but their situation was not an enviable one:

> *Necessity moved these migrants north from southwestern communities during a decade that witnessed major regional social and economic benefits from the New Deal. Since they were Mexicans and seasonal migrants, they had no other recourse but to depart as poverty stricken as when they arrived. Federal state relief was not extended to them, and the opportunity to escape the migratory cycle through the resettlement program was beyond their reach . . . [T]hose Mexicans who became permanent residents in the Northwest and elsewhere had no significant choice but to retreat into the backwaters of the depressed rural communities of the 1930s* (Gamboa 1990, 21).

Out of sight, out of mind—early Mexican migrants in Oregon and the offspring of early settlers remained shadows in official historical annals. This changed with World War II with the institutionalization of the Mexican Farm Labor Program, popularly known as the *bracero* program, which brought a good deal of publicity to Mexican immigrant workers. Experiences of early immigrants paved a path for the sustained presence of *mexicanos* in Oregon, and contributed to the gradual "browning" of the state.

Braceros Come to Oregon

The natural fertility of the Willamette Valley in western Oregon had attracted farmers since pioneer days of the mid-nineteenth century. By the 1940s, Oregon's fertile soils, aided by irrigation and rural electrification to the east, had turned the state into an agricultural cornucopia. These commercially valuable, perishable crops required "a large pool of labor in order to rush crops to market at the optimum point of maturity and command the highest prices" (Gamboa 1990, 5). Over the years, local labor had been supplemented to a small extent by workers from the Southwest and Mexico, but now a shortage of farm labor was about to impede the state's ability to harvest and get its fresh crops—now considered munitions of war—to market. As World

War II progressed, available young men enlisted or were drafted; other men and women flocked to urban centers, away from agricultural communities, to join the more lucrative war production industry. A crisis indeed was in the making across all the major food-producing regions of the country.

In the name of patriotism, calls were issued to the citizenry at large asking them to step up to fill the labor gap in fields across Oregon. Against forceful community opposition, farmers in eastern Oregon received clearance from the president to employ uprooted and interned Japanese American farmers, who were prohibited from buying or leasing land in their new resettlement environment (Gamboa 1990; see related experience in Sakurai, this volume). In other areas, optimism for local participation and feelings of rural independence and self-sufficiency mixed with a strong resistance to Mexican labor. *The Monmouth Herald,* speaking for a small town west of Salem, Oregon, observed: "It now appears that with the complete cooperation of townspeople the situation will be relieved and may be entirely licked" (June 17, 1943). Appeals went out to Women's Clubs, labor unions, schoolchildren, and civilian defense and other community groups to rise to the call, as well as to business establishments to share their workers. For those who remained at home, harvesting crops to feed America's soldiers and allied troops was a noble way to demonstrate civic pride and loyalty; imported labor seemed an anathema to national pride. *The Monmouth Herald* stance on Mexican labor was unequivocally clear: "Local authorities as well as people generally are opposed to bringing in Mexican labor, which was already picking crops in California, except as a last resort. Many people have expressed their opinions that the use of Mexican labor is not to be sought as it is believed that our own people are patriotic enough and anxious to lend assistance to the great task facing us this season" (June 17, 1943).

One month later *The Herald* may not have changed its position about Mexican labor, but it certainly was open to the possibility of *bracero* labor in Polk County: "Elmer McClure, overseer, of the State Grange, who was in Monmouth Wednesday on his way to Benton County Pamona meeting at Alsea, said that Mexican labor is available to farmers and orchardists in Polk County" (July 15, 1943).

One week later it announced: "Five hundred Mexicans will join housewives, children, and a large number for evening work [*sic*] who are otherwise employed in day-time." These Mexicans, *The Herald* observed, were part of the fifty thousand allocated to the United States by the Mexican government, four thousand of whom would make up Oregon's quota. The newspaper assuaged public concerns by assuring that "in every community where they have been used they are exceedingly well pleased with them and have requested more than could be allotted to them. . . .They are turning out very efficient work after they have had a chance to learn how the work should be done when they are not familiar with the work assigned them" (July 22, 1943). Implicit in early articles was the concern—real or imagined—that Mexicans were deficient in their knowledge of farm labor, an idea that may very well have been instilled by disgruntled farmers whose past free-wheeling recruitment practices had been interrupted by the inopportune intrusion of the Mexican and U.S. governments (Scruggs 1988; Gamboa 1990):

> *Somebody in our government with a lot of high ideals went to the Mexican government and made an agreement to send laborers to the United States. They arranged to have a contract which would deal with each laborer as a free agent and put in all sorts of conditions which the farmer who had to hire him had to agree to. . . . But instead of sending over experienced farm laborers, the Mexican government gathered a lot of ne'er-do-wells and hobos (*Northwest Farm News*, Feb. 4 1943).*

If journalists ten miles east of Monmouth, in Salem, were convinced by arguments of this sort, they certainly had experienced a change of heart by July of that year, though reference to social characteristics of Mexicans implied earlier fears went beyond worries about farm work skills: "The *Oregon Statesman* has to revise its fears regarding the use of Mexicans for farm labor. The report from all over the states where the Mexicans are employed are uniformly good. The men are chosen from the farming region of Mexico, are friendly and cooperative, and their work is very satisfactory" (July 18, 1943).

Increasing numbers of workers were arriving in the heart of the Willamette Valley: in Woodburn, Salem, and Dayton in Marion County, and in Monmouth and Independence in Polk County. Polk County received its first cadre of five hundred *braceros* in July 1943 (*Independence Enterprise*, July 23, 1943).

Housing presented a special problem. One plan to house workers at an unused sewage disposal plant in Salem was scrapped when the War Food Administration promised to make an alternate camp site available. Even as this new plan—with the site location still unknown—was approved, locals resisted having imported workers living anywhere near them: "The proposed ground is state-owned and is close enough to the city to be within reach of certain services of sanitation and supply. It is not in the center of a thickly populated area" (*Oregon Statesman*, August 13, 1943). North River Road residents called a meeting where they objected to housing Mexican workers in their area and considered ways to deal with racial issues: "[I]f Mexicans come here they will be used in comparatively few hop yards and prune orchards, all of them large establishments which will use full crews of the dark-skinned laborers, and will keep them separated from other workers" (*Oregon Statesman*, August 13, 1943).

Small growers also were resistant to Mexican labor, but rather than focusing on the issue of race, their expressed concern was that locals, who had done their patriotic duty by taking up the slack, would be replaced by Mexican labor and made to feel unappreciated. The *Oregon Statesman* assures Salem citizens: "This would not relieve local people of the responsibility of carrying the most of the burden. It would merely be a small supplement to the local labor forces, but one which may be badly needed" (July 18, 1943). Repeated articles acknowledging the need for Mexican laborers pointed out the *bracero* agreement's provision stipulating that Mexicans would not replace local workers (Rasmussen 1951). However these well-publicized fears and reservations did not impede the importation of Mexican labor to Oregon. The first group of Mexican laborers, who arrived in July 1943, immediately went to work harvesting hops and prunes. By August 1943, 585 newly arrived *braceros* were housed in a "tent city" west of the Salem fairgrounds (*Oregon Statesman*, Aug. 25, 1943). It was typical of labor camps throughout Oregon: "The *braceros* were housed together, sometimes in mobile tent camps or in permanent farm labor camps that dotted the farming areas from Ontario to Salem and Hood River to Medford. As a rule, six workers lived together in a 16x16-foot tent that was furnished with folding cots, one blanket per person, and heating stoves when available" (Gamboa 1995a, 41).

As *braceros* became a reality in Oregon farming communities, newspapers played an important role in changing the attitudes of local residents toward these once unwelcome guests workers. The *Oregon Statesman* wrote on August 25, 1943, "County Agent Nibler said that, judging from the experiences of other Oregon communities in which Mexican groups have worked this year, they will prove to be excellent workers and quiet citizens who will have little inclination to visit in nearby cities, though they are free to do so and may occasionally come in to buy clothing or make other small purchases." Obviously the writer walks a fine line as he or she addresses the divergent interests of discriminating citizens and pragmatic businessmen willing to overlook social status in the interest of commerce.

Quickly the press passed from reluctant acceptance to enthusiastic commendation. "'Good Neighbors' Here to Aid Farmers"—an August 29 headline on the first page of the *Oregon Statesman* is accompanied ironically by a large photo captioned "foreign army of invited invaders," marching like a troop of trained soldiers down Capitol Street. In general, the press given to *braceros*, once they arrived and proved their mettle, is quite positive. However this coverage may have been influenced by the Emergency Farm Labor Services Office (EFLSO), which administered certain aspects of the Mexican Farm Labor Program out of the Agricultural Extension Office at Oregon State University, then known as the Oregon State College. Part of its job was to mediate between this federally funded program and rural communities. To this end, it carefully orchestrated a publicity campaign that included extensive use of flyers, news releases, photographs, radio advertisements, and farm-labor radio programs. Carefully worded broadcasts encouraged citizens to toe the line—a line clearly drawn by the State Department—in this time of war. And toeing that line included accepting foreign workers.

Well-publicized Mexican Independence Day celebrations with red, white, and green streamers, the Mexican flag raised alongside the U.S. banner, Mexican food, and choruses of "Viva Mexico" and "Viva los Estados Unidos!"(*Oregon Statesman*, Sept. 17, 1943 and Sept. 26, 1943) were held at Woodburn, Dayton, and Salem camps in the Willamette Valley. In Dayton, "Girls from the war food administration office in Portland acted as partners" at the celebration dance (*Oregon Statesman*, September 19, 1943). Several journalists expressed mild surprise about the men's orderly behavior, suggesting that it ran counter to their preconceived notions of how Mexican workers might behave: "According to reports, the men have been satisfactory and diligent workers. They stand field work in the hot sun better than the average Oregonian . . . After showers and their night meal, they deport themselves in an orderly manner" (*Oregon Statesman*, September 26, 1943). Another writes, "And though they celebrated with song and shopping sprees, the end of the day found not one in any sort of difficulty—a rare record for any group of men bound together simply because of their common interest in work" (*Oregon Statesman*, September 17, 1943).

Though some two hundred fifty workers remained in Oregon through the first winter season (*Oregon Statesman*, December 24, 1943), most were on their way home by October. Every *bracero* who worked in Oregon carried a letter of gratitude and greetings to their fellow countryman signed by Governor Earl Snell and William Schoenfeld, dean and director of agriculture at Oregon State College:

Neighbors of the Republic of Mexico, Greetings: The farmers of the State of Oregon salute you. They are grateful to you and your fellow countrymen who have labored in the production of the crops of this country. . . . We hope that your associations here have been congenial and that you have found it as profitable to you as it has been to us. . . . If similar cooperation in the war effort should seem desirable again, we would consider it a privilege to welcome you back to the state (Independence Enterprise, October 8, 1943*).*

The next year new camps were established in the western states to help avoid the "racial flare-ups" that had occurred the previous year (*Oregon Statesman,* March 10, 1944). Eager to bring back a cadre of efficient workers who "completed a three-week harvest in two weeks," the Horst hop ranch in Salem applied for five hundred *braceros* shortly after their departure (*Oregon Statesman,* November 4, 1943). Preparing for this new wave of imported workers, a member of the county agricultural committee reported to the Salem Lions Club that these workers "need to be here again . . . They come purely as a wartime answer to a food harvest problem and they were called upon when it became apparent other labor could not save the entire fall harvest" (*Oregon Statesman,* March 17, 1944). That year there were camps in the Hood River Valley, Malheur and other counties of central Oregon, and the Rogue River Valley and Klamath County in southern Oregon. The largest concentrations were at Salem, Independence, and Dayton hops and prune farms in the Willamette Valley of western Oregon.

In a foreign country far from their families, surrounded by people whose language they did not speak, living with strangers in uninviting camps, and eating strange food, *braceros* had little to do when they left the fields. According to Erasmo Gamboa, *braceros* were "treated worse than Italian and German prisoners of war held in northwestern farm labor camps" (1990, 129). Oregonian women took the responsibility for creating a bridge between Mexican workers and the communities they served. In April 1944, Mrs. George Phalen talked to the Women's Salem Club "about the work done with the Mexico land army which has been here for the past two years. The local people, she said, taught them English and at the same time acquired a speaking knowledge of Spanish" (*Oregon Statesman,* April 29, 1944). The club women helped plan the Independence Day celebration in Salem and sponsored musical events that were also attended by a few locals, to show signs of greater acceptance. *Braceros* returned in 1945, but anticipating an end to the war, the message of the Emergency Farm Labor Office was clear: "Just as fast as men and women from the war plants show a desire to take over the jobs the Mexicans are now doing, the Mexicans will be repatriated" (*Farm Labor News Notes*, August 16, 1945, 2). But the growers preferred to hire Mexican nationals. They certainly valued them over Jamaicans, whom they tagged as "troublemakers" (Gamboa 1990). Given the historical prejudice towards black people in the state, this comes as no surprise. However, they also preferred Mexican nationals to white migrants. An editorial in *The Oregonian* minces no words: "Fruit growers of the Hood River Valley, hop growers of the Salem area and other of the state's agricultural community have experienced almost unanimous satisfaction with the southern workers. Some declare their preference of the Mexicans to the jalopy brigade of white migrants that followed the crops in pre-war days" (Sept. 29, 1943).

An article in the *Farm Labor News Notes* makes the following derogatory reference to "jalopy riding" families: "Roy Donaldson, farm labor assistant at Hillsboro, reports that contrary to popular opinion [cited] two weeks ago, cessation of hostilities abroad so far has not resulted in any influx of job seekers on the Washington County farm front. He says, rather, workers seem to have vanished, as some farm-labor people forecast. Roads seem to be filled with an endless ribbon of old jalopies bedecked with bedding, vacation equipment, and carefree motorists" (Aug. 27, 1945).

The alleged passivity of Mexican workers and their supposed "inherent" capacity for stoop labor had become legendary among growers, and this argument was used frequently to justify hiring them over other workers. A more realistic motive was probably that farmers could pay Mexican workers, particularly those not protected by the binational labor contract, lower wages; white migrant workers also had options not available to Mexican workers and were more likely to abandon the fields when better job opportunities arose. Whatever the incentive for employers, local communities did not like hiring Mexicans over whites, particularly as wartime industry jobs dried up and workers returned to their rural communities only to encounter job discrimination. For example, "At the Dayton Farm Labor Camp in Oregon, nineteen Anglo families circulated a petition urging that Mexican contract workers be excluded from the camp on the grounds that whites remained unemployed while farmers hired the *braceros*" (Gamboa 1990, 64).

Whenever possible the EFLSO made every effort to assure that the crops got picked by domestic workers and volunteers. In 1945, one hundred patients at the U.S. Naval Hospital in Corvallis worked as hay hands in Benton and Polk counties; and four hundred G.I.s from Camp Adair, just north of Corvallis, gave up their Independence Day furlough to work at a hops farm in the area. Throughout Oregon thousands of elementary school children helped pick crops as "Victory Farm Volunteers." In Milton-Freewater, forty-five stores and businesses closed for several days so clerks and stenographers could work on farms; one ninety-year-old joined them. When thirteen hundred expected Mexican nationals did not show up because the Mexican government put a hold on recruitment for a week, prisoners of war were used to replace them (*Farm Labor News Notes,* July 23, 1945; July 30, 1945; August 6, 1945; September 13, 1945).

Between 1943 and 1947 approximately 15,136 Mexican nationals brought their *brazos* to do contractual farm labor in Oregon (Gamboa 1993). Their collective arms "thinned 25 percent and harvested 40 percent of the sugar beets, thinned 50 percent and picked 10 percent of the apples, and thinned 60 percent and picked 30 percent of the pear crop. They also harvested 25 percent of the asparagus, 20 percent of the onion crop, 60 percent of the cucumbers, and 60 percent of the peas" (Gamboa 1990, 57). This work did not always get done without a good measure of conflict and response by *braceros.* Demonstrating a strong sense of agency, despite constraining conditions, they frequently engaged in strikes and work stoppages to protest ill treatment, bad food, low wages, and other forms of exploitation. In fact, no sooner had they arrived in Oregon than a platoon of workers in Medford staged a work stoppage to protest the fact that they were being paid by the box instead of by the hour. The conflict was resolved when "[t]he growers then agreed to pay them 75 cents an hour instead of 8 and 10 cents a box" (*Oregon Statesman,* August 13, 1943). Without the contractual protections insisted upon by the Mexican government, such actions would not have been possible.

While the *bracero* program was extended until 1964, Oregon growers were reluctant to employ *braceros* after 1948 (Gamboa 1990). However, *braceros* were indeed brought to Oregon in 1952, when 1,014 picked crops in Umatilla and Jackson counties and in Hood River and Medford (*The Oregonian,* May 17, 1953). And in 1958 *braceros* were again brought to Medford to harvest the pear crop (Oregon Legislative Assembly Interim Committee 1958). Administrative changes in the *bracero* program introduced in 1948 (Gamboa 1990) and assertive work stoppages made Oregon growers reluctant to hire *braceros,* but particularly unsettling was the new requirement that they would have to pay the full cost of transporting workers from the interior of Mexico (Gamboa 1990; Loprinzi 1991). Given the high cost of transportation for so great a distance, growers in Oregon began to look for a new source of labor.

During the 1940s illegal migration from Mexico ran parallel to contractual labor migration, and by the fifties undocumented workers were squeezing Mexican Americans out of farm labor in the Lower Rio Grande Valley (Fuller 1953). At the same time land consolidation, irrigation, and mechanization signifigantly reduced the number of jobs (Wells 1976; Loprinzi 1991). As workers displaced by illegal immigration gradually made their way to the Northwest, Oregon farmers, who had become very fond of Mexican labor, found a new work force. Not unlike *braceros* before them, this new group of farm workers arrived on time to cultivate and harvest, and left when the season was over, creating few wrinkles in the social fabric of the state. These migrants were joined by former *braceros*; their formal contract program had ended, but they continued to come, illegally, to places they had visited as contract workers. "In this sense, the *bracero* program never really ended, it simply went underground" (Cornelius 1978, 18). The grandchildren and great-grandchildren of these *mexicanos* form today's third and fourth generation of Hispanics in Oregon.

From Sojourners to Settlers 1950-1980

When Oregon growers decided to diminish their reliance on the *bracero* program in 1948 they declared the unbending will of Oregon agribusiness to get and keep its labor on its own terms. In the post-*bracero* period of the 1950s, concerted recruitment practices, which took labor contractors to economically depressed areas of Mexico and the Southwest, together with the tight operation of income-generating labor camps, formed the foundation of a highly structured process that guaranteed workers during the peak season, and encouraged their return on a yearly basis (Dash 1996). Connie García, a teacher in the small Willamette Valley town of Independence, settled with her migrant family in 1961. She gives us an idea of the control tactics employed in this system:

> We came to Horst Ranch and moved into the main labor camp. At that time, Horst Ranch had several labor campsites, but the main one was quite large. It had two community baths and outhouses, a "community center," a small park, and even a restaurant. We were assigned a section. Each family worked a couple of acres of asparagus, and we were paid a percentage of what that piece produced. Sharecropping is what it was. Another percentage

was withheld until the season was over. If we didn't stay to finish the season, we didn't get the "bonus" as it was called (LOHP).

The contracting process was crucial for managing this exploitative system. In many cases the contractors, or their sub-contractors, were themselves *mexicanos* from the Rio Grande Valley in Texas whose knowledge of the region's social conditions and people gave them certain advantages in selecting from the migratory labor pool. Contracted groups of families, called crews, were transported in large trucks with canvas-covered beds and delivered as a cohort to various sites along the migrant trail. Some contractors delivered the workers to farmers who paid a per-head fee for each migrant. Other contractors were paid a lump sum to act as employers, pay out wages, take care of paperwork, and keep records. The employer/contractor deducted additional fees at the rate of 5-11 cents per hour that were distributed among the contractor, sub-contractors, and crew leaders. Average weekly earnings for a family, from which transportation and rental fees were also deducted, were $84; expenses amounted to $69. In camp, workers often had credit accounts at local stores and taverns that were arranged by contractors, who collected a cut from merchants (Oregon Legislative Assembly Interim Committee 1958). Some contractors lent money to workers at high interest rates and made additional money by "dabbl[ing] in markets of prostitution, drugs and gambling" (Loprinzi 1991, 40). At the end of the long seven-and-a-half-month season a fortunate family would return to Texas with $235 to sustain them for the remaining three and a half months of the year (Oregon Bureau of Labor 1958, 9-10).

The shared vicissitudes of migrant life had a profound bonding effect on families. This in turn benefited contractors, upon whom employers could count to deliver a quota of workers at the opportune moment. Among migrant families their capacity for work was their only possession; frequently they felt beholden to the contractor for finding them jobs, and showed their loyalty by joining his labor caravan year after year. Because they rarely had access to private modes of transportation, opportunities for breaking away from this pattern were scarce. Family cohorts guaranteed substantial numbers of workers and facilitated bookkeeping and paying wages. More important, the system functioned as a control mechanism, for a man obligated to shelter and feed a family, which found himself in an unfamiliar environment far from the usual support networks and unable to speak English, was less likely to engage in disruptive labor actions or, equally important, to break away from the migrant stream. Furthermore, family crews were delivered yearly to the same farms thereby creating a sense of connection and perhaps even a sense of reciprocal obligation on the part of farm workers.

A rumor mill sounded an alluring siren call that fed the dreams of families like the Leos who came to Independence in 1954:

> *Word came from other farm workers that they were hiring plenty of workers up in Oregon in some place called the Willamette Valley. From what they were told, it sounded something like a paradise. The weather was always mild and never too hot, the landowners paid more, and there were plenty of opportunities for housing, and basically the water flowed like wine. It was all too good to be true. And when they got there they found it was. The employers didn't pay any more, it was often too cold and rainy for a human to be working outside, and there weren't that many more jobs. It was all just a rumor. But they decided to stay anyway since they were already there. There, they were given less than good housing for a price of fifteen dollars a month. All nine of them lived there and when each child got old enough to work, they would. This age was about five or six years old* (LOHP).

When Hipólito García's father decided to make the move from Texas to Independence in the early 1960s the rumor had the ring of promise, for it was made by the man to whom their family was about to turn over their lives. Hipólito's son reported, in the family history he provided for the Independence oral history project:

> *[O]ne of the reasons they decided to move to Oregon was because they were told, by a contractor, that with all the children that my grandfather had, they would be able to make a lot of money. They were told that they would most likely make enough money to survive in Oregon and also make enough to return to Texas for the next crop season . . . When they first arrived in Independence they stayed in Green Villa Farms and picked asparagus and also irrigated the crops. When they were finished picking those crops they went to another camp that same year in Independence called the Long Ranch where they picked pole beans. When the winter came his family realized they did not have enough money to return to Texas. They realized that what the contractor had told them wasn't true* (LOHP).

President Harry Truman, in response to pressure from labor unions, the NAACP, and numerous religious and social reform groups, formed the Commission on Migratory Labor in 1950. The next year the commission reported that migrant families in Colorado were making an average wage of $1,424 per year, including work tendered by women and children of the family. The report stressed that migrant workers enjoyed none of the protections guaranteed other workers in the United States such as the right to organize, unemployment insurance, or minimum wage (cited in Fuller 1953). The lives of migrants were governed by "uncertainty, insecurity, poverty and filth" (Fuller 1953, 11). And they were subject to all matter of calamities: "A truckload of workers smashes up and many are killed; an ex-chicken coop catches fire and migrants living in it are burned to death; laborers of migrant families are reported to have died from malnutrition and neglect" (Fuller 1953, 11).

The new spirit of migrant labor reform that overtook the United States in the 1950s significantly affected Oregon, with its heavy dependency on migrant farm labor. This is not to say that migrant workers had been completely neglected before that date. The Oregon State Council of Churches had been actively ministering to migrants as early as the 1940s with educational and recreational activities, radio programs, and summer programs for children (Gamboa 1995b). The Council became a strong political voice in advocating for social change for migrant workers. It successfully lobbied the state legislature to establish an Interim Committee on Migrant Affairs and for legislation beneficial to migrant workers. Subsequently a statewide survey by the Interagency Committee on Migratory Labor in 1959 considered a broad range of topics, and resulted in passage of four bills that covered labor contracting, worker transportation, housing standards, and an education pilot program for migrant children. The Bureau of Labor assessed their work:

> *There is no question that Oregon has passed the most comprehensive and balanced and studied legislative program for the welfare of migrants ever enacted by any state at one time. . . . Lest Oregon sound like a Utopia for migrants, let it be said that many problems remain unsolved and that even the problems for which there now seems to be some hope of solution will require attention year-in and year-out for the foreseeable future.* (Current and Infante 1959, 162-63).

The Catholic Archdiocese also became involved in ministering to the spiritual needs of *mexicanos* in Oregon, the majority of whom were Catholic. In 1952, the Oregon Diocese recruited its first priest, Father Ernesto Bravo, from Mexico (Loprinzi 1991), though the Catholic Migrant Ministry Office might have been a bit reluctant to advocate for migrant workers and risk antagonizing farmers, many of who were members of the church and contributors to its coffers. Eventually, as the Catholic Church became transformed by the liberal reforms of Vatican II, and its clergy increasingly influenced by the new ideas of Latin American Liberation Theology, it became a catalyst for political activism among settled-out *mexicanos* and migrant farm workers. Catholic parishes like St. Luke's in Woodburn "started to emerge as the hub of the growing Mexican-American community" (Gamboa 1995b, 48).

Migrant reform also arrived in the field of health, and rightly so, as health problems besieged migrant workers, who more often than not had little choice but to accept death. Mary Theil, whose family moved to Eastern Oregon in the 1930s, recalls:

> *If you got sick, you died if it was a disease that would take your life. In fact, we lost three that way. They got sick and all you did was try to take care of them the best you could. We did get to a doctor. The doctors would tell you if you didn't have the money, they wouldn't take you. We did take a baby to a doctor with measles, and my mother didn't know how to bring the fever down and things of that nature, and the doctor turned her away. So she brought the baby back and it died that night* (Gamboa and Buan 1995, 135).

In 1963 the federal Migrant Health Act established migrant health programs throughout the country. Migrant workers and families in the Oregon Migrant Health Project (OMHP) were diagnosed and treated; throughout Oregon nurses found families suffering from skin infections, bedbug and lice infestations, and diarrhea. Oversight of sanitation in the camps was also part of the Oregon Project as health problems were exacerbated by substandard conditions such as filthy toilet and shower facilities, lack of drainage, dirty mattresses, polluted drinking water, and lack of refrigeration. In field after field, inspectors found workers sharing a single drinking cup, which contributed to the spread of infectious diseases (Oregon State Board of Health 1965). On occasion inspectors were successful in shutting down substandard labor camps.

"Rugged Camp Living Causes Vicious Circle"—the title of an article in a series by graduate student David Laing—describes life in camp: "Each year the better part of 2,500 people lead a miserable existence in Polk County. While here their standard of living is far below that of permanent residents." Laing believed the growers were unmotivated "to come to the rescue of a group of people from whom society needs but cannot seem to find room for. They take refuge in the old myth which claims that every individual can make his way, no matter what the odds are against him." Laing also thought workers themselves "are passive and unwilling to do anything for themselves . . . and trapped in a vicious cycle" (*Independence Enterprise,* August 6, 1964). To the contrary, recollections of early settlers in the Willamette Valley speak powerfully about strategies employed to confront their living conditions as they made the transition from the migrant stream to permanent residency during the 1850s and '60s. Their stories are filled with determined acts of agency and self-determination.

The life of the migrant child, Raul Pena recalls, was a life of adventure, an adventure that involved the entire family. For a child that thought "going north" meant a trip to Plainview, Texas, rolling across the vast Western landscape was exciting and educational. He remembered winning a geography bee, not because he was the smartest kid in his class in Reynosa, Texas, but because he identified the names of the state capitals, and knew details about them after passing through scores of states and their capitals. His buddies, overjoyed that a Mexican kid had won the contest, hoisted him on their shoulders and paraded through the auditorium.

When migrants arrived in Oregon their reception was often unpleasant: "When Raul Leo Sr. and Anna were putting the children to bed they heard a noise outside the window. They both went out to check and what they found was a letter tacked to their door reading 'leave wetbacks'" (LOHP). Discrimination could also be found among some educators. "One of the concepts expressed by some schools was that the Spanish-American child is mentally inferior. One official even went out on an unscientific limb as follows, 'I have noticed that if the children are more on the Indian side, they are slower in learning than those who are more on the Spanish side'" (Infante and Current 1958, supplement, 7). In one county the practice of "price-jacking" was common, with prices of staples increasing by 15 percent once migrants arrived. In another county one tavern made a practice of refusing service to "Spanish American" migrants, though other migrants were not turned away. The law-enforcement official in this same county counseled "businessmen and townspeople to handle the 'Mexicans' with extreme caution and give them no chance to start anything. As far as he is concerned, all 'Mexicans' are dangerous" (Current and Infante 1959, 116). At another location, a town officer, speaking of migrant youth, affirmed: "If we see the young boys dating white girls, we tell them to go only with their own" (Current and Infante 1959, 123). In 1962 Gilbert López reported to the *Oregon Journal* that "transient workers in the Boise Valley area of Eastern Oregon were unable to meet socially because of discrimination against them by bar and club owners." Everywhere they turned, he reported, "they are met with signs stating 'No Mexicans allowed'" (July 19, 1962).

However *mexicanos* were accustomed to a life of segregation and deeply entrenched racial discrimination in Texas; they were seeking change. In the state of Texas a legacy of Jim Crow laws applied also to Mexicans. David Montejano addresses this subject in his award-winning study on Mexican Americans in Texas:

"Jim Crow" may appear to be an odd description of the situation of Mexicans in Texas. There were no constitutionally sanctioned "separate but equal" provisions for Mexicans as there was for blacks. According to the prevailing jurisprudence, Mexicans were "Caucasian." But in political and sociological terms, blacks and Mexicans were basically seen as different aspects of the same race problem. In the farm areas of south and west Texas, the Caucasian schools were nearly always divided into "Anglo schools" and "Mexican schools," the towns into "white towns" and "little Mexicos," and even the churches and cemeteries followed this seemingly natural division of people. This was not a natural phenomenon, however, but the cumulative effect of local administrative policies. In the farm districts, the result was a separation as complete—and as de jure—as any in the Jim Crow South (1987, 262).

Under these conditions, "people stayed on their side of town," (interview, Raul Peña) and speaking Spanish in public was akin to committing a crime.

Connie García's memories give a vivid image of the life of a Mexican child in a Texas school:

The next year I joined my older brothers and sister in school. All I remember of that experience is that we were all herded into one room with a whole bunch of other kids and we moved around a lot, singing "picking up posies, puttin' them in a basket, picking up posies, puttin' them in a basket." I think we really weren't in a school, because the following year, my mom walked me to school and we met with the principal. His name was Mr. Barron. He told my mom to tell me I was not to speak Spanish at school at all. We then went down a corridor to a room down the far end. The teacher took me in and sat me down, and there I stayed, completely mute, silent for almost three years (Chicana Literary Group 2000, n.p.).

Relative to Texas, Oregon indeed was a welcome change. For Elena Peña living and attending school in Oregon was exciting: "The teachers were so nice to us. We weren't used to this in Texas. We were even afraid to speak Spanish because we thought we were going to get spanked. To me that was really different. We would speak Spanish whenever we wanted. . . . The school system was better. They treated us nicer. There was a lot more curriculum. . . . That's when I got the idea of what going on field trips was about" (Interview, April 15, 2004). These changes had a lot to do with her family settling in Independence. "My dad saw how happy we were, that we were speaking more English and more involved in school, and he was more involved in school. In Texas he didn't feel welcome." She found joy in interacting with Anglos, out of the question in race-conscious Texas; likewise her mother enjoyed exchanges with Anglo women because "they were so nice to her."

Elena's arrival in Oregon was also memorable. There was a rush for mattresses, only to find that they were crawling with bedbugs. Her parents refused to allow their children to sleep on the infested mattresses, so they spent the night in their truck. The next day, her father negotiated with their employer to allow them and another family to camp out by the river. After a week of camping, sleeping in their truck and in a tent, work at that farm was completed and the two families moved on to another crop. Ms. Peña stresses how their own vehicle gave her family a measure of independence as well as additional money, because they did not have to give the contractor a cut of their wages. These developments sped up the process of settling out in a shorter period of time. Years after arriving in Independence, her father bought a small house on an acre of property where he and his wife still live. Their daughter Elena lives with her husband Raul in their own home next door. It might be tempting to infer that Ms. Peña was a good candidate for complete assimilation, but her strong identity as a Chicana and a life of involvement and service to the *mexicano* community in Polk County belie such a speculation.

The "browning" of Oregon, though indeed gradual, has taken place over a long period of time, for Latinos—primarily of Mexican origin—have been present in Oregon in significant numbers since the 1940s. Migration from Texas to Oregon and settling out persisted in mid-twentieth century. By 1965, sixty-three families had left the migrant stream to settle in the Independence area. Twenty lived in housing provided by their employers on ranches; twelve were renting; six lived with other families; and twenty five were in the process of purchasing homes. For the latter, the migratory life style was indeed coming to an end (*Independence Enterprise*, April 22, 1965). Though the stream of *mexicanos* continued arriving as migrant workers, in the '70s more migrants to Oregon came from Mexico (Loprinzi 1991).

Like Independence, Woodburn became a target for Mexican-origin population in the early fifties. By the end of this decade there were sufficient *mexicanos* to make it a profitable venture for the local theater to run Spanish movies once a week. "Spanish Americans" from all over the state traveled to get their drivers' licenses in Woodburn, the only state office to contract Spanish-speaking employees and administer the drivers' license test in Spanish (Current and Infante 1959). By the sixties the Chamber of Commerce organized its first Mexican fiesta "for the purpose of recognizing 'the many Spanish-speaking peoples in the area for the harvest season'" (Dash and Hawkinson 2001, 92-93). Today Woodburn has the largest Hispanic population of the state, and is the epicenter from which much of the state's activism on behalf of *mexicanos* and Latinos continues to emerge.

Eastern Oregon continued to draw *mexicanos* throughout the second half of the twentieth century. In 1954 Nyssa held its first Mexican fiesta, and by 1959 it had a baseball team organized by migrants from Eagle Pass, Texas, a bilingual mimeographed newspaper, and Spanish-language broadcasts (Current and Infante 1959). By 1964 there were 330 settled-out families in Malheur County (Oregon State Board of Health 1964, 9), forcing school districts to give some thought to how they could best serve migrant children. The Nyssa School District encouraged *mexicano* parents to send their children to school: "We believe your children should attend schools while they reside in this Community. We have no prejudice against any Nationality, Race or Creed. A child is a child as far as we are concerned and we treat them all alike. . . . You may be assured that your children and you, if you accompany them for registration, will be treated courteously and kindly (Oregon Legislative Assembly Interim Committee 1958, 54). By the 2000 census Malheur County had the state's second-largest concentration of Hispanics.

Raul Peña, who migrated with his family from Texas to Independence, recently retired from the Oregon Department of Labor, where he worked as a labor compliance officer. Looking back at his journey, he pondered:

Yeah, we were poor. Actually, I didn't know we were poor but my father sure knew it. If I had stayed in Texas my life would have been very different. I would probably still be working in the fields, or I would be pushing drugs or in jail for pushing drugs, or I would be dead. Coming to Oregon increased my life chances. But what I learned as a child of migrants is to value work. My father taught me that no matter what the job was, I was being paid for it, and I was obliged to do it the very best I could. "If your boss asks you to dig a ditch," my father told me, "ask how deep and how wide" (Interview, April 15, 2004).

Maria Magaña migrated north from Mexico with her family, "like animals in a trailer truck" (Interview, May 2003), with nine other families to Jefferson, Oregon. When they arrived there were no jobs, but the contractor kept charging them for rent and other expenses. With another family the Magañas headed to Woodburn, where they connected with a different contractor, who found them work in the strawberry harvest. The whole family worked to get ahead and eventually bought a car.

Just as relocated migrant families had coped before, they formed a small bonded community with other Mexican families on which they could rely for mutual support. Eight families pooled their finances and labor in construction to build a shared neighborhood within a few years of their arrival in Oregon. As the oldest of four children, Maria helped her widowed mother, who worked in the fields to support the family. "Study and work, study and work, study and work" (Interview) was what she recalls about that period of her life. After graduating from high school, marrying, and staying home with her children, she eventually left her "very machista" husband. She supported her family with two jobs, one in the daytime and one at night, sleeping only four hours. Today Ms. Magaña works as a teacher's aide and owns her own business that provides commercial cleaning services. Though she is disappointed that she has not been able to complete college, her first son has just received his Bachelor's degree. Maria Magaña proudly proclaims: "I have always worked and have not asked the Americans for anything, because I have exerted myself to get where I am. All of my life I have worked for the little that I have, and I have done it with my own sweat" (Interview).

Works Cited

Boyd, Bob. 1995. "Vaqueros on the High Desert Rangeland." *In* Erasmo Gamboa and Carolyn Buan eds. *Nosotros: The Hispanic People of Oregon.* Portland: Oregon Council for the Humanities.

Chicana Literary Group. 2000. *Our Words.* Pen Readers and Writers Program. Milpa Press.

Cornelius, Wayne A. 1978. *Mexican Migration to the United States: Causes, Consequences, and the U.S. Responses.* Cambridge, MA: Center for International Studies, Massachusetts Institute for Technology.

Current, Tom, and Mark Martinez Infante. 1959. *. . . and Migrant Problems Demand Attention.* Bureau of Labor, Migrant Labor Division, Final Report of the 1958-59 Migrant Farm Labor Studies in Oregon.

Dash, Robert. 1996. "Mexican Labor and Oregon Agriculture: The Changing Terrain of Conflict." *Agriculture and Human Values.* 13:4 (Fall 1996):10-20.

Dash, Robert, and Robert E. Hawkinson. 2001. "Mexicans and 'Business as Usual': Small Town Politics in Oregon." *Aztlan: A Journal of Chicano Studies* 26:2 (Fall 2001):87-121.

Elguezabal, Mary Ann Dority. 1980. "Chicano History of Nyssa & Ontario." Unpb. paper. Nyssa Public Library.

Fuller, Varden. 1953. *No Work Today!* Public Affairs Pamphlet No. 190. New York: Public Affairs Committee, Inc.

Gamboa, Erasmo. 1990. *Mexican Labor and World War II: Braceros in the Pacific Northwest, 1942-1947.* Austin: University of Texas Press.

_____. 1991. "Mexican Mule Packers and Oregon's Second Regiment Mounted Volunteers, 1885-1856." *Oregon Historical Quarterly* 92 (Spring 1991):41-59.

_____. 1993. "Oregon's Hispanic Heritage." In Gordon B. Dodds, ed. *Varieties of Hope: An Anthology of Oregon Prose.* Corvallis, OR: Oregon State University Press.

_____. 1995a. "The Bracero Program." *In* Erasmo Gamboa and Carolyn Buan eds. *Nosotros: The Hispanic People of Oregon.* Portland: Oregon Council for the Humanities.

_____. 1995b. "El Movimiento: Oregon's Mexican-American Civil Rights Movement." *In* Erasmo Gamboa and Carolyn Buan eds. *Nosotros: The Hispanic People of Oregon.* Portland: Oregon Council for the Humanities.

Gamboa, Erasmo, and Carolyn Buan, eds. 1995. *Nosotros: The Hispanic People of Oregon: Essays and Recollections.* Portland: Oregon Council for the Humanities.

Infante, Mark Martinez, and Tom Current. 1958. *We Talked to the Migrants: Preliminary Report, July 1958.* Salem: Oregon Bureau of Labor.

Loprinzi, Colleen Marie. 1991. Hispanic Migrant Labor in Oregon, 1940-1990. M.A. Thesis: Portland State University.

Montejano, David. 1987. *Anglos and Mexicans in the Making of Texas, 1836-1986.* Austin: University of Texas Press.

Oregon Bureau of Labor. 1958. *'Vamonos pal Norte' (Let's Go North): A Social Profile of the Spanish Speaking Migratory Farm Labor.*

Oregon Interagency Committee on Migratory Labor. 1966. *Report of the Interagency Committee on Migratory Labor for 1959-61.* (Includes reports through 1966.)

Oregon Legislative Assembly Interim Committee on Migratory Labor. 1958. *Migratory Labor in Oregon.*

Oregon State Board of Health. *Oregon Migrant Health Project.* Annual Reports 1961, 1964-65, 1968, 1970, 1971.

Péon, Máximo. 1966. *Como viven los mexicanos en los Estados Unidos.* Mexico, D.F.: Costa-Amic.

Perspectives on Migrant Labor in Oregon. 1968. Proceedings of conference held May 14, 1968, Corvallis.

Peterson del Mar, David. 2003. *Oregon's Promise: An Interpretive History.* Corvallis: Oregon State University Press.

Rasmussen, Wayne. 1951. *A History of the Emergency Farm Labor Supply Program, 1943-1947.* Ag. Monographs No. 13. USDA Bureau of Agricultural Economics. (In Oregon State University Archives.)

Reisler, Mark. 1976. *By the Sweat of Their Brow: Mexican Immigrant Labor in the United States, 1900-1940.* Westport, CN, and London: Greenwood Press.

Saenz, Rogelio. "Interregional Migration Patterns of Chicanos: The Core, Periphery, and Frontier." *Social Science Quarterly* 72:1 (March 1991):135-148.

Scruggs, Otey. 1988. *Braceros, "Wetbacks," and the Farm Labor Problem: Mexican Agricultural Labor in the United States 1942-1954.* New York: Garland Publishing, Inc.

Wells, Miriam J. "Emigrants From the Migrant Stream: Environment and Incentives in Relocation." *Aztlán* 7:2 (Summer 1976): 267-291.

Newspapers, Journals, and Reports Consulted:

El Relámpago (Archives, Knight Library, University of Oregon)
Farm Labor News Notes. Oregon State University Archives.
The Independence Enterprise
The Monmouth Herald
Northwest Farm News, State of Washington Archives
Oregon Farm Labor Report 1943, Oregon State University Archives
The Oregon Journal
The Oregon Statesman
The Oregonian

Oral History Projects Consulted:

Latino Oral History Project. Independence Historical Museum Archives, Independence, Oregon. (LOHP)

Latinas in Oregon. Oregon Council for the Humanities Hispanic Oral History Project, 1992-1993, Oregon Historical Library (HOHP)

The Gila River runs through hot, dry desert in southern Arizona, near one of the camps where Japanese Americans were interned during World War II. Patti Sakurai describes her visit to the camp where they struggled to farm and develop community. Her words remind us of historical events and the physical reality of a place where the air is still "dense with the presence of those who once lived here."

In Wind and Sand:
Landscape and the Reading of Gila River Internment Camp

Patti Sakurai

S unday, May 28, 2000. Arizona. Seated two by two on chartered buses, rocking with the dips and turns in the road, the chatter of voices mixing in with the drone of the engine, I am flashing back to past rides on school buses: the excitement and the chaos, the teasing and the social angst, the desire simply to be home. But looking at the faces around me, the contrast is readily apparent. Unlike my former classmates, almost all of us are Asian American, most of us well beyond our grade-school days, most of us academics here for an Asian American Studies conference in Scottsdale. Behavior is calm and civil—no angry bus driver has to pull over and scold anyone for running around the bus or otherwise misbehaving. Yet old as we are, we are indeed on a field trip.

We are headed to Gila River, about fifty miles southeast of Phoenix, having been granted permission by the Gila River Indian Community to visit the site of the World War II internment camp that was placed on their land by the U.S. government to hold Japanese Americans for the duration of the war. We are told that the Gila River Indian Community has declared the site sacred land, a fact that hits me hard for its grace and for the myriad resonances it sets off, given the Gila River Indian Community's own relationship with this land and experiences with the U.S. government—histories that started long before the construction of the internment camps and that continue into the present day.

This information also sets me thinking about the internees' time on this land and their relationship to the landscapes that surrounded them. As a humanities scholar who has studied the internment, so much of my attention has focused on the facts and figures, the legal issues, the violations of civil and human rights, and the impact of all these on the lives of the internees, particularly as told through their written narratives and oral histories. As a Sansei (a third-generation Japanese American), I have also tried to sort out my own family's experiences during the period. But this long-overdue trip to one of the ten War Relocation Authority (WRA) camp sites brings a physicality to this history that is truly new and overwhelming to me. As the Arizona desert whisks by my window, my stomach tightens with the thought: Could this be the road the internees themselves traveled all those decades ago? What was it like on their buses? Was there much talking? An occasional anxious laugh even? Or did they sit in silence, each in his or her own thoughts? When they stared out their windows at this desert, did any of them see beauty? Or, given the circumstances, could the desert only have looked hostile to them? How striking the differences in our journeys. Ours, a finite day trip taken in air-conditioned comfort. Theirs, a forced displacement from their homes, marked by crowded trains and buses headed for unfamiliar terrain for who knew how long. Riding to camp, I am sure that they, more deeply than I could ever imagine, simply wanted to be home.

Upon our arrival at the reservation, we are greeted by members of the Gila River Indian Community and fed a wonderful lunch (another sharp contrast to what awaited the internees). Then it is time to get back on the buses and ride to the camp site itself, or rather, camp sites, as Gila River was divided into two areas—Butte and Canal camps. We head to Canal first (due to time constraints, sadly, we never make it to Butte). When we finally get there, we emerge from the buses to a landscape that at first glance appears little different from all that we have seen on the way in, the barracks and various buildings long torn down, the ground pretty much reclaimed by the desert.

But as we start to walk around, upon closer inspection, we see signs of the former occupants—an old concrete foundation here, an apparent pathway there. Like many others, I am fascinated by the concrete fish ponds that are scattered around the landscape, some elegant and simple, others elaborate with alcoves and tunnels in which fish could hide and enjoy some shade. Some would have been partially or wholly under barracks, apparently offering the fish additional shade and the occupants above a bit of a cooling effect. As we walk around, we come across remnants of rock gardens, old pipes, and at one point, a decorative mosaic pattern in the dirt—bottle caps the improvised material of choice, as I recall, both beautifully innovative and telling of the makeshift conditions of camp life.

Gila River officially opened on July 20, 1942, and closed on November 10, 1945.[1] At its peak, the camp held 13,348 Japanese Americans, making it the fourth-largest "city" in Arizona at the time, behind Phoenix, Tuscon, and Poston—another Arizona internment camp (Daniels et al. 1991, xxi). Looking across the expanse, I try to visualize the buildings, the rows of barracks, the people held here, the routines of what had become their daily lives. Overcrowding for a time was no small matter; some internees were temporarily housed wherever they could find space, including mess halls and latrines (Commission on Wartime Relocation and Internment of Civilians 1997, 160). Regular barracks were divided into four rooms measuring twenty by twenty-five feet, each room housing a family or group of people thrown together by the circumstances (at some other camps, room dimensions were even smaller). Privacy, clearly, was not easy to come by. A number of internee accounts describe the initial open rows of toilets without any dividers between them as being particularly daunting and humiliating. But internees gathered scrap lumber and did what they could to make their quarters livable. One woman's account of an engagement gift implies much about material conditions at the camps in general: "To a friend who became engaged, we gave nails—many of them bent—precious nails preserved in fruit wrappings, snitched from our fathers' meager supply or found by sifting through the sand in the windbreak where scrap lumber was piled" (Commission on Wartime Relocation and Internment of Civilians 1997, 161). Meals at all the WRA camps revolved around a mess hall instead of a family dinner table, and communal latrines and showers were the standard. As one former internee described it, "Camp life was highly regimented and it was rushing to the wash basin to beat other groups, rushing to the mess hall for breakfast, lunch and dinner. When a human being is placed in captivity, survival is the key"

(Commission on Wartime Relocation and Internment of Civilians 1997, 169). Eventually, internees at Gila River formed a camp government, opened a cooperative store, built and furnished schools, cleared and leveled sports fields. Some even started small businesses, for which they were paid nineteen dollars a month (the WRA pay scale was twelve dollars a month for unskilled labor, sixteen for skilled labor, and nineteen for professionals: Commission on Wartime Relocation and Internment of Civilians 1997, 166, 169). Still, such internee-built "amenities" could hardly make up for the extreme temperatures, the incessant sand and dust storms, the separated families, or the simple fact that they were not there by choice. Additionally, many had lost homes, personal belongings, family heirlooms, farms, and businesses that had taken years if not decades of work to establish. It may have seemed to some that the internees were able to create a sense of normalcy within the camps, but their responses to their displacement were much more complicated and heterogeneous than that surface appearance might indicate.

Contributing to the image of normalcy at the time was a 1942 article published in the *Phoenix Republic*, bringing news of the internees' activities to the Arizona public, explaining the inner workings of this instant "city." Along with all the other details—the churches, the schools, the "barber shops, beauty shops, shoe repair shops" (Simmons and Meyer 1943, 209) and even the Boy Scouts—the article notes that "an outstanding vegetable farm and a garnishing factory have sprung up overnight at Rivers" (Simmons and Meyer 1943, 206).[2] With water supplied by the San Carlos Reservoir, internees produced a wide variety of vegetables, providing food for themselves as well as shipping their produce to other camps. Farming at other camps soon followed, and collectively, they produced 85 percent of the produce they consumed and sold 2.5 million pounds (Commission on Wartime Relocation and Internment of Civilians 1997, 168). All of the camps eventually raised

hogs, and some raised poultry and beef as well. At Gila River, they raised pigs, cattle, and chickens, and even ran a dairy (Commission on Wartime Relocation and Internment of Civilians 1997, 168). Later, due to wartime labor shortages, officials allowed Gila River internees to be trucked out daily to work in the cotton fields outside of camp (Weglyn 1976, 99).

Of course, the internees were not the first to farm in the area. Members of the Gila River Indian Community—made up of the Akimel O'odham (Pima) and Pee Posh (Maricopa)—have a long agricultural history in the area, their predecessors, the HuHuKam, farming in the Gila River Valley as far back as 300 B.C. (Gila River 2005, 1). Indeed, the *Phoenix Republic* article cited above notes that the land on which the internees were farming had previously been used for alfalfa (Simmons and Meyer 1943, 210), though interestingly no mention is made of the people who had been growing the alfalfa before the internees got there.

Nor were the internees the first Japanese Americans to farm in Arizona. Japanese Americans began immigrating to Arizona in significant numbers in the late 1800s. Early contract laborers usually did not settle in Arizona, but rather migrated, following opportunities for work. Others did come to settle, however, working various low-paying jobs (as cooks, domestic workers, farm workers, etc.), opening small businesses, or running their own farms (Walz 1997, 2). Many of the Issei (first-generation Japanese immigrants) came from farming backgrounds in Japan, and this was strongly reflected in their work histories on the West Coast. For example, in the first decade of the twentieth century, around two-thirds of the Japanese Americans in California were farm laborers (Chan 1991, 38).[3] By 1910, thirty-nine thousand Japanese Americans worked in agriculture, around six thousand of them working their own farms, mostly as tenant farmers with small truck farms (Takaki 1998, 193; Commission on Wartime Relocation and Internment of Civilians 1997, 43). Farming independently, however, was no small feat, especially given intentional barriers such as Arizona's 1917 Alien Land Law, which made it illegal for Asian immigrants to own land (Chan 1991, 47). The law was later extended in effect to include leasing land as well (Walz 1997, 8). Some Issei managed to work their way around the laws by buying or leasing land in their U.S.-born Nisei children's names or finding a white American willing to enter into a lease or purchase arrangement on their behalf. In 1925, around 46 percent of employed Japanese Americans still worked in agriculture (Takaki 1998, 192-93). Collectively, Japanese American farmers and farm workers, along with other Asian immigrant groups, had a tremendous impact on the development of agriculture in Arizona and the West as a whole.[4]

As Eric Walz writes in an article on pre-war Japanese immigrant settlement in Arizona's Maricopa County, "Japanese farmers became known throughout the valley for the abundance and quality of their specialty crops. . . . Farming a proportionately larger number of acres than their population size would indicate, being the first to grow and ship certain important crops, and developing innovative farm practices are concrete measures of the community's relative importance" (Walz 1997, 6-7). This impact was echoed elsewhere in the West. In *Asian Americans: An Interpretive History*, Sucheng Chan (1991) notes that, by 1917, Japanese farmers in California "produced almost 90 percent of the state's output of celery, asparagus, onions, tomatoes, berries, and cantaloupes; more than 70 percent of the floricultural products; 50 percent of the seeds; 45 percent of the sugar beets; 40 percent of the leafy vegetables; and 35 percent of the grapes" (38). Japanese American farmers brought experience and agricultural techniques from their homelands, created associations and networks of financial support, and were able to rely on family labor and citizen children through which they could access land.[5] Their timing was especially good. From the late 1800s on, shifts and developments in agricultural markets, industrialization and increasing demands for produce from urban populations, the expansion of irrigation networks, the advent of the refrigerated boxcar, and the continued expansion of railway transportation all contributed to the success of a number of Japanese American farmers (Takaki 1998, 189).

But their economic success was no guarantee of social acceptance. While some outside the Japanese American community praised the quality of their produce and supported the Issei farmers with their business, anti-Asian and anti-Japanese sentiment among others was quite apparent. A parade in Glendale, Arizona, in 1934 clearly illustrated those animosities. Hundreds of white farmers gathered for the event to make their views clear, one of their banners proclaiming,

We Don't Need Asiatics
Jap Moving Day August 25th, We Mean It
Move Out By Saturday Noon August 25th,
Or Be Moved (Walz 1997, 10-11).

In the weeks following, Japanese immigrants and their families had their homes bombed, their property destroyed, and their lives threatened with gunfire as they tried to protect themselves and their crops (Walz 1997, 11). Such violent acts reflected regional and national anti-Asian attitudes that had been in place since the mid-1800s, traceable through the discriminatory local, state, and federal legislation and court rulings passed over the years. While these laws and rulings are too numerous to list here, examples include the 1854 California Supreme Court ruling (*People v Hall*) that Asians could not testify in court against white defendants, expanding an already existing law that likewise barred African American and Native Americans from testifying. In 1882 Congress passed the Chinese Exclusion Act and in 1924 halted Asian immigration. Asians could not marry a white person in many states, own or lease land as mentioned above. Riots and violence against Asian immigrants were not uncommon during the period, and whole communities were destroyed, people killed, and workers run out of town. Much of the hostility was tied to economic conditions and labor competition. Fifteen Chinese immigrants were lynched, four shot, and two wounded by a mob in Los Angeles in 1871. In September 1885, white coal miners attacked a group of Chinese workers in Rock Springs, Wyoming, after they did not join plans for a strike, killing twenty-eight of them, wounding fifteen, and burning down their living quarters (Chan 1991, 49). White mobs forced hundreds of Asian Indian workers out of Bellingham and Everett, Washington, in 1907, Korean workers out of Hemet, California, in 1913, and Japanese out of Turlock, California, in 1921 (Takaki 1998, 297; Chan 1991, 48-53). A mob of four hundred attacked Filipino workers at the Northern Monterey Filipino Club in California, beating dozens and killing two in 1930 (Chan 1991, 53).[6]

Nationalism also fueled anti-Asian sentiment and notions of a threatening "yellow peril." A racialized minority considered "unassimilable" by many Americans, Asian immigrants often had a hard time finding acceptance in their adopted country. Drawing on the 1790 Naturalization Law that preserved naturalized citizenship for white immigrants only, U.S. courts barred Asians from becoming naturalized citizens no matter how long in the country or what their intentions of settling—a practice that generally held until naturalization laws were changed in 1952. This in turn limited their political power, since as non-citizens they could not vote. Of the Japanese, the California State Attorney General argued before Congress in 1924 "They are different in color; different in ideals; different in race; . . . They speak a different language; they worship a different God. They have not in common with the Caucasian a single trait. . . . This is a Government of the white race" (qtd. in Modell 1973, 5).

The above history considered, the relationship between Asian immigrants and U.S. soil takes on at least two interconnected dimensions: their physical labor on the land and their ongoing struggle to create a sense of place and national belonging for themselves in often hostile terrain. By the time of the Japanese American internment during World War II, the Grower-Shipper Vegetable Association had no qualms admitting in the *Saturday Evening Post* in May 1942: "We've been charged with wanting to get rid of the Japs for selfish reasons. We might as well be honest. We do. It's a question of whether the white man lives on the Pacific Coast or the brown man. They came into this valley to work, and they stayed to take over . . . If all the Japs were removed tomorrow, we'd never miss them in two weeks, because the white farmers can take over and produce everything the Jap grows" (qtd. in Takaki 1998, 389). The Japanese American internment did not occur in isolation but was part of an ongoing history of anti-Asian sentiment, economic competition, and racialized nationalism. While the impact of the war and alleged security fears cannot be dismissed, such pre-existing anti-Asian attitudes and conditions make the argument that the Japanese American internment was solely a matter of "wartime necessity" rather suspect indeed.[7]

In the days just after the bombing of Pearl Harbor, over two thousand Issei were taken from their homes by the FBI in Hawaii and on the mainland, and most were eventually sent to Department of Justice prison camps separate from their families. None were ever formally charged with a crime, espionage, or treason, but rather held on mere suspicion. A community leadership role or occupation in industries such as fishing was enough for the government to justify arrest and prolonged incarceration (no act of sabotage by a Japanese American during the period has ever been substantiated). Ideas about national belonging remained clearly tied to static notions of race, as seen in the often-quoted January 1942 *Los Angeles Times* staff editorial: "A viper is nonetheless a viper wherever the egg is hatched—so a Japanese American, born of Japanese parents—grows up to be a Japanese, not an American" (qtd. in Takaki 1998, 388). After the bombing and well before the internment, all Nisei, despite their U.S. citizenship by birth, were designated 4-C, "enemy aliens," and Nisei soldiers already in the U.S. armed forces were kicked out (notably, exceptions were made for those in the Military Intelligence Service, whose translation skills were too vital to the war effort, and, as the war went on, not only were Nisei allowed back into the armed forces, they were later drafted, including from within the internment camps).

With the signing of Executive Order 9066 on February 19, 1942, President Franklin Delano Roosevelt allowed for the forced displacement of all Japanese Americans from the West Coast and the internment of 120,313 Japanese Americans, two-thirds of whom were U.S. citizens by birth (conspicuously referred to as "non-aliens" rather than as "citizens" in the internment notices and other government documents). Starting in March, Japanese Americans living in the military's exclusion zone were given only a few days' notice to get their affairs in order and told to report to a designated location with only what they could carry. Individuals with as little as one-sixteenth Japanese blood were legally included in the action—a rare individual indeed, given the history of anti-miscegenation laws and sentiment in the U.S. Japanese American infants and children adopted by non-Japanese families were taken from their adoptive parents only to be put into orphanages run within the internment camps. Even Issei veterans who had served in the U.S. armed forces during World War I were not exempt. While some Japanese Americans were bused to temporary assembly centers—racetracks and fairgrounds converted into makeshift housing—others went directly to one of the WRA internment camps: Tule Lake and Manzanar, California; Gila River and Poston, Arizona; Heart Mountain, Wyoming; Minidoka, Idaho; Rohwer and Jerome, Arkansas; Amache, Colorado, and Topaz, Utah. The fact that there was not a mass internment in Hawaii was a telling point to many, given that Hawaii was the site of the actual Japanese attack, not the U.S. mainland, undercutting the government's arguments concerning national security. Still, well over a thousand individuals of Japanese descent were arrested and held in Hawaii, 1,118 of those eventually sent to WRA camps on the mainland (Commission on Wartime Relocation and Internment of Civilians 1997, 150).[8]

Given that the military's exclusion zone ended in southern Arizona, the approximately six hundred Japanese Americans living in northern Arizona at the beginning of World War II were not forced into internment camps. But escaping internment did not mean life for them was easy. For example, on top of the general anti-Japanese hostility amplified by the war, the state passed legislation severely restricting commercial transactions with Japanese Americans. As Michi Weglyn details in *Years of Infamy* (1976), in order for a Japanese American to buy anything at all, including food items, he or she would have to publish a notice of intent three times and file a copy with the Secretary of State. In one case, showing that the law was taken quite seriously, the state fined Standard Oil $1,000 for selling gasoline to a Nisei. In the face of such barriers and outright hostility, many "were faced with virtual extinction, economically and otherwise" (Weglyn 1976, 99-100). Such conditions were not limited to Arizona, and the various accounts of beatings, refusals of service, and other hostile acts make clear that the "outside" was no haven (Weglyn 1976, 100). At the same time, the presence of animosity and discrimination hardly validates the often-heard argument that the internment was primarily for the internees' own protection. Documentation (government reports, letters, memos, etc.) surrounding the original motives behind the internment make the inaccuracy of such explanations quite clear. Moreover, as so many have pointed out, the guns of the guards around camp perimeters were pointed inward at the internees, not out.

Their point is driven home by several incidents. At Gila River, a guard shot and wounded a mentally unstable internee (Commission on Wartime Relocation and Internment of Civilians 1997, 176). An internee at Manzanar was also shot and wounded when he went outside the camp's barbed wire fence to collect scrap wood for some shelves (Commission on Wartime Relocation and Internment of Civilians 1997, 175). And while shootings were not commonplace, there were a number of notable cases in which other internees were actually killed by guards. Probably best known is the incident at Manzanar in December 1942. A crowd had gathered in protest over the arrest of a fellow internee and refused to disperse. Guards ended up throwing tear gas canisters into the crowd and in the subsequent chaos, opened fire, killing two and wounding nine (Chan 1991, 129). Another internee was shot and killed during an argument with a guard at Tule Lake (Commission on Wartime Relocation and Internment of Civilians 1997, 175), and at Topaz, an elderly internee who wandered too close to the barbed wire fence was shot and killed when it was assumed he was trying to escape (Chan 1991, 129-30). Given that Topaz, like Gila River, was surrounded by desert, I have to wonder to where exactly did the guard think the old man was going to escape?

Standing in the noonday sun at Gila River, I find it hard to imagine trying to make this place a home under such conditions, both natural and man-made. Still, some managed to do what they could. Besides the fish ponds, there are other indentations in the landscape, similar in size, but without the concrete or sense of intentional aesthetic design. An older man in our group explains that they were spaces dug out under the barracks in which internees could escape the heat. Groups of older men and younger boys would compete over the apparently gendered space. Looking at the holes, envisioning the

barracks overhead, I have to wonder if the heat was the only motivation for digging and fighting over them, each dusty hole the equivalent of a coveted extra room in which to play and socialize.

These physical markers tell me that, despite the conditions, and perhaps despite their own intentions even, the internees did put down roots here, however shallow or temporary, simply in the process of living and trying to make this space livable. One former internee described their impact on the land around them: "[W]hen we entered camp, it was a barren desert. When we left camp, it was a garden that had been built without tools, it was green around the camp with vegetation, flowers, and also with artificial lakes, and that's how we left it" (Commission on Wartime Relocation and Internment of Civilians 1997, 161).

In her essay, "Time and Landscape," Barbara Bender writes, "*Landscape is time materialized.* Or, better, *Landscape is time materializing:* landscapes, like time, never stand still." (2002, S103, emphasis in original). Landscape is a physical manifestation of time, the relationship between them intricate and ongoing—anything but abstract. The landscape of Gila River is marked with the internees' time on it, their history, but walking around Gila River, speculating which of these markers, if any, will remain decades, even centuries from now, I also understand that this will not always be so.

Bender goes on to assert that "*Landscapes and time can never be 'out there':* *they are always subjective.* . . . [T]he engagement with landscape and time is historically particular, imbricated in social relations and deeply political" (2002, S103, 104, emphasis in original). While we might think of time and place as simple objective realities, our relationships with them, how we read and understand them, are fluid, subjective, and complex. The significance of a particular landscape is what we make of it. The very act of reflecting on the past shifts time and brings history into the present. My own need to make sense of this landscape, to connect with this particular history, inevitably colors how I see the Gila River landscape and the use I make of it here. The U.S. government had their particular lens when it came to this place. I have mine. Where I stand, the air is dense with the presence of those who once lived here. This is indeed sacred ground.

In the heat of July 1942, the land at Gila River did not distinguish between "citizen" and "non-citizen," "loyal" and "disloyal," "American" and "enemy alien," but the U.S. government obviously did.[9] In this sense, the internees' prewar dual relationship to the land—physically working the soil while at the same time struggling to belong to the land as a nation—continued in camp. Whatever the internees' original intentions, I come to read these ponds and gardens, the pathways and plantings, as small acts of resistance, the internees trying to make themselves at home in the face of a government that seemed determined to deny them one, attempting to assert some agency in relation to their environment in the face of a situation over which they ultimately had little control.[10] There is a certain irony to the act, internees putting down roots in a camp in the desert on a reservation, when they had been put there precisely because they were believed incapable of doing so—these "enemy aliens," these "unassimilable foreigners."

What began as a reflection on the internees' relationship with Gila River turns out really to be about a number of different relationships—the internees' relationship with a specific piece of land while they were forced to occupy it, their broader historical relationship with the land as a geopolitical, national space, and my own relationship to both of these, my own need to find a sense of place in this history.[11] I was born well after the internment, but as a part of my extended family and community's collective memory, it is a part of my memory as well. Growing up, I remember listening to the conversations among Issei and Nisei. Sometimes, at a certain point in the conversation, the tone of one of their voices would change, and someone would quietly ask, "Were you in camp?" With the subject of the war years open, I would see the air around them shift, watch them transport themselves to another place and time, and feel like I, not they, had somehow disappeared. Such exchanges seem rarer now as so many of the Issei have passed and the Nisei are themselves passing on. When I first started in Asian American Studies, the primary concern was over the loss of the Issei and their first-person accounts of history. It is heartbreaking to realize that we are now facing the same dilemma with the Nisei, my own parents' mortality no small consideration with this thought.

While members of my extended family were interned, my own parents were not. At the time, my father was a young boy living in Kersey, Colorado, outside the exclusion zone, tenant farming with his family. When asked about the period, he recalls bans on Japanese Americans owning short-wave radios, knives, and flashlights, not being allowed to gather for meetings, weddings, and funerals without a white authority present, and his parents taking in a number of Japanese American families who had fled the West Coast. Over a decade before my parents met, my mother and her family were among those fleeing the West Coast for Colorado. They had been living in Santa Monica, California; with more and more restrictions being imposed on Japanese Americans and rumors of the internment beginning to circulate, my maternal grandparents decided they should go. They sent my mother and her brother ahead of them with relatives to Colorado, packed the rest of her siblings and a cousin with whatever else they could fit into their pickup truck, and took off to join them, leaving the rest of home behind. They chose Colorado as they already had some relatives living there, and stayed on even after the war, never returning to California. My maternal grandfather, a gardener by trade, eventually opened a landscaping business in Denver. Both sides of my family have strong roots working the soil in this country.

No horticulturalist myself, as we continue walking around Gila River, I cannot tell which plants are indigenous to this area and which might be remnants from an internee's garden. Still, I would like to think some of those transplants took root and survived, came to coexist well in their new environment. Of course the hope is not really about plants or the landscape. It is about the survival of memory, acknowledging some of this history, paying homage to those who lived through it—and those who did not. In *Strangers from a Different Shore*, Ronald Takaki ends his chapter on the World War II period with a poem by internee Keiho Soga:

When the war is over
And after we are gone
Who will visit
This lonely grave in the wild
Where my friend lies buried? (Soga 1982, 64)

It seems an appropriate way to end here as well. Over eighteen hundred internees died while in WRA camps (Commission on Wartime Relocation and Internment of Civilians 1997, 150). Looking around at the seemingly infinite desert, it is both easy and incredibly hard to picture dying out here, so far away from home. While graves at Gila River have since been moved and relocated, I figuratively visit them here. The desert continues to overtake the remnants of the camp, perhaps just as it should. It is not the desert's responsibility to remember. It is ours.

References

Bender, Barbara. 2002. "Time and Landscape." *Current Anthropology* 43 (Supplement, August-October 2002): S103-S112.

Bulosan, Carlos. 1946. *America Is in the Heart*. Reprinted, Seattle: University of Washington Press, 1973.

Chan, Sucheng. 1991. *Asian Americans: An Interpretive History*. Boston: Twayne Publishers.

Commission on Wartime Relocation and Internment of Civilians. 1983, 1984. *Personal Justice Denied: The Report of the Commission on Wartime Relocation and Internment of Civilians*. Washington, D.C., and Seattle: Civil Liberties Public Education Fund and the University of Washington Press, 1997.

Daniels, Roger, Sandra C. Taylor, and Harry H. L. Kitano (eds.). 1991. *Japanese Americans: From Relocation to Redress*. Revised Edition. Seattle: University of Washington Press.

Gila River Indian Community Web site. "Akimel O'Odham/Pee Posh: 'People of the River.'" Accessed 26 February 2005. <http://www.gric.nsn.us/history/hist_home.html>

Modell, John (ed.). 1973. Introduction. *The Kikuchi Diary*. Reprinted, Chicago: University of Illinois Press, 1993. 1-39.

Simmons, Gurdon, and Ralph Louis Meyer (eds.). 1943. "A Little Tokyo in Arizona." *This is Your America*. New York: Literary Classics, Inc. 206-210. Originally in *Phoenix Republic* as "Evacuees Operate Factory Vegetable Farm at Rivers," 1942.

Soga, Keiho. 1983. "When the War Is Over." *Poets Behind Barbed Wire*. Ed. and trans. Jiro Nakano and Kay Nakano. Honolulu: Bamboo Ridge Press. 64.

Takaki, Ronald. 1998. *Strangers from a Different Shore*. Revised Edition. Boston: Little, Brown and Company.

Walz, Eric. 1997. "The Issei Community in Maricopa County: Development and Persistence in the Valley of the Sun, 1900-1940." *The Journal of Arizona History* 38 (Spring 1997): 1-33.

Weglyn, Michi. 1976. *Years of Infamy: America's Untold Story of America's Concentration Camps*. New York: Morrow Quill Paperbacks.

As a young man David Mas Masumoto returned to farm in the Central Valley of California where he grew up. Home to immigrants, farm families and weeds, the valley is 400 miles long, 50 miles wide, carved by the Sacramento River flowing south and San Joaquin River flowing north to the San Francisco Bay delta. Masumoto might call these fertile lands, once dominated by extensive wetlands, "The Other California," hidden and invisible to outsiders. In these "letters" to his grandmother, he calls up the names and attributes of weeds growing on the farm, affirming ownership of and familiarity with the place where his family struggled to set roots and make home. April: Spring Weeds is adapted from an essay by Mas Masumoto which appeared in Letters to the Valley, A Harvest of Memories, Heyday Books, 2004.

April: Spring Weeds

David Mas Masumoto

Dear Baachan/Grandma,

Morning Glory. Spanish clover. Pineapple weed.

Spring appears each year with the sudden green blanket of luscious weeds. They sound innocent, even playful, and some children still make scissors from the flowers and stems of filaree. But you knew these plants well, nothing new for your callused hands.

I remember on the first warm day of the new spring watching you search for your favorite shovel stored in the barn since last fall. The one with the smooth handle well oiled by your hands over the years. The sleek metal was perfectly adapted to the dry climates of California's Central Valley, where annual rainfall often totals in the single digits. Most of our weeds here are shallow rooted. Shovels just need to glide beneath the surface, swimming in the sandy loam soil, slicing weeds, severing roots. In a single afternoon of work, you erased the brown tinge of winter rust from the shovel face, the steel gray and silver polished by a thousand strokes in the soft, moist earth.

The shovel once had a sharp tip, the point worn down as the land worked you and Jiichan. We had a hard-pan farm, cheap land filled with rocks. Hard pan, a compressed layer of clay that behaves more like rock than dirt. Hard pan, huge sheets of stone, yards wide and long, weighing thousands of pounds. Hard pan symbolized the character of our piece of farm land, almost impossible to grow things on and difficult for water to penetrate and resulting in cheap land for poor immigrant farmers with little cash for down payments. Even weeds don't like hard-pan ground.

I think they should proclaim hard pan the official rock of the Central Valley of California, a hard rock in a hard land for hardy immigrants. What others cursed, the Issei (first generation Japanese in America) and the Nisei (second generation) saw as opportunity—to plant roots in American soil. Dad gambled and bought our farm in 1948, a piece of dirt full of hard pan. For two years he cleared the rocks piece by piece, wagon load after wagon load, until vines could be planted. Years before the fox tails made their way along the field's edges; I believe the appearance of wild barley was a good sign, nature's way of acknowledging and complimenting dad's years of labor.

And decades later the weeds grew prolific as our farm family grew and evolved. They say that the first generation immigrants worked the land with their strong backs. Then the next generation began to buy land and farm with stubborn heads. My generation were given the choice to stay on the farm or the chance to go on to college and leave. Most ran away, escaping the prickly lettuce and burning nettle of farm life. In my little community of Del Rey, an unincorporated town of about a thousand, just south of Fresno, we once had a thriving Japanese American population with a Buddhist temple and community of forty farm families. I'm the only Japanese American to return to the farm. Baachan, you and mom and dad gave me the resources to leave for college; I like to think you also provided me with the opportunity to come home and discover the weeds for myself.

Mare's tail. Lambs quarter. Cheeseweed.

These weeds lie in ambush all winter, gathering strength with each rainstorm and finally bursting, well, everywhere. They're good at disguising themselves: initially as cute, slender shoots that paint the earth with a light, emerald hue. Trick me into a smile as I stand in the sunshine, breathing in the start of a year, surrounded by new life. The sly weeds take advantage of my trance—delicate and innocent one day, a growing menace the next. Yet with the first shovel of earth turned over, Baachan, you shared a recognition with our valley's thousands of farmers and gardeners: breaking winter's crust to plant, water, and harvest—and the feel of something plowed back into the soul. We begin the journey with weeds, a rite of passage, the ritual we call spring. We treat ourselves to a glorious moment, even if in denial—after all, aren't weeds part of the good earth too?

Italian rye grass. Miners lettuce. Burclover.

The green of rye grass shimmers in the light. With a slight dew, it shines and dances in the early morning sun, glistening to make the earth feel alive. Burclover, a low-growing weed that can be a source for nitrogen, a kind plant, gentle and unobtrusive. I've learned to live with these weeds, good companions to vines and trees. Juicy fruits should be grown in soils covered with green; weed-free "moonscapes" will never add to the flavor of my farm.

Baachan, did you ever think of yourself as a weed, an alien to this valley, a foreigner who may not have always felt welcomed? You and Jiichan could not own land because of a racist law preventing "Orientals" from buying land while others—from Germany, Sweden, Italy—planted roots in California's soil. When Jiichan arrived in 1899, his Armenian neighbors were initially classified as "Asiatics," but when you came as a picture bride in 1918, authorities had already ruled Armenians were Caucasian and could become land owners, while Japanese Americans were exiled to work these fields.

And the weeds stood witness to the traumatic turning point in history when you were scarred by the upheaval of World War II evacuation, exiling all Japanese Americans from the West Coast. Later, when you both returned from the Arizona deserts in 1946 to Fresno, Jiichan was a broken old man in his sixties. I believe as the bombs fell on Pearl Harbor, his dreams were crushed, then withered behind the barbed wire of Gila River Internment Center. You two were among the last ones released from the Relocation Camps, not because they kept you those extra months but rather because you didn't know where to go. One son killed in Europe fighting for America, two other sons drafted in the U.S. army, only a teenage daughter left with you in the desert. But you came back to this valley to weed.

Baachan, you remained terrified for decades, fearing "they would take things away." Even when Dad bought our farm in 1948, you grew angry and scolded him, "We can lose everything. Again." Perhaps all you could count on were the weeds and hard work. Eventually the family accepted, adapted, and adopted: our farm survived because we became native to a place. Tenacious, stubborn, persistent. Like weeds?

Catsear. Summer lupine. Yarrow.

A philosopher/gardener once proclaimed that a weed was simply a plant whose virtues we had yet to discover. A weed was just something growing in the wrong place at the wrong time. I'd like to see that philosopher's farm: morning glory choking peach tree roots, fox tail drinking up irrigation water, and pigweed gorging itself in the shade of an anemic vine. It would probably drive you and me crazy.

Yet perhaps there's some truth in it: Not all things foreign to a field are weeds. (A convenient rationalization since I've given up trying to dominate all that's growing on our farm.) The trick you taught me is to redefine what I call a weed. A neighbor calls his: "native grasses." I like that term. Not as evil as weeds. Acknowledges that most of us here (like the vast majority of our weeds) came from somewhere else and forged a place in this soil. With the magic of time, we became natives, calling this land home as if we too would always be here, just as the weeds would always be with us.

So now I learn their proper names. Shepherd's purse blooms near Valentine's Day and has tiny heart-shaped leaves. Chickweeds have a miniature white flower, the first blossoms of a new year. Even fiddlenecks,

mostly tolerable because they will dry out by the middle of summer. Someone once asked if I planted those colorful wildflowers. Wild to think my weeds become someone's flowers.

Naming weeds adds life to our fields. I laughed at myself after Marcy convinced me to plant Queen Anne's lace in our flower bed and a visitor from the East Coast could not believe we actually planted weeds that flourish along eastern roadsides. Or recalled an old neighbor who came by to harvest our purslane; he claimed it was wonderful to eat as a salad. Or when I read that dandelions were first prized as salad greens, a step up, perhaps, from purslane?

By knowing these names I claim ownership. Names provide a familiarity, knowledge specific to a place. I plan on staying here for a while so I'll take the time to learn names. The power of language to personalize, to create identity, to find comfort. By calling weeds by their names I'm committing myself to stay put here for a while. Baachan, is this your secret to creating home?

Baachan, you knew weeds better than most of us because you hand shoveled them all. You understood that all farmers and gardeners struggle with some of them—despite their hidden virtues—because we also try to grow other things. Peaches and raisins put food on the table, not lamb's quarters or mare's tails.

And weeds kept you strong, with bulging biceps. "Eggs," we grandkids called them as you flexed your arms as you worked a shovel, attacking the weeds. Hard physical work as you carved out a place where you belonged, knowing it was only staking a claim. Watching and working side by side with you, I finally understood the ephemeral nature of working the land. Nothing is permanent. The land will always outlive us and so will the weeds. But we still must work our shovels.

Sand burr. Puncture vine. Sow thistle.

But there are weeds we don't tolerate, do we, Baachan? These are evil, treacherous to a farm, sinister to a family farmer. Find puncture vine thorns in a raisin crop and entire truck loads will fail inspection. Sand burrs scattered in a bin full of raisins and they must be removed by hand, one at a time with zero tolerance. We work the entire year, weathering storms and heat, dodging late-season rains and yet a simple weed and its seeds—the thorns—scattered throughout a field can ruin a year's labor.

So we walk the fields keeping a watch for these weeds. I've grown accustomed to such a vigil, leaping out of the pickup when driving by and noticing these pale green leaves or the odd-shaped plants. A chill sweeps across my back and a shiver at the first recognition of these evil plants—I can destroy one but are there more lurking nearby? We are intolerant, but not from prejudice, for we have had numerous bad experiences and learned from hard lessons with these weeds.

You had a special name for some weeds; you called them *abunai kusa*, which in Japanese means "dangerous grass." If puncture vines were evil weeds, then johnsongrass and Bermuda grass are classified as "dangerous" because they can choke a tree's root system and shade out a grapevine. These weeds were dangerous because they could gradually harm a farm, sucking life from the land and the farmer.

But your secret was teaching which weeds we can also live with. Life is too short to worry about them. Now I am learning to recognize the weeds in my life, and which are indeed *abunai kusa*.

Your grandson,

Mas

In Taos, where John Nichols lives, and in other towns of northern New Mexico, water is delivered to small farmers and some households by irrigation ditches called acequias. *His "acequia and property connected [him] to four hundred years of history, and to the people, culture, and community that had revolved around the water for all that time. They connected [him] to a tradition rich in grass and orchards and animals and healthy neighborhoods. They connected [him] to a language rich in history and personality and soul."*

Aamodt, Schmaamodt:
Who Really Gets the Water?

John Nichols

Speech given on July 18, 2004, at Nambe, New Mexico, to protest the controversial Aamodt water rights adjudication in the Pojoaque/Nambe/ Tesuque Basin near Santa Fe.

When I arrived in Taos thirty-five years ago I bought a little adobe house in the Upper Ranchitos part of town. It was on an acre and a half of land that was fed by two irrigation ditches. I came from the east and knew absolutely nothing about *acequias* or water laws in New Mexico. The only things I had going for me were that I could speak Spanish after a fashion and I was eager to learn.

I had been in my new house for about two weeks when I got a letter from the New Mexico State Engineer's office. It was an offer of judgment on the water rights of my land, and was part of a massive adjudication suit that is still going on today. Back then I had no idea what the State Engineer was talking about, and of course my heart fell into my toes because I thought I was being sued in some way that would tangle me up with lawyers, land me in jail, and take away the land that I had owned for about five minutes, total.

Welcome to *Nuevo Méjico, tierra del encanto.*

About two minutes after my heart fell into my toes, the Mayordomo of the Pacheco Ditch, Eloy Pacheco, showed up at my house to inform me that all the *parciantes* were going to clean that ditch on Saturday. So I went in town and bought a shovel, and showed up on Saturday to clean the *acequia.* I had never worked on a chain gang before, and I had never worked so hard in my life. It wasn't a very long or difficult ditch, but there were about forty of us who worked hard all day long cleaning up that artery, plugging the *perrito* holes, burning the grass, chopping out *jaras*, and cursing the *viejitos* who just leaned on their shovels shouting "Vuelta!" every few minutes and babbling to each other about how hard they used to work in the good old days, when men were really men and the *acequias* truly meant something. I was the only *gavacho* on the crew, and that was the first time I met all my neighbors together, and I had a blast, complaining, bitching about the work, listening to filthy jokes, and to all the *chisme* and *mitote* of the neighborhood and of Taos. I picked up a lot of history, too. Stories galore. And plenty of laughter.

The old guys are mostly gone now. Adolfo Lavadie, Alfonso Tejada, Eloy Pacheco. Phil Miera is still kicking, however. The young people like Jerry Pacheco and his brother Bobby and Joe Cordova are getting older like me. I'll be sixty-four next week. But the *acequias* are still running with water every spring and summer . . . and the adjudication suit is still going on. Nobody knows when the adjudication will eventually run its course, but it may cause considerable damage to the *acequia* system that created the valley in the first place.

Water is what connected me to my little plot of land, and to my neighbors, to my community, and ultimately to the larger world of New Mexico. There was a half acre of pasture in front of my house, irrigated by the Pacheco Ditch. The half-acre pasture in back was irrigated by the Lovatos Ditch. Near the house was a small garden area that I watered off a hand-dug well beside my house. The house was also connected to a community water users association for domestic use.

The first thing I did in Taos was plant a garden, and for twenty years I had a beautiful garden. Every year I grew corn and green beans and carrots and beets and squash and broccoli and peas and sunflowers and I even tried to grow watermelons a couple of times, but they never got bigger than baseballs. I had more pears and apples than I knew what to do with in the autumn. And I had chickens and turkeys, also. My neighbor, Tom Trujillo, put his horse in my front pasture, and then in my back pasture, and I spent more time talking to that horse than Tom ever did. In the spring and summer I let the grass grow in the two fields, and then Tom would bale it for his animals. I fixed my fences, and cleaned my little irrigation channels, and carefully irrigated all the living space on that property.

I got so that I really loved watering that land. I loved it because it gave me common ground with all my neighbors. We gathered at meetings to discuss the *acequias*, and during and after those meetings we discussed everything else. We got to know each other. We became friends. I got to palaver with the mayordomos, and that was fun. I treasured friends like Tom Trujillo and Bernardo Trujillo and Eloy Pacheco and Phil Miera. There were lots of fights and tense times. The Lovato Ditch runs through Pueblo land, and so we were always talking with people at the Pueblo about ditch problems. In dry summers, when the Pueblo River was really low, we had a heckuva time getting enough water. You could bet that some idiot on the Molino Ditch would divert so much of the river through their *compuerta* that the Pacheco Ditch would run dry. Then our hotheads would go over and kick out their diversion dam, and the next thing you know they'd be threatening to attack us with rifles.

In a real wet year, with a bad spring runoff, naturally our *compuerta* would get blown out in the flood. I say *compuerta* with a grain of salt, because what we called a *compuerta* was basically a lot of rocks, old tires, downed trees, and railroad ties, black plastic and chicken wire, with maybe a dead horse thrown in in order to divert some of the flow into the *acequia*. I would stand waist deep in ice-cold water trying to tie down all that stuff with cables and metal fence posts, and I'd snarl over at Alfonso Tejada or Eloy Pacheco or Adolfo Lavadie or Jerry Pacheco, "Aint there a better way of doing this?" And they'd just shrug and say, "Well, we been doing it like this for four hundred years. And so far it seems to work." People didn't have very much money, but they knew how to get the job done.

The *acequias* and my property connected me to that four hundred years, and to the people, culture, and community that had revolved around the water for all that time. They connected me to a tradition rich in grass and orchards and animals and healthy neighborhoods. They connected me to a language rich in history and personality and soul.

Of course, it wasn't always easy to keep those connections healthy. For me, those two *acequias* that fed water to my property were sometimes one wonderful disaster after another. Some years the muskrats went absolutely postal and we had to form emergency brigades to try and repair the ditch banks between Tom Trujillo's property and Sebastian's bar. Occasionally those water dogs would hit my ditch bank like roto-rooters going berserk, and although I'm not the bloodthirsty type, I actually wound up trying to shoot them from the kitchen window before the ditch bank collapsed and drowned Tom Trujillo's horse.

Because we had such a primitive *compuerta* on the Pacheco Ditch, it wasn't really feasible to kick out the diversion dam, so water often ran all winter. Sometimes it froze low in the ditch. The water rose, and froze again, and rose, and froze again, and pretty soon the ice forced the water over the top of the banks into my front field and Tom Trujillo's front field, and it froze really solid. Then one day all the kids in the neighborhood came skating. They brought with them dozens of dogs. And the dogs immediately attacked my chickens and killed all of them while I was taking a nap. There is no end to the tragedies that can be caused by water.

Sometimes, by mistake, I would leave open a *compuerta* in my back field and again, at night, somebody would throw the entire Pueblo River into a *veinita* six inches deep, and when I woke up in the morning the chickens would be roosting on top of their shed, their eggs would be floating in the Kingdom Hall Church parking lot next door, and my outhouse would be transformed into an overflowing septic tank.

When I say "*compuerta* in the back field," I should explain that for me a "*compuerta* in my back field was just a hole I chopped in the side of the ditch with a shovel. It used to amaze me to watch how my neighbors irrigated compared to myself. Me, because my backfield was at the end of the ditch, I always got the water last, and usually at night. It was only a half acre of grass with a lateral going through it. You'd think I could just cut one little opening and flood the field. I mean, that's how my neighbors did it. I'd watch old Adolfo Lavadie, a little bent-over grasshopper of a *viejito*, at his fields. He'd make one little shovel cut, plop the dirt in the proper spot, then lean on his shovel and watch the water calmly flood five acres without a hitch. Me, I'd chop one path, irrigate forty square feet, then chop another path, irrigate another forty square feet, chop a third path, irrigate another forty feet—what was the matter with me? I would never figure out the Euclidian geometry necessary to laying down a perfect sheet of water across the grass. I finally figured out it was the genes cultivated during those past four hundred years of creating and caretaking the *acequias* that gave my neighbors such an advantage.

I remember once a cow died on Indian land and fell into the Lovatos ditch and blocked it. But we weren't allowed on Indian land without permission from the Pueblo. So we went out to the Pueblo and the Governor's office said they'd send a crew to get rid of the cow. But they never sent the crew. So we went back to the Pueblo and they told us not to worry, the crew would be there that afternoon. And that afternoon a bunch of us waited on the road outside the fence near the rotting cow, but the Pueblo crew never showed up. Of course, you could bet if we jumped the fence and started shoveling out the cow on our own, that's when the Pueblo crew probably would've showed up and they would have accused us of trespassing on federal land, and we all would have wound up in the government prison at Leavenworth, Kansas. So, we tried once again to speak with the Governor, the War Chief, and who knows who else, and they promised to deal with the cow.

But nothing happened. So finally I went down there with a buddy, we tied kerchiefs over our noses, and shoveled out that cow. I think it was probably the most unpleasant task I ever performed on a New Mexico *acequia*. And afterwards I figured out that the Pueblo was probably laughing at us the whole time. I mean, right from the git-go they weren't idiotic enough to place themselves knee deep in bovine gore, and they were probably trying to figure out: What had taken us so long to catch on to that fact and jump the fence and break the law, and get rid of their rotten cow for them?

Of course, one of the most detestable jobs on the *acequia* is collecting the money. The ditch fees. The yearly dues. The work fees to hire *peones* if the *parciante no quiere limpiar la acequia* herself . . . or himself. In my experience on the Pacheco Ditch it was always Eloy Pacheco, the mayordomo, who performed this invaluable service. He was pretty informal. He'd known everybody for seventy years and he had his ways. Sometimes he got the money, sometimes he didn't. It was a frustrating job. Then I was elected a commissioner on the ditch, and the other commissioners decided to make me the treasurer. Thanks a lot, you guys. You could say that the record keeping up until then had been fairly lax, and my orders were to clean it up because the state was starting to really poke its nose into *acequia* business because of the ongoing adjudication suit. They also decided that I should collect the money. Me? I gulped, said okay, and went about the task with the zeal of a born-again tax collector. I hated the job, I was terrified of the job, but I realized the money was really important to the well-being of the *acequia*, and also to keeping people involved as modern times began to weaken the commitment many were beginning to feel toward the land.

"Hey, Effie Sebastian," I would say on the phone, "where's our twenty dollars?"

"*A la chingada con your viente pesos*," Effie would shout back. She's eighty-five years old. "I don't use the water anymore, so *a mi no me importa* if I lose it."

"Don't be a *pendeja*, Effie. *Sin derechos de agua tu terreno no vale nada.*"

"*Tú no vales nada, gringo*," Effie would shout, and hang up the phone. So I dialed her again.

"We gotta have the money, Effie. We have to hire a backhoe to dig out a cave-in over by Archie Anglada's."

"Why do I have to pay to dig out a cave-in at Archie Anglada's?"

"Because you're a *parciante* on the *acequia*, *viejita*."

"Who you calling *viejita*, *nene*?"

"Please. *Por favor. Dios te lo pagará después.*"

"Tell God He can pay my ditch fees for me *now*, *bobo*."

And she'd hang up the phone once more.

Eventually, I got the money. It was just a ritual we were going through. I imagine people have been going through that ritual since time immemorial. Still, as the years passed on it was tougher to get the money. People complained more, they had more excuses, they weren't as enthusiastic, they were starting to lose interest. The old guys on the *acequia* died off. The families sold their animals. There weren't so many gardens any more. Newcomers moved in and built houses where there'd once been fields and the newcomers weren't so interested in the water. Each year when we went to clean the *acequia*, there were less *peones* to do the work. Homeowners would not want to go themselves, and they would hire young boys, cheap, to do the work, but the boys couldn't really do the work. And it became more difficult to find people willing to work for the prices offered. And some years, while I still had my property on the *acequia*, when we went to clean the ditch in the springtime we'd only have, maybe, fifteen people. And you can't do a very good job that way. So we'd have to raise the fees, collect the money, and hire a backhoe to do part of the job. A backhoe is a wondrous machine that can replace fifteen, twenty, twenty-five people working together in the same amount of time. But the backhoe is run by a single person, who's usually not even connected to the *acequia*, to its history, or to the community that for centuries has drawn its life blood off that artery. So the backhoe can be the beginning of the end for much of what makes the *acequia*, and its water, truly valuable. When the backhoe becomes a necessity on a ditch, then it's a good bet the *acequia* is going to lose its water. *Parciantes* will sell it to a business, to a hotel, to be used in flushing toilets. And after a while the community on the *acequia* won't be so interactive. People won't work together so much anymore. They won't know each other as well. They'll lose their connections. And the community itself will begin to come unglued.

Interestingly, this all goes back to that first letter I received from the State Engineer, in the summer of 1969, that offer of adjudication of water rights on the Pacheco Ditch for my acre and a half of land. Of course, I had no idea what they were talking about, but pretty soon I would learn. The adjudication was, and still is, an attempt to legally define every drop of water in the Upper Rio Grande watershed. It was launched up in Taos not long after the Aamodt adjudication suit was started down here in the Nambe/Pojoaque area.

Concurrent with the adjudication, the state was also trying to partition San Juan-Chama Diversion water to various areas of New Mexico, including Taos. For our valley, the plan was to give us 12,000 acre feet of water to be impounded in a dam called the Indian Camp Dam, that would be built just south of Taos. In order to build the dam and contract with the Bureau of Reclamation and the state we were told that we had to form a conservancy district in order to tax the people in the Taos Valley for all the good fortune slated to come our way as a result of the dam.

At first, everybody was for the Indian Camp Dam, because who do you know in New Mexico who isn't for more water? In a state this dry you'd have to be crazy to say "No" to more flow. But pretty soon a lot of local folks realized that even if the dam was subsidized in part by the government, the cost to locals would still be pretty steep, given that this is a real poor area. But after that realization people really rebelled when they began looking into the legal powers of a conservancy district, and they concluded that in all likelihood the control of water in this valley would pass from the individual communities and *acequia* systems to politically appointed boards who would very likely shift much of the water in this area into development endeavors. And, given the nature of the development endeavors in New Mexico during the twentieth century, the local farmers and ranchers and other residents figured they were going to get screwed.

So they formed an organization called the Tres Rios Association to fight against the Indian Camp Dam, the Bureau of Reclamation, the State Engineer's office, the conservancy district, and many of the bankers and lawyers and developers and business people in the Taos Valley. The Tres Rios Association was made up of almost all the *acequias* in our valley and most of the people on those *acequias*. The battle lasted for a good part of nine years, and it created a fair amount of bad blood in the Taos valley. It pretty much pitted the development future against the sustainable past, and it certainly put the history, and custom, and culture of the Taos area up for grabs. The San Juan Chama water slated for the Indian Camp Dam was tied into the adjudication of all the water rights in the valley.

It is not an accident that most of the leaders of the Tres Rios Association were elderly gentlemen and women, and many of the meetings were conducted in Spanish. Many of those leaders are gone today, and the Taos valley—and myself—misses them dearly. They were not radicals, they were not people who wanted to ask for trouble, nor were they ostriches who decided to stick their heads in the sand in order to avoid facing the realities of modern growth and change. They were people deeply rooted in the culture and history that had shaped New Mexico for centuries. They were Republicans and Democrats, they were farmers and teachers, they were veterans and pacifists. Some had herded sheep, others had worked at Los Alamos. There were grade school principals and people who worked on the county roads and men who built houses and women who ran little grocery stores.

The oral history of the Taos valley was repeated, explained, and venerated at every meeting. All feuds in the valley could be present in the background of any meeting. All the politics of the valley were present at every meeting and heatedly debated by the various participants. At the meeting were people who loved each other, and people who hated each other, but the really important thing was that the people dealt with each other as a community. That is the way democracy is supposed to work, with all the participants personally involved.

There was a time, during the heat of the battle against the conservancy district in Taos, that I had tacked up, on every wall in my little adobe house, the State Engineer's hydrographic survey maps of every irrigated piece of land in the Taos Valley. I knew by heart all the *acequias*, their locations, and many of the pieces of land that they irrigated. I had a big telephone-book-sized list of all the *parciantes*. I knew many of those *parciantes* personally. It was the most intimate kind of map you could have of my home area. When I looked at all those parcels of irrigated land and the people who owned them I was learning an entire town. It was like being in medical school and dissecting a body. It was like memorizing the Bible. It was like learning the entire history of a people that had become an important part of my own history and vice versa. It's one way I put down roots. That's how communities remain strong, when their people have that connection, those roots, that obligation.

The Tres Rios Association raised a lot of money to pay for lawyers. The leaders went back and forth to Santa Fe and back and forth to Santa Fe and back and forth to Santa Fe. The old timers' tenacity amazed me. They hired people to do research and then they listened to the result of the research. They attended countless court hearings. Sometimes our meetings were chaotic and full of dissension. Sometimes nobody came to the meeting, so the leaders called another meeting, and nobody came to it, so they called a third meeting . . . and all of a sudden *everybody* came.

Eventually, despite our protests, the District Court formed the Taos conservancy district anyway. So we appealed the verdict and kept fighting. And a few years later the state Supreme Court overturned that District Court decision. And in the end the conservancy district and the Indian Camp Dam did not arrive in Taos. But the adjudication never quit. And, of course, development has gone on anyway, although it received a serious setback when Taos shot down the conservancy.

Ever since, people have been struggling to maintain the traditional *acequias* and community water structures and all they represent. The adjudication suit is a difficult and cantankerous beast. It is an attempt to once and for all impose an American legal system on an area that has operated on largely Spanish custom for the last few centuries. The adjudication wants to clear things up so that water can be bought and sold with impunity, clearing the way for modern growth and development. It wants to make it possible to evolve from so-called "inefficient" and antiquated ways into the fast-paced twenty-first century.

In the process, the adjudication suit has pitted people against each other and one *acequia* against another *acequia* in a scramble for more advantageous priority dates. Indigenous Latino irrigators are placed against irrigators from the Pueblo, which entered the adjudication asking for enormous amounts of water. The State, the Feds, and the passel of lawyers seem to have grown fat over this. In Taos, the old Tres Rios Association was replaced by a group called the Taos Valley Acequia Association which continues to represent the often impoverished *parciantes* on most of the ditches in the Taos Valley. Many people still don't understand this convoluted process.

Now: Ever since I came to New Mexico in 1969 I have read articles in the newspapers about *Aamodt vs. the State of New Mexico*. It was your 800-pound gorilla down here in Nambe like the Indian Camp Dam and the conservancy district were Taos's 800-pound gorilla up there. I never really understood what was happening in Aamodt, the same way that for years nobody really understood what was happening with the adjudication, the Indian Camp Dam, the conservancy district, and the San Juan-Chama diversion water in Taos.

I don't know what your experience has been down here, but up in Taos years ago, official representatives would arrive from the State Engineer's Office—like Paul Bloom, or Eluid Martínez (who eventually became the State Engineer)—and they would call meetings to explain to us the conservancy district, the proposed dam, the San Juan Chama Diversion Project, the adjudication suit, and also Einstein's Theory of Relativity. And after Paul Bloom and Eluid Martínez had spent five hours explaining all these things in both Spanish and English to maybe a hundred small farmers and teachers and construction workers and cabinet makers sitting in the auditorium of the Garcia Middle School, there would be a long pause. And then one of those small farmers would stand up and say, "That's all very well, *pero no lo hacemos así aquí en Taos*—but we don't do things that way here in Taos."

And after a while the government authorities and the Bureau of Reclamation and the state and federal *tiburones* (I mean *abogados*) and local development sharks realized that they were talking to a wall.

And the wall never collapsed.

One reason the wall did not collapse is that the people of Taos realized the adjudication, the San Juan Chama Diversion, the Indian Camp Dam and conservancy district were probably going to ream them completely. Individual community *acequias* were going to lose their autonomy to a politically appointed conservancy board: i.e., we were going to lose control of our water systems. And we were going to have imposed upon us an open-ended taxation system over which we had no control. We weren't even going to be allowed to vote for the conservancy board that would govern us because the powers that be recognized that if we were given the opportunity to vote we would elect a board that would immediately dissolve the conservancy and that would end the Indian Camp Dam project.

The Tres Rios Association studied the history of other major water projects along the Rio Grande, especially the Elephant Butte Dam and the Middle Rio Grande Conservancy District, and it discovered that in every case water projects that were advertised as ways to help local farmers grow more and better crops for economic profit wound up instead by running indigenous people off the land in favor of agribusiness corporations and urban/suburban development.

A fascinating study of this process was done way back in 1936 by a Middle Rio Grande Regional Conservator, Hugh Calkins, in a document called *A Reconnaissance Survey of Human Dependency on Resources in the Rio Grande Watershed*. Calkins explains that before Elephant Butte Dam 70 percent of the 889 farms in the area were "owned by their operators," a large majority of whom were "Spanish-Americans." He described the farms and people as self-sufficient and relatively stable. Then the dam and irrigation district arrived and suddenly bankruptcy and loss of farmers "became a constant threat." And in the end, "The irrigation project . . . was the instrument by which this essentially self-sufficing area was opened to commercial exploitation. The establishment . . . of a legal claim upon the resources of the area and the labor of its inhabitants . . . led to the dispossession of the natives, and their replacement by American settlers financed by American capital . . . Through the construction of a costly irrigation project . . . an additional land area of 100,000 acres was made available for agriculture use," but "the native population, unable to meet the new high cash costs, was in large measure displaced from 50,000 acres it had owned."

A noted sociologist, Dr. Clark Knowlton, who testified at several 1970s conservancy hearings in Taos, had previously written: "Every major irrigation or water conservation project along the Rio Grande River . . . has been responsible for land alienation on an extensive scale. The Spanish-Americans have been replaced by Anglo-American farmers. Their subsistence agriculture has made way for a highly commercial, partially subsidized, and basically insecure agriculture, made possible by government programs. Little thought has ever been given to the rights and land use patterns of the Spanish-Americans in planning water projects in New Mexico and in neighboring states."

Needless to say, little or no thought has been given to the rights and land use patterns of Native Americans during this same epoch, until recently. And even then it often seems that today Pueblo rights are merely being touted as a way to partition and confuse indigenous communities in a form of divide and conquer, weakening both sides, so that eventually most of the water will end up in golf courses for rich tourists, luxury hotels, developments like Las Campanas of Santa Fe, and in frantic urban development from which native and Latino and all working-class New Mexicans will be excluded.

The proposed settlement agreement and regional water system being offered to the people of the Pojoaque/Tesuque/Nambe area reads to me like a nightmare of antagonistic and far-fetched water development. For starters, all the water proposed for future use in this area only exists on paper. It will cost a fortune to develop a regional system, but nobody can tell if the water really exists for this system or how much it will actually cost. I read in newspapers that the government will pay "most" of the estimated 280 million dollars for the system. During the conservancy and dam battle in Taos we were told that the government would pay something like 96.5 percent of the costs, but we figured out that that last 3.5 percent plus maintenance of the dam would not only be exorbitant for the relatively poor population, but it was open-ended with no guarantee there wouldn't be endless cost overruns.

Today, in the Southwest, we are locked in a severe drought. Global warming is a fact of existence. In the last few years I have read a hundred articles by scientists, sociologists, hydrologists, political and demographic analysts declaring that most of the major wars of the twenty-first century will be fought over water. It's not just in New Mexico, it's everywhere. U.S. America's Ogalalla aquifer is draining way down; the Aral Sea in Uzbekistan has half evaporated and is a disaster area. And you know that Israel will never give Palestine its own state because something like 70 percent of Israel's water comes from the West Bank.

I think if I had current irrigation rights or access to well water I would not in a million years give them up for paper water projected to cost me a fortune with no guarantee of future delivery in the first place. At the rate we're going, the state of New Mexico could very well sink 280 million dollars into a regional water system that'll just wind up drawing sand from the Rio Grande. The whole gambit is a rush to more urban development in a desert state already buggered by nonsensical growth, which seems like a formula for Land Enchantment suicide. History teaches us that for sure the regional water system project is not geared to benefit the working men or women of this valley, or folks of modest means. It is more like a grand ploy to stimulate outrageous growth-oriented commercial development for the rich, and as such just another criminal boondoggle in a global world economy eager to self-destruct. I apologize to Indian water users who have been short-changed for centuries by the outside world, but we are now living in times that cannot tolerate more development insanity like golf courses and luxury hotels in the desert, which ultimately will destroy the biology that nurtures all of us.

Do you remember the '80s under Ronald Reagan, when the savings and loan industry collapsed, much of it because huge loans in the oil and gas industry were being given based on a collateral of future production that never materialized when the energy industry tanked? This disaster cost American taxpayers untold billions. Well, even as I speak, given the drought, global warming, and expanding human population, future water, as collateral for proposed regional systems and urban development, is becoming a pipe dream. Edward Abbey once said, "Growth for sake of growth is the ideology of the cancer cell." We should be stopping all growth, going on emergency water rations, and completely retooling the economic philosophy that guides our behavior. Instead, we keep frantically trying to tread water and expand our numbers in a lake that increasingly is running out of H_2O.

A major serious problem confronting us all is philosophical. It's all about ideology. It's about our attitude toward our own lives of material well-being. If we need to keep consuming as we do, if we need to keep driving gas-guzzling SUVs as we do, if we need to live in big houses with air-conditioning as some of us do, if we need to have lots of gimcracks and geegaws and entertainment centers and vacations in Mexico or Hawaii . . . if, in short, we need to be typical American consumers in a world where our habits are causing twenty-seven thousand species to go extinct each year and a forest the size of New York State to be logged each year and almost three billion people elsewhere on the globe to live on less than 2 dollars a day . . . then there's no point to resisting the proposed regional water system to settle the Aamodt cast. Because as far as I can tell the settlement is an attempt to keep up U.S. America's excessive material lifestyle against all evidence that that lifestyle is destroying the planet we live on.

Resisting the settlement should indicate a desire to call a halt to the growth and the consumption that threatens life on earth. But so far not many U.S. Americans have been willing to change our lifestyles to bring about a more sustainable order.

So my feeling is this:

The development future being offered us in New Mexico and around the world is grim indeed. Here in northern New Mexico we still have partial access to a precious way of life. From my outsider's perspective, the current solutions offered to Aamodt seem negative for all parties concerned. If possible, I would band everyone together in this valley to demand a more benevolent social, economic, and environmental solution that does not destroy the infrastructure that took hundreds of years to produce by crushing it under a massive water project that has enough costs and other hidden variables in it to sink a battleship.

Authorities have told you that if you don't accept the current settlement, you'll lose everything: I'd guess that's BS. Thirty years ago Helen Ingram wrote a book called *Politics in Water Resource Development* in which she explained how water projects are sold to communities. I quote:

> *Support for a water project is justified by magnifying the need and benefits of water projects. It is claimed that projects will foster all sorts of goals, grandiose or particular, even if these goals may be contradictory . . . Economic and social advantage is promised to all sorts of groups, even if their interests conflict . . . Crisis in terms of water scarcity or floods is exploited to create consent. Backers of projects claim that an emergency situation exists. Projects are said to be essential to economic survival. At the very least, it is asserted that continued growth of a locality hinges upon the particular development being pushed . . . Projects are made to pass experts' tests even if there is little agreement among the experts on the soundness of these tests.*"

And so forth.

The fact is: If many people in this area believe the current solutions to Aamodt are unjust, unfair, and untenable, the fight ought to go on until a more equitable, and a more sane conclusion is realized.

You know, it's been a while since I've walked the length of an *acequia* in Taos. Today, I live in a small house, I have no irrigated land, I'm not a commissioner any more. But I think often of the Pacheco and the Lovatos ditches that used to give me water. I can see myself walking along the bank with a shovel, checking it out, looking for problems. I walk through yards and little back fields. There's Lucy Mares's house and her daughter Stella's trailer. And Vidal Cisneros's big purple martin birdhouse, and Shorty's Mower Service garage. Indian ponies on Pueblo land shy away from me, they never come over for handouts. Peacocks are strutting by Isabel Vigil's corrals, and her little donkey starts braying. Tom Trujillo's old horse is standing knee deep in grass in his daughter Frances's front field. And they're singing gospel hymns in the Good News church that's right behind Sebastian's old bar. A rusted truck is sinking on its axles in Adolfo Lavadie's two-acre plot. And somebody's hanging out wash by Archie Anglada's trailer. One of the Pacheco boys is shooting at a prairie dog in their garden: "*Órale, bro', cuidadito!*" And we're gonna have to chop down all these *jaras* behind

the Miera's field also. And I better call the Cordovas and tell them it looks like there's a hole in the fence where the sheep could move through to the Romero's pasture where the alfalfa would bloat those idiot sheep to death in fifteen minutes. And when can we get a crew to repair the *desague* just below Medina's corrals—?

Water can still be like that in Taos, in northern New Mexico: up close and personal. Nobody is making much money from irrigating small pastures and little gardens from *acequias* and old wells drilled long ago. People don't hang onto the *acequias* or their little wells and fight for them because of all the *profit* involved anymore. No: We hang onto this way of life and fight for it because water and the local organizations that dispense it are the blood that keeps our communities alive.

In Taos, people say this: "*Buen abogado, mal vecino.*"

They also say: "*Sin agua, no hay vida.*"

When Reies Tijerina was up north fighting for the land grants I would see signs everywhere that said: "*Tierra o muerte.*"

And I myself always end every talk I give by saying "*Hasta la victoria, siempre!*"

Contributing Authors

John P. Bieter Jr. is an assistant professor of history in the College of Social Sciences and Public Affairs, Boise State University. Along with other works in Basque history, Bieter co-authored *An Enduring Legacy: The Story of Basques in Idaho.* Bieter lived and studied in the Basque region of Spain for three years and currently serves as the Executive Director of the Cenarrusa Center for Basque Studies in Boise, Idaho.

Dolly (Skungwaii) Garza is a Haida/Tlingit Indian from Ketchikan, Alaska. Garza has a Ph.D. in Marine Policy from the University of Delaware. She is a professor with the University of Alaska Sea Grant Marine Advisory Program. As an outreach educator Garza works with tribes in marine mammal co-management, and educates the public about the value and uses of traditional foods and food gathering by Native peoples. Garza knows that her Ph.D. pales in comparison to the decades and generational knowledge held by many Natives. She works with locals and relies on the traditional knowledge as she represents local interests in resource management arenas.

Erlinda Gonzales-Berry is Chair of the Department of Ethnic Studies at Oregon State University. She has published extensively on Chicano/a and Latina/o literature and culture. She has served on the board of the New Mexico Endowment for the Humanities, the executive board of American Departments of Foreign Languages, the Advisory Board on the Languages and Literatures of the Americas, and the National Advisory Board of the Recovering the U.S. Latino Literary Heritage Project. In 1990 Gonzales-Berry was the recipient of a Fulbright Award, which took her to Germany to teach Latino literature at the University of Johannes Guttenburg in Germersheim.

Steven Hackel is an associate professor of history at the University of California at Riverside. The focus of his research has been early California history, particularly in the Monterey Bay Area. He has recently published *Children of Coyote, Missionaries of Saint Francis: Indian-Spanish Relations in Colonial California, 1769-1850.* He is writing a biography of Junípero Serra and is general editor of the Early California Population Project.

David R. Hatch is Ike Martin's great-grandson, Nick Hatch's grandson, Ken Hatch's son, and Peter Hatch's dad. He is not a biologist, but his brother Keith is, so folks often mistake him for a biologist. Actually he's an engineer for the City of Portland. He also served on the Siletz Tribal Council and is one of the founding members of the Elakha Alliance, which is dedicated to restoring the sea otter in order to restore the near-shore ecosystems.

Deanna Paniataaq Kingston is a Native Alaskan from the King Island community. She is an associate professor of anthropology at Oregon State University. Following her masters and doctoral research examining King Island traditions, she has developed collaborative grants from the National Science Foundation and various arctic research groups to explore the culture, biogeography, and traditional ecological knowledge on King Island and Alaska more broadly. Kingston serves on multiple advisory boards that advocate for Native people in the Pacific Northwest and Alaska and is advisor to several Native American student groups.

Judith L. Li is a recently retired associate professor in the Department of Fisheries and Wildlife at Oregon State University. She is a stream ecologist by training, with particular interests in invertebrate food webs. Her interests in cultural ecology have been sparked by a course she teaches entitled "Multicultural Perspectives in Natural Resources," which received a gold award from Agricultural Distance Educators and Communicators. Her ethnic roots as a second-generation Chinese American have led her to study the role of Chinese in California, where she grew up.

Jim LeMonds is a freelance writer and editor who has lived his entire life in the heart of timber country in Castle Rock, Washington. He is the author of numerous newspaper and magazine articles, as well as two books: *South of Seattle: Notes on Life in the Northwest Woods* and *Deadfall: Generations of Logging in the Pacific Northwest.*

Irene Martin was born in England, raised in Canada, and has lived in the U.S. for over thirty years. Her background as a repeated immigrant as well as now belonging to a family that has been part of the fishing community of the Columbia River since the 1870s gives her two very different perspectives. Martin is the author of several books, including *Legacy and Testament, the Story of Columbia River Gillnetters; The Beach of Heaven, a History of Wahkiakum County; Lewis and Clark in the Land of the Wahkiakums,* and *Sea Fire, Tales of Jesus and Fishing.* She is currently at work on a history of the Columbia River Packers Association/Bumble Bee Seafoods.

David Mas Masumoto is an organic peach and grape farmer and the award-winning author of *Harvest Son, Planting Roots in American Soil; Epitaph For A Peach: Four Seasons on My Family Farm;* and *Four Seasons in Five Senses, Things Worth Savoring.* He has also written several other books about the Japanese American experience and received the James Clavell Japanese American National Literacy Award in 1986.

Margaret Mathewson is an anthropologist and ethnobotanist. She has studied with traditional Native weavers in California, and has been practicing Western fiber arts and basketry for twenty-five years. Her graduate training was at U.C. Berkeley, with a postdoctoral fellowship at the Smithsonian. Mathewson is an adjunct assistant professor at Oregon State University, and also works for a number of Oregon and California tribes in their cultural and education programs.

John Nichols is the author of eleven novels and eight works of nonfiction. He is most noted for his novels *The Sterile Cuckoo* and *The Milagro Beanfield War*. Nichols has long been active in land and water issues in northern New Mexico and has lived in Taos, New Mexico, since 1969. In 2003 he received the Wallace Stegner Award from the University of Colorado's Center of the American West.

Patti Sakurai is a third-generation Japanese American who was born and raised in Southern California. She came to the field of ethnic studies by way of her graduate studies in literature. Her areas of research have included Asian American literature of the 1960s and '70s and literature arising from the Japanese American internment of World War II.

Charles Wilkinson is a Distinguished University Professor and Moses Lasky Professor of Law at University of Colorado at Boulder in the School of Law. He has written twelve texts on law, public land law, and Indian law, and numerous books for the public, including *Eagle Bird, Crossing the Next Meridian*, and more recently, *Messages From Frank's Landing: A Story of Salmon, Treaties, and the Indian Way*. His numerous awards for teaching, conservation work, and collaborations with tribes include the National Conservation Award from the National Wildlife Society and university awards from Colorado, Oregon, and Michigan. Over his career Wilkinson has been appointed to numerous committees for federal agencies, and continues to serve as negotiator and mediator for tribes.

Notes

Introduction

1. Flores, Dan. 1999. "Place, An Argument for Bioregional History" in Dale D. Goble and Paul W. Hirt, editors, *Northwest Lands, Northwest Peoples: Readings in Environmental History*. Seattle: University of Washington Press, p. 41.

2. Discussed eloquently in the introduction of *The Colors of Nature: Culture, Identity and the Natural World* by Alison Deming and Lauret Savoy. 2002. Minneapolis, MN: Milkweed Editions, 210p.

3. For example, Goble and Hirt's *Northwest Lands, Northwest Peoples: Readings in Environmental History* (see note 1); Richard Manning's *Grassland: The History, Biology, Politics and Promise of the American Prairie* (Penguin Books reissue, 1997); Donald Worster's *Dust Bowl: The Southern Plains in the 1930s* (Oxford University Press paperback reprint, 2004).

4. Such as Charles Wilkinson's *Crossing the Next Meridian: Land, Water, and the Future of the West* (Island Press paperback reprint, 1993); Richard White's *The Organic Machine: The Remaking of the Columbia River* (Hill and Wang paperback reprint, 1996); Jim Lichatowich's *Salmon Without Rivers: A History of the Pacific Salmon Crisis* (Island Press, paperback, 2001).

5. Chan, Sucheng. "Introduction" in S. Chan, C. H. Daniels, M. T. Garcia, and T. P. Wilson, editors. 1994. *Peoples of Color in the American West*. Lexington, MA: D. C. Heath & Co., p. 11.

6. Alvin Josephy Jr.'s *The Nez Perce Indians and the Opening of the Northwest* (Mariner Books paperback, 1997); Robert H. Ruby and John A. Brown's *The Chinook Indians: Traders of the Lower Columbia River* (University of Oklahoma Press paperback reprint, 1988); Robert F. Heizer and Alan J. Almquist's *The Other Californians: Prejudice and Discrimination under Spain, Mexico, and the United States to 1920* (University of California Press paperback edition, 1977); Douglas Monroy's *Thrown Among Strangers: The Making of Mexican Culture in Frontier California* (University of California Press paperback reprint edition, 1993).

7. Robert F. Heizer and Albert B. Elsasser's *The Natural World of the California Indians* (University of California Press paperback reprint, 1981); Courtland Smith's *Salmon Fishers of the Columbia* (Oregon State University Press, 1980); to some extent Patricia Limerick's *The Legacy of Conquest; The Unbroken Past of the American West* (W. W. Norton paperback reprint, 1987).

8. Yi-Fu Tuan. 1974, 1990. *Topophilia: A Study of Environmental Perception, Attitudes, and Values*. New York: Columbia University Press.

9. Elaborated by Dan Flores in "Spirit of Place and the Value of Nature in the American West" in *A Sense of the American West: An Environmental History Anthology* edited by James E. Sherow (University of New Mexico Press paperpack, 1998).

Walrus Hunting in a Changing Arctic

1. This flight to *Ugiuvak* was a reconnaissance trip, funded under a National Science Foundation grant (OPP-0328234) entitled "Documenting the Cultural Geography, Biogeography, and Traditional Ecological Knowledge of King Island,

Alaska," the purpose of which was to assess the condition of the buildings on the island for fieldwork in 2005 and 2006.

2. Uncle Gabe passed away on February 5, 2006. He will be missed very much, not only by his family, but by the community as a whole. Gabe served on the tribal council (and had been chief at the time of his death) and on the board of the King Island Native Corporation for many years; he was one of our song leaders; and he was our community representative to the Eskimo Walrus Commission. I would like to dedicate this chapter to his memory, especially since he gave a very long interview about walrus hunting in 2004.

3. Bogojavlensky (1969:30-33) gives population figures for *Ugiuvak* ranging from one hundred (made in the summer months when the *Ugiuvangmiut* were usually elsewhere trading) to 210 in 1940.

4. See, for example, the hunting summary for King Island in the online database on the State of Alaska Department of Commerce's Community Information Summaries: http://www.dced.state.akus/dca/commdb/CF_CIS.htm

5. This project was supported under a grant from the Pacific Walrus Conservation Fund, National Fish and Wildlife Foundation, under Project Number 1997-0292-005 (Co-PI's Jesse Ford, Deanna Kingston, and Selina Heppell) and Kingston's travel to Nome was supported by the National Science Foundation Arctic Social Science Program, under grant # OPP-0096985.

6. Several of the nineteen walrus hunters interviewed wished to remain anonymous, which stems from a cultural value of humility in which people do not want to claim to know more than others. In these cases, we created a pseudonym based on the order in which we interviewed them. "Mr. Four," for example, was the fourth hunter we interviewed.

7. In the early 20th century, *Ugiuvangmiut* began to use rifles that they received in trade for their carvings and other sea mammal resources.

8. During a project (funded under NSF Grant #9400929) to document images seen on archival film footage of *Ugiuvangmiut* in 1937-38, another community member and I noted that a typical Ugiuvak skinboat held about thirty-five people, including all the food and gear that they needed for spending the summer in Nome or elsewhere on the mainland.

9. For more extended discussions about how these policies caused the depopulation of *Ugiuvak*, see Bogojavlensky (1969:39-42), Kingston (1999:182-202), and Braem (2004).

10. In the past, the population on *Ugiuvak* was about one hundred to one hundred fifty people, which means that there were probably a total of about thirty or so able-bodied men. Today, the King Island Native Community estimates that there are at least four hundred *Ugiuvangmiut*, based on the fact that there are about two hundred or more "enrolled" members of the community and many more that are not enrolled. In my family alone, there are over one hundred people descended from my mother's parents.

Comanaging Sea Otter
1. www.r7.fws.gov/fisheries/mmm/pdf/vision.pdf

Shifting Patterns of Land Use in Monterey, California, before 1850
1. Stephen A. Dietz, Thomas L. Jackson et al., *Final Report of Archaeological Excavations at Nineteen Archaeological Sites for the Stage 1 Pacific Grove-Monterey*

176 Notes: *Land Use in Monterey*

Consolidation Project of the Regional Sewerage System, II (Berkeley, California, 1981), part 2, 661-66.
   2. Quotes: William Bryant and J. D. Borthwick in M. Kat Anderson, Michael G. Barbour, and Valerie Whitworth, "A World of Balance and Plenty: Land, Plants, Animals, and Humans in a Pre-European California," in *Contested Eden: California Before the Gold Rush*, edited by Ramón A. Gutiérrez and Richard J. Orsi (Berkeley, University of California Press, 1998), 12-47, at 14. On the changing ecology of the Monterey region, see Burton L. Gordon, *Monterey Bay Area: Natural History and Cultural Imprints*, 3rd ed. (Pacific Grove, California, The Boxwood Press, 1996). This essay is based on sections from my larger work, *Children of Coyote, Missionaries of Saint Francis: Indian-Spanish Relations in Colonial California, 1769-1850* (Chapel Hill, University of North Carolina Press, 2005). For a collection of articles that discuss how California Indians modified their environment to increase food yields, see Thomas C. Blackburn and Kat Anderson, eds., *Before the Wilderness: Environmental Management by Native Californians*, (Menlo Park, California, Ballena Press, 1993).
   3. The Scotts Valley archaeological site (CA-SCR-177) has been dated to around 10,000 B.C. Robert Cartier and Victoria Bobo, "Early Peoples of Monterey Bay: The Scotts Valley Site," in *A Gathering of Voices: The Native Peoples of the Central California Coast, Santa Cruz County History Journal* (No. 5, 2002), 109-116. See Dorothy Patch and Terry Jones, "Paleoenvironmental Change at Elkhorn Slough: Implications for Human Adaptive Strategies," *Journal of California and Great Basin Anthropology*, 6:1 (1984): 19-43, Table 1, page 26. Joseph L. Chartkoff and Kerry Kona Chartkoff, *The Archaeology of California* (Stanford, Stanford University Press, 1984), 4.
   4. Over the past decades, archaeologists have proposed several different chronologies for California prehistory. Here I adopt the dates and periodization of Breschini and Haversat, who have done much work on the Monterey region. While this periodization seems at odds with that of other regions of the California coast, it sees most consistent with the archaeological record for the Monterey region. See Gary S. Breschini and Trudy Haversat, "Baseline Archaeological Studies at Rancho San Carlos, Carmel Valley, Monterey County, California," reprinted as *Coyote Press Archives of California Prehistory*, (No. 36, 1992), 7, note 3.
   5. Jon M. Erlandson and Roger H. Colten, *Hunter-Gatherers of Early Holocene Coastal California* (Los Angeles, Cotsen Institute of Archaeology, 1991).
   6. Chartkoff and Chartkoff, *The Archaeology of California*, 38-50.
   7. Ibid., 68-69.
   8. Ibid., 75.
   9. Dietz and Jackson, "Stage 1 Pacific Grove-Monterey," volume 2, part 2, pages 692 and 700-702; and Stephen A. Dietz, William R. Hildebrandt, Terry L. Jones et al., *Archaeological Investigations at Elkhorn Slough: CA-MNT-229: A Middle Period Site on the Central California Coast*, Papers in Northern California Anthropology, No. 3 (Berkeley, California, 1988), 424. Note that Dietz and Jackson place this transformation two thousand years ago; Dietz, Hildebrandt, and Jones argue that it occurred more recently, about one thousand years ago.
   10. Chartkoff and Chartkoff, *The Archaeology of California*, 148.
   11. On the flora and fauna of Central California and the Monterey region, see the Costanoan and Esselen entries in the *Handbook of North American Indians*, vol. 8: *California*, edited by Robert F. Heizer and William C. Sturtevant (Washington,

D.C., Smithsonian Institution, 1978); Robert F. Heizer and Albert B. Elsasser, *The Natural World of the California Indians* (Berkeley, University of California Press, 1980); and Rebecca Allen, *Native Americans at Mission Santa Cruz, 1791-1834: Interpreting the Archaeological Record, Perspectives in California Archaeology*, Vol. 5, Senior Series Editor, Jeanne E. Arnold, Institute of Archaeology, University of California, Los Angeles, 1998, 21-22. See also appendices, C through G, in Dietz and Jackson et al., "Pacific Grove-Monterey Consolidation Project."

12. Sherburne F. Cook, *The Population of the California Indians, 1769-1970* (Berkeley, University of California Press, 1976), 43. Estimates of the aboriginal population in Alta California have changed over time. Some scholars have placed the pre-contact population of California as high as 1,000,000. The methodologies that Cook and others have used to estimate pre-contact populations are the subject of John D. Daniels, "The Indian Population of North America in 1492," *William and Mary Quarterly*, 3d. Ser., 49 (1992), 298-320. On Indian languages in California, see Michael J. Moratto, *California Archaeology* (New York, Academic Press, 1984; reprint, Salinas, Calif., Coyote Press, 2004), 530-74; and William F. Shipley, "Native Languages of California," in Heizer, ed., *California*, 80-90. See also Chartkoff and Chartkoff, *The Archaeology of California*, 203.

13. Heizer and Elsasser, *The Natural World of the California Indians*; Julia G. Costello and David Hornbeck, "Alta California: An Overview," in *Columbian Consequences*, ed. David Hurst Thomas, vol. 2: *Archaeological and Historical Perspectives on the Spanish Borderlands West*, 304-08; James T. Davis, "Trade Routes and Economic Exchange among the Indians of California," *Reports of the University of California Archaeological Survey*, No. 54 (Berkeley, 1961).

14. Based upon the number of Indians baptized in the missions in this area and the assumption that an additional percentage was not baptized, the aboriginal population of the Monterey Bay region seems to have been approximately 2,800 in 1769.

15. Costanoan is a Penutian language whereas Esselen is Hokan. For brief discussions of the linguistic variations among the Indians of California, see Shipley, "Native Languages of California," in Heizer, ed., *California*, 80-90.

16. This paragraph as well as the one that follows rely heavily on Dietz and Jackson et al., "Pacific Grove-Monterey Consolidation," 657-667.

17. Mission San Carlos "Libro de Cuentas, Inventario de la Mision," 14a, LDS Film 0913303, cited hereafter as San Carlos Account Book. This document has irregular and at times illegible page numbers.

18. San Carlos Account Book, "Ganado y Vacuno." No clear page number.

19. San Carlos Account Book, 9.

20. Zephyrin Engelhardt, *Mission San Carlos Borromeo (Carmelo): The Father of the Missions* (Mission Santa Barbara, Santa Barbara, California, 1934), 245.

21. Elinor G. K. Melville, *A Plague of Sheep* (Cambridge, Mass., Cambridge University Press, 2003), 6-7, and especially 47-59 for the four stages of this process. Ungulates are "herbivores with hard horny hooves," Melville, *A Plague of Sheep*, 6.

22. Junípero Serra, Report on the Missions, Monterey, July 1, 1784, Antonine Tibesar, ed. and trans., 4 vols. (Washington, D.C., Academy of American Franciscan History 1955-1966), 4: 275.

23. Allen, *Native Americans at Mission Santa Cruz*, 42-43.

24. Serra, Report on the Missions, Monterey, July 1, 1784, *Writings of Junípero Serra*, 4:273.

25. San Carlos Account Book, 17a. Nearly all of the harvest was in corn, wheat, and barley. The majority of gentiles that year attained baptism in late summer, fall, and early winter, during and after the harvest.

26. Serra, Report on the Missions, Monterey, July 1, 1784, *Writings of Junípero Serra*, 4:271.

27. San Carlos Account Book, 17a.

28. Accumulating scholarship points to the variability of climate in Alta California and its potentially drastic impact upon native subsistence. See Lester B. Rowntree, "Drought During California's Mission Period, 1769-1834," *Journal of California and Great Basin Anthropology* 7:1 (1985): 7-20; H. C. Fritts and G. A. Gordon, "Reconstructed Annual Precipitation for California," in *Climate from Tree Rings*, eds. M. K. Hughes, P. M. Kelly, J. R. Pilcher, and V. C. LaMarche Jr. (Cambridge University Press, 1982), 185-91; Larson, "California Climatic Reconstructions," *Journal of Interdisciplinary History* 25:2 (Autumn 1994): 225-53; Daniel O. Larson, John R. Johnson, and Joel C. Michaelson, "Missionization among the Coastal Chumash of Central California: A Study of Risk Minimization Strategies," *American Anthropologist* 96:2 (June 1994): 263-99. See also Roy A. Salls, "The Fisheries of Mission Nuestra Señora de la Soledad, Monterey County, California," in *Research in Economic Anthropology* (Vol. 11, 1989), ed. Barry L. Isaac (Greenwich Conn, JAI Press, 1989), 251-84, especially 267-68.

29. Letter of Joseph María Beltrán, May 2, 1798, AGN Californias 21, Expediente 12:400a-401b. By the mid 1790s when the drought struck, the introduced animals' needs exceeded the carrying capacity of the land. The crash that ensued conforms to stage 3 of the cycles of ungulate irruptions described by Melville, *A Plague of Sheep*, 53-55.

30. Testimony of soldiers, AGN Californias 21, Expediente 12:414a-419a.

31. Ibid.

32. During the drought and the following decade, nearly eight hundred Indians came to the Franciscan missions of the region, and more than half of those went to Mission San Carlos.

33. Robert Archibald, *Economic Aspects of the California Missions* (Washington, D.C., Academy of American Franciscan History, 1978), 179 and 181.

Lost China Camps

1. Sandy Lydon's *Chinese Gold; the Chinese in the Monterey Bay Region* was invaluable for this essay.

2. Lydon cites two sources for these possibilities: "aulon" from *Pacific Sentinental*, Nov. 15, 1856; "orejones" from Fish Commission, 1883. p. 425.

3. In 1879 a provision in the California constitution prohibited Chinese from fishing in coastal waters.

Clifton Gillnetters

1. Martha McKeown, *The Trail Led North* (New York: Macmillan, 1948), p. 78.

2. For the early history of the Columbia River fishing and canning industry, see Irene Martin, *Legacy and Testament* (Pullman, Wa.: Washington State University Press, 1994), pp. 18-22.

3. Interview with John Vlastelicia by Jim Bergeron, Nov. 10, 1988, p. 6. Astoria, Columbia River Maritime Museum.

4. Ibid., p. 13.

5. Letter from Jack and Georgia Marincovich, December 2004, to author; interview with Jack Marincovich by Irene Martin, Jan. 31, 2005.

6. Anon., *Columbia River Fishermen's Protective Union* (Astoria, Ore.: G.W. Snyder, 1890), pp. 16-17.

7. Kent Martin, "Ethnic Identity and the Fishermen of Skamokawa." Paper for Rutgers University Ph. D. Program, April 1975, p. 17. In author's possession.

8. The thumbnail sketch of Clifton has been put together from an interview of four Clifton fishermen—Delwin Barendse, Brian Davis, Jack Marincovich, Dave Lindstrom—conducted Jan. 31, 2005 by Irene Martin, and several printed sources. These include "Clifton—A Historic Fishing Community," in *The Bumble Bee*, Jan.-Feb. 1946, p. 5; Steve Bagwell, "Remembering a Bygone Era, Clifton and Bradwood: A Time When People Truly Lived Off the Land." *The Columbia River Gillnetter*, Summer/Fall 1990, pp. 21-23; Samuel Soter, "Clifton, Oregon: A Place and Time," *Cumtux*, vol. 24, no. 1, Winter 2004, pp. 2-13; Linda Wilson, "Clifton," in *Longview Daily News*, Mar. 23, 1983, p. B1.

9. Interview with Jack Marincovich by Irene Martin, Jan. 31, 2005, p. 3.

10. Interview with Clarence Demase by Irene Martin, Jan. 28, 2005, p. 3.

11. Interview with Jack Marincovich by Jim Bergeron, Nov. 2, 1988, p. 31. Astoria, Columbia River Maritime Museum.

12. Interview with John McGowan by Irene Martin, Mar. 31, 1985, p. 24. Astoria, Columbia River Maritime Museum.

13. Label on Gillnetter's Delight wine bottle.

14. Kent Martin, "Ethnic Identity," op. cit., pp. 23-24.

15. Interview by Irene Martin with four Clifton fishermen, Jan. 31, 2005, p. 1.

Logger Poetry and Music

1. Robert Swanson. 1992. *Rhymes of a Western Logger: The Collect Poems of Robert Swanson*. Madeira Park, British Columbia: Harbour Publishing.

2. Robert Walls. 1997. *The Making of the American Logger: Traditional Culture and Public Imagery in the Realm of the Bunyanesque*. Bloomington, Indiana: Indiana University Press.

3. John Springer. 1851. *Forest Life and Forest Trees*. New York: Harper and Brothers.

4. Ibid.

5. Franz Lee Rickaby. 1926. *Ballads and Songs of the Shanty-Boy*. Cambridge: Harvard University Press (reprinted in Baltimore: Clearfield Company, 1993).

6. http://dlib.home.nyu/dram/Objid/5157

7. Walls 1997.

8. http://www.mainepoetry.com/mainepoets-p3.html

9. Mary Killebrew. "I Never Died: The Words, Music and Influence of Joe Hill." http://www.pbs.org/joehill/voices/article.html

10. Joe Hill. 1912. "Where the Fraser River Flows." *Little Red Songbook: Songs to Fan the Flames of Discontent*. Chicago: Industrial Workers of the World.

11. Valentine Huhta (T-Bone Slim). "The Lumberjack's Prayer." http://www.fortunecity.com/tinpan/parton/2/ljackpray.html

12. "Fifty Thousand Lumberjacks." *Little Red Songbook: Songs to Fan the Flames of Discontent*. Chicago: Industrial Workers of the World, 1917.

13. Rickaby 1926.

14. Walls, 1997.
15. http://disneyshorts.toonzone.net/years/1958/paulbunyan.html
16. James Stevens. "The Frozen Logger." http://hbingham.com/humor/frozen-logger.htm
17. Woody Guthrie. "Lumber Is King." http://employees.csbsju.edu/dlarson/Writings/HTML%20copies/Lumber%20is%20king.htm
18. Swanson, 1992.
19. Buzz Martin. 1968. "Sick of Settin' Chokers." Ripcord Music. Portland, Oregon.
20. Otto Oja. Interview. Cathlamet, Washington, March 3, 2004.
21. "Buzz Martin—The Man to See and Hear." *Loggers World*, October 1968.
22. Jens Lund. Phone interview. Olympia, Washington, December 11, 2003.
23. Lund 2003.
24. Craig Jenkins and Terry McKinnis. 1990. *Endangered Species*. C&T Music. Deadwood, Oregon.
25. Sunny Hancock. 1991. "Ode to the Spotted Owl." *Dry Crik Review*. Lemon Cover, California.
26. Todd Cinnamon. 1992. "Timberman." http://bari.iww.org/iu120/local/Timberman.html
27. Darryl Cherney and Judi Bari. 1989. "Potter Valley Mill." http://bari.iww.org/iu120/local/PVMill.html
28. Hank Nelson. Phone interview. Wasilla, Alaska, April 4, 2004.
29. Nelson 2004.
30. Nelson 2004.
31. A section titled "Songs of the West" in *The Golden Encyclopedia of Folk Music* (Hal Leonard, Owensville, Indiana, 1985) lists seven songs about cowboys, but none about loggers. *American Ballads and Folks Songs* (John Lomax, New York: Macmillan, 1934) offers twenty-four tunes about cowboys, only five about timber workers.
32. Robert Walls. E-mail interview. Lafayette, New York, November 19, 2003.
33. Oja 2004.
34. Lund 2003.
35. "NFA Timber Facts." www.afrc.ws/timberfacts/99JuneTF.pdf

From Sojourners to Settlers

1. The use of identity labels is a very complex issue. *Mexicano*, when speaking in Spanish, is the one term that is universally accepted by people of Mexican origin in Oregon. Hence, I have chosen to use this term throughout this paper. I deliberately wish to call attention to the original language in which it is used; hence I designate this language in which it is used. I designate this language switch through the use of the lower case, which is standard practice in Spanish writing.
2. In an atmosphere of strong anti-immigrant sentiment immediately after World War I, restrictive regulations were enacted that, among other control measures, set quotas for all countries save those in the Western Hemisphere. This left the door open, so to speak, to the continued entry of Mexican labor. Many Americans believed that the restrictions should apply also to the Caribbean, Mexico, and South America, giving rise to animated debates in Congress and the media.
3. In 1942 Mexico and the United States established a contract labor program which brought Mexican workers to the United States to ease the labor shortage

induced by the war in the agriculture and railroad industries. The program, popularly known as the Bracero Program, was extended for agriculture workers after the war, and it remained in effect intil 1964.

4. In Oregon the primary employing war industries included ports of embarkation, ship building yards, and aluminum plants.

5. Wayne Rasmussen addresses this issue in his 1951 history of the Emergency Farm Labor Supply Program: "Almost immediately after the Commanding General of the Western Defense Command had announced that all people of Japanese descent would be evacuated from the West Coast, large-scale agricultural interests, particularly sugar-beet growers in the Rocky Mountain United States, requested that the evacuees be made available for work in the beet fields and in other season agricultural work" (101).

6. This claim may be a bit exaggerated if one considers that the screening process was rigorous and "ensured that only able, experienced, and healthy individuals received contracts" (Gamboa 1990, 52).

7. While not ever explicitly spelled out in the media, prejudice towards Mexicans comes as no surprise given the lack of diversity in the state, as well as its history of exclusionary laws pertinent to Chinese and African Americans. In 1944 a law was passed in the Oregon Territory that prohibited the entry of African Americans. This law was included in the statues of the State of Oregon as well (Peterson del Mar 2003).

8. Racial discrimination was certainly an issue that braceros had to contend with, and one that the Mexican government grappled with throughout the length of the program. Gamboa finds that such discrimination indeed was present in the Northwest. He cites one particular case in Medford, Oregon, where a Mexican worker was beaten by five young men, then arrested and charged with drinking in public when in fact he was staggering from the beating he had just received (1990).

9. One of the provisions of the labor contract stipulated that workers would be free to purchase personal items wherever they chose. The Mexican government no doubt insisted on this provision in order to avoid the kinds of abuses practiced by hacienda *tiendas de raya* [company stores] with which it was too familiar.

10. Gamboa points out the irony implicit in the high praise given to Mexican workers even as the latter were creating all manner of problems for their employers through frequent work stoppages and "bootlegging." The latter term was used to refer to the practice of taking side jobs at farms that had no contract labor; these jobs were attractive because they paid cash at the end of the day. "Skipping" or deserting their contractual positions was another common practice that resulted from worker dissatisfaction with food, housing, low wages, and ill treatment by employers. Gamboa states that it is "estimated that 10 percent of all braceros abandoned contracts" (1990, 68).

11. It also carries a photo of a bracero playing the guitar as one of his companions reads a girlie magazine titled *Burlesk*. Given that racialized discourse tends to project men of color as lascivious characters from whom women of the dominant culture must be protected, inclusion of the latter suggests to this reader some residual ambivalence regarding Oregon's "good neighbors."

12. In addition to administering contract labor from Mexico, the EFLSO was in charge of domestic interstate migrant labor as well as local emergency volunteer and hired workers.

13. See *bracero* collection in the Oregon State University Historical Archives.

14. These celebrations were sponsored by the Emergency Farm Labor Office, and were planned and carried out in conjunction with residents and leaders of the various communities (Oregon Farm Labor Report 1943, OSUA). The costs for these celebrations, however, were born primarily by the workers themselves who were charged an entrance fee of $1.00 to $3.00 (Gamboa 1990).

15. It appears that many U.S. Americans saw Mexicans as nothing more than laborers. Máximo Peón, in his memoirs of his stint as a railroad bracero, assures us that Mexican nationals, anxious as they were to accumulate dollars to take home, were also reflective human beings, conscious of the role they were playing in helping the United States and its allies win the war: "Among the braceros there were a few who were disoriented, but the majority was filled with a notorious enthusiasm for our cousins who we hoped would win the war" (1966, 46, translation by the author). Peón encourages his compatriots: "What I am trying to say is that we should not go only for the dollar, but rather with the mystical and humanitarian ideal of supporting our country and enthusiastically help increase the production of our neighboring and allied country, of sustaining the war effort and helping the civil population as well as those who do combat on the war front, so they do not experience need because of a labor shortage" (45).

16. According to Gamboa these kinds of racial incidents happened primarily at sites that included Jamaican workers. "To some extent, employers simply resisted the Jamaicans because they were black and their very presence among other workers led to disruptive racial problems and jealousies over jobs" (1990, 64).

17. The issue of hiring Mexicans over locals had already been dealt with in Oregon in 1944 when the cannery workers' union opposed the hiring of Mexicans in canneries: "'Not because of opposition to Mexicans as fellow workers would objections be raised,' representatives of the union declared, but 'because we are convinced that there is enough labor right here to handle the job if the labor in turn, is handled correctly'" (*Oregon Statesman*, July 28, 1944). In Washington and Idaho the hiring of *braceros* over locals in canning companies resulted in open protests by the affected communities (Gamboa 1990).

18. Reisler's summary of the arguments of defenders of Mexican labor highlights the essentializing rhetoric that made Mexicans the ideal farm worker in the minds of growers: "Not only did the Mexican's mental outlook attune him to outdoor work, but his physical attributes allowed him to be a perfect stoop laborer. Because the Mexican was small in size, agile, and wiry, growers explained, his ability in the fruit, vegetable, sugar beet, and cotton fields far excelled that of the white man" (1976, 138).

19. Reverberations of problems at the Texas border apparently were being felt in Oregon. One newspaper, for example, noted that Mexican nationals were to be available but perhaps in fewer numbers than the previous year (*Monmouth Herald*, March 8, 1944).

20. It is important to note that the Mexican government was not satisfied with just writing these protections into the contract, but helped enforce them through their consulate offices in the United States. For further discussion on this topic, see Gamboa 1990.

21. This was true in Oregon as it was throughout the Southwest and Midwest. *The Oregonian*, in demeaning language typical of that period, noted that in addition to *braceros* growers could also count on undocumented workers: "In addition to the Mexicans brought into this country legally, Oregon gets its share of the illegal

hordes of 'wetbacks' who sneak across the border to collect the American dollars U.S. farmers are glad to pay them" (May 17, 1953).

22. A report issued by the Oregon Bureau of Labor in 1958 found that there were four major contractors operating in Oregon who together handled 5,750 workers. In addition there were nine lesser contractors who handled 1,735 workers.

23. In its 1958 report, the Oregon Legislative Interim Committee on Migratory Labor attempted to tease out the distinction between labor contractors and crew leaders: "The purpose of the distinction is to ensure encouragement of the crew as a source of labor for Oregon. The detailed difference between the crew leader and the labor contractor is primarily legal. Customary usage of the terms varies in the United States and in different sections of Oregon. Generally speaking the crew leader is one who in addition to working in the crops himself aids the crew as spokesman and the farmer as foreman. The contractor usually seeks to handle a job for the farmer at a fixed price and then pays his workers less, keeping the difference for himself" (15).

24. As Elena Peña observed, "[T]hey always looked for hardest-working families."

25. A poignant memory for Elena Peña regarding her family's first trip was spending the entire night wrestling blankets from fellow travelers as they slept piled together in the back of the truck.

26. This particular finding by the Oregon Bureau of Labor in its 1958 preliminary report apparently created quite a flap in the state. The 1959 report addresses this issue: "In pursuing the regular survey of farm labor contractors and crew leaders, we came across a beneath-the-surface situation involving marijuana peddling, prostitution, and other things which make better headlines than the vast amount of statistical information which was really our major contribution. . . . The unfortunate effect, of course, was that it created a defense psychology on the part of the rural residents and farmers who quite rightly felt innocent of the activities described on the front pages of the papers" (Current and Infante 1959, 161-62).

27. Apparently this practice was not uncommon. In 1978 migrants brought a class-action suit against two brothers, charging them with "fraud, false advertising, breach of contract and minimum wage violations." The brothers had offered workers high wages, quality housing with hot water, televisions, recreation facilities, and more perks, which proved to be false promises (Loprinzi 1991, 58).

28. For a touching story of these conditions see Tomás Rivera's *And the Earth Did Not Swallow Him* (Houston: Arte Publico Press, 1995).

29. A report issued by the Oregon Legislative Assembly Interim Committee in 1958 found that in 1957, Oregon ranked sixth in the nation as a user of migratory labor.

30. Our reading of the reports mentioned above, even those that reveal a marked empathy for migrant workers, suggests that a preponderance of the blame for substandard labor and living conditions is laid at the feet of contractors, thereby tending to mitigate grower responsibility.

31. Loprinzi's assessment of the Migrant Health Project upon its cancellation in 1970 was that it was "the best program that had thus far existed for migrants" (1991, 74). This speaks well for the program, as Loprinzi's sense of government and especially politician's actions is that they talked the talk, but when it came time to act, they tended to bend before the powerful farm lobbies.

32. Loprinzi finds the lack of concern among farmers to stem from their lack of direct contact with workers, "because the use of contractors often allowed small

and large farmers alike to be unconcerned" (1991, 49). In fairness to small farmers, who she thought were manipulated by large growers, who made politicians and the public believe that the plight of the struggling small farmer was the plight of all farmers, she adds: "As the small farmer continued to struggle, and the larger farmer profit, farmworker conditions remained a low priority" (49). The words of one farmer, who spoke at a conference on migrant labor at Oregon State University, offer another perspective on the issue of farmer responsibility: "Within my financial ability, I can do things about wages, housing, and working conditions. I cannot do much for the chronic wino or the unskilled, uneducated father of eight children under the age of ten. Their problems are not agriculture's, and when society recognizes that I would hope society can stop shirking its collective duty by pointing its finger at farmers in order to expunge its own responsibility" (*Perspectives on Migrant Labor in Oregon* 1968, 13).

33. It was the kind of environment that the Peñas and Ms. García describe that prompted the Mexican government to refuse to send *braceros* to Texas for so many years.

34. Loprinzi (1991) notes that families who operated independently of contractors faced challenges that did not affect contract workers, such as arriving without funds and not being able to find work or not being able to buy items on credit. Despite these drawbacks, one report indicates that, in 1957, of the total 111,760 Spanish-speaking workers running the migrant circuit to Oregon, 2,945 (not counting children) came independently of contractors (Oregon Bureau of Labor 1958, 9-10).

35. We must caution the propensity for this language to function as a code that shores up traditional racializing practices in this country.

36. The Interagency Committee on Migrant Labor noted, in what could be interpreted as a mildly acerbic and warning tone, this settling-out pattern and called attention to the problems it augured for Oregon: "Some of the migrant workers who have been coming to Oregon the past few years have selected to stay here. As citizens of the United States this is their privilege. However, the transition poses some problems for the state and its communities. Having spent most of their lives working in agriculture, they are not prepared to obtain jobs other than that type of work. Beginning in November the workers find little to do. It is after a lean Thanksgiving and a bleak Christmas they can again be used in preparing for another berry and bean season" (Annual Report 1966, 14).

37. During the harvest season it was not uncommon for *mexicanos* from both sides of the U.S./Mexico border to gather in the Woodburn area, where jobs were plentiful for a short period of time.

In Wind and Sand

1. While I focus on Gila River here as a means of discussing the internment in general, there were significant differences among the WRA camps as well, though I do not address them in this paper. Further, the Department of Justice and INS camps, not discussed in this paper, were quite different from the WRA camps.

2. The camp's other major industry noted in the article, making camouflage nets, also holds some interesting resonances in terms of landscape, resonances I leave unexplored here.

3. California was the first state to pass an alien land law in 1913, followed by numerous other states, including Washington, Louisiana, New Mexico, Idaho, Oregon, and Kansas (Chan 1991, 47).

4. I hope it goes without saying that the issue of agricultural development is multilayered and hardly unproblematic, especially given the history of colonization in North America and treatment/displacement of indigenous peoples. Further, the Japanese and other Asian immigrant groups also had a tremendous impact on the development of agriculture in Hawaii, having been initially recruited as contract laborers to work on various plantations. Hence their history is interconnected with that of another indigenous population, Native Hawaiians, and processes of U.S. colonization there as well.

5. Their gender ratio, while still skewed toward men, was significantly less so than it was for other Asian immigrant groups, due in large part to U.S.-Japan diplomatic relations and immigration legislation allowing Japanese male immigrants to send for wives before the Immigration Act of 1924 stopped Asian immigration altogether. As a result, Japanese Americans were more likely to be able to start families and then own or lease land in their citizen children's names more often than members of other Asian groups.

6. For a longer account of anti-Asian legislation, public sentiment, and violence, see Chan (1991), chapter, "Hostility and Conflict" (45-61). Carlos Bulosan's *America Is in the Heart* is also notable for its documentation of violence and hostility against Filipino migrant workers in the 1930s and '40s.

7. More recently, in the wake of 9/11 and concerns about national security, some social critics such as Michelle Malkin have revisited the Japanese internment, arguing that it was in fact a justified and necessary act in the interest of national security in a time of war, much to the anger and dismay of the Japanese American community and all of those who felt that its status as an inexcusable gross violation of civil and human rights had been relatively settled in the eyes of history.

8. Related histories are those of the removal and treatment of indigenous populations in the Aleutian islands, Alaska (Commission on Wartime Relocation and Internment of Civilians 1997, 317-59) and the forced removal and shipment of over two thousand Latin Americans of Japanese descent, most of them Peruvians, to the Crystal City, Texas INS camp (Commission on Wartime Relocation and Internment of Civilians 1997, 305-14).

9. Seen in this light, the term "naturalization" seems all the more interesting, given that processes of determining national belonging are hardly "natural" per se.

10. Contrary to popular belief, there were more overt acts of resistance in which those who protested the internment and their subsequent treatment, risked their lives and futures to make their views known. Aside from those who took part in public protests and strikes, others, such Fred Korematsu, Min Yasui, Gordon Hirabayashi, and the Heart Mountain draft resisters come to mind.

11. Obviously, this paper merely touches the surface of Japanese American and broader Asian American history. Much is left out, such as the story of the segregated all-Nisei 442nd Regimental Combat Team, which joined with Nisei from Hawaii to become the most decorated unit in U.S. history. They also suffered the war's highest casualty rate.

Recommended readings from the editor's library with a little help from friends

We learn about places most intimately and personally by being there, taking in the landscape, meeting the people, hearing their stories. Thank goodness we can begin to understand the spirit of a place in other, more convenient ways, by reading what others have to say, what their experiences have been, what histories are there. This list expands the narratives of our anthology and encourages the reader to develop a personal interest in these cultures and places. It includes several titles written by authors included in the volume because many were writings that inspired this collective effort.

Pacific Northwest and Alaska

Barker, James H. 1993. *Always Getting Ready Upterrlainarluta; Yup'ik Eskimo Subsistence in Southwest Alaska*. Seattle: University of Washington Press. 143 p.

Capoeman, Pauline K. (ed.). 1990. *Land of the Quinault*. Taholah, Washington: Quinault Indian Nation. 315 p.

Douthit, Nathan. 2002. *Uncertain Encounters; Indians and Whites at Peace and War in Southern Oregon 1820s-1860s*. Corvallis: Oregon State University Press. 248 p.

Hess, Bill. 1999. *Gift of the Whale; the Inupiat Bowhead Hunt, a Sacred Tradition*. Seattle, Washington: Sasquatch Books. 224 p.

Kasner, Leone Letson. 1976. *Siletz: Survival for an Artifact*. Dallas, Oregon: Itemizer-Observer. 82p.

Krupnik, Igor, and Dyanna Jolly (eds.). 2002. *The Earth is Faster Now: Indigenous Observations of Arctic Environmental Change*. Arctic Research Consortium of the United States.

Ruby, Robert H., and John A. Brown. 1976. *The Chinook Indians; Traders of the Lower Columbia River*. Norman: University of Oklahoma Press. 349p.

———. 1981. *Indians of the Pacific Northwest*. 1981. Norman: University of Oklahoma. 294 p.

Smith, Courtland L. 1979. *Salmon Fishers of the Columbia*. Corvallis: Oregon State University Press. 117 p.

Stewart, Hilary. 1977. *Indian Fishing; Early Methods on the Northwest Coast*. Seattle: University of Washington Press. 181 p.

Tamura, Linda. 1993. *The Hood River Issei; An Oral History of Japanese Settlers in Oregon's Hood River Valley*. Urbana: University of Illinois Press. 337 p.

Wilkinson, Charles. 2000. *Messages from Frank's Landing; A Story of Salmon, Treaties, and the Indian Way*. Seattle: University of Washington Press. 118 p.

Wohlworth, Charles. 2004. *The Whale and the Supercomputer: On the Northern Front of Climate Change*. New York: North Point Press.

California

Barbour, Michael, Bruce Pavlik, Frank Drysdale, and Susan Lindstrom. 1993. *California's Changing Landscapes; Diversity and Conservation of California Vegetation.* Sacramento: California Native Plant Society. 244p.

Blackburn, Thomas C., and Kat Anderson (eds.). 1993. *Before the Wilderness; Environmental Management by Native Californians.* Menlo Park, California: Ballena Press. 476 p.

Hackel, Steven W. 2005. *Children of Coyote, Missionaries of Saint Francis.* Chapel Hill, North Carolina: University of North Carolina Press. 496p.

Heizer, Robert F., and Alan F. Almquist. 1971. *The Other Californians; Prejudice and Discrimination under Spain, Mexico, and the United States to 1920.* Berkeley: University of California Press. 278 p.

Heizer, Robert F., and Albert B. Elsasser. 1980. *The Natural World of the California Indians.* Berkeley: University of California Press. 271 p.

Luke, Timothy J., and Gary Y. Okihiro. 1985. *Japanese Legacy; Farming and Community Life in California's Santa Clara Valley.* Local History Studies Volume 31. Cupertino: California History Center. 156 p.

Lydon, Sandy. 1985. *Chinese Gold; The Chinese in the Monterey Bay Region.* Capitola, California: Capitola Book Company. 550 p.

Margolin, Malcolm. 1978. *The Ohlone Way; Indian Life in the San Francisco-Monterey Bay Area.* Berkeley, California: Heyday Books. 182 p.

Masumoto, David Mas. 1987. *Country Voices.* Del Rey, California: Inaka Countryside Publications.

———. 1999. *Harvest Son; Planting Roots in American Soil.* New York: W. W. Norton. 299p.

Ortiz, Beverly R., as told by Julia F. Parker. 1991. *It Will Live Forever; Traditional Yosemite Indian Acorn Preparation.* Berkeley, California: Heyday Books. 148 p.

Wyatt, David, 1997. *Five Fires: Race, Catastrophe, and the Shaping of California.* Reading, Massachusetts: Addison-Wesley Publishing Co. 288 p.

Southwest

Crawford, Stanley. 1988. *Mayordomo; Chronicle of an Acequia in Northern New Mexico.* Albuquerque: University of New Mexico Press. 231 p.

Gonzales-Berry, Erlinda, and David R. Maciel. 2000. *The Contested Homeland; A Chicano History of New Mexico* Albuquerque: University of New Mexico Press. 314 p.

Nichols, John. 1974. *The Milagro Beanfield War.* New York: Ballantine Books. 629 p.

Rivera, Jose A. 1998. *Acequia Culture; Water, Land and Community in the Southwest.* Albuquerque: University of New Mexico Press. 243 p.

Wilkinson, Charles F. 1992. *Crossing the Next Meridian; Land, Water, and the Future of the West.* Washington, D.C.: Island Press. 376 p.

And Other Books of Interest . . .

Andrews, Ralph. 1994. *The Glory Days of Logging.* Lancaster, Pennsylvania: Schiffer Publishing. 176 p.

David, Marilyn. 1990. *Mexican Voices/American Dreams; An Oral History of Mexican immigration to the United States.* New York: Henry Holt and Co. 446p.

Deming, Alison H., and Lauret E. Savoy (ed.). 2002. *The Colors of Nature; Culture, Identity, and the Natural World.* Minneapolis, Minnesota: Milkweed Editions. 210p.

Dietrich, William. 1993. *The Final Forest.* New York Penguin Books. 303 p.

Etulain, Richard W (ed.). 1991. *Basques of the Pacific Northwest.* Pocatello: Idaho State University Press. 95 p.

Heilman, Robert. 1995. *Overstory Zero: Real Life in Timber Country.* Seattle, Washington: Sasquatch Books. 221 p.

Swanson, Robert. 1992. *Rhymes of a Western Logger.* Madeira Park, B.C.: Harbour Publishing Company. 192 p.

———. 1993. *Whistle Punks and Widow-Makers.* Madeira Park, B.C.: Harbour Publishing Company. 160 p.

Takaki, Ronald. 1993. *A Different Mirror; A History of Multicultural America.* Boston, Massachusetts: Little, Brown & Company. 508 p.

———. 1989. *Strangers from a Different Shore; A History of Asian Americans.* New York: Penguin Books. 570 p.